CHRISTIANITY EXPLORED

CHRISTIANITY EXPLORED

Brenda Courtie and Margaret Johnson

LION EDUCATIONAL

Text copyright © 1990 Brenda Courtie and Margaret Johnson
This edition copyright © 1990 Lion Publishing

Published by
Lion Publishing plc
Sandy Lane West, Oxford, England
ISBN 0 7459 1800 X
Albatross Books Pty Ltd
PO Box 320, Sutherland, NSW 2232, Australia
ISBN 0 7324 0199 2

First edition 1990
Reprinted 1992, 1993

Acknowledgements
Bible quotations are from the *Good News Bible*, copyright
1966, 1971 and 1976 American Bible Society, published by
the Bible Societies and Collins

Quotations from *The Alternative Service Book 1980* © Central
Board of Finance, Church of England. Reproduced with
permission.

The authors and publisher wish to thank the following for
permission to use copyright material:
Christian Education Movement: pages 189, 192, Stephen
Orchard and Fiona Williams Hulbert, *Christian Pilgrimage*
William Collins, Sons and Co. Ltd: page 218, Sheila Cassidy,
Audacity to Believe; page 76, Billy Graham, *The Holy Spirit*;
page 30, C. S. Lewis, *Mere Christianity*
Robert Hale Limited: page 67, Michael Legat, *Writing for
Pleasure and Profit*
Hodder and Stoughton Publishers: page 182, Corrie Ten
Boom, *In My Father's House*
Inter-Varsity Press: page 101, Helen Roseveare, *Give Me This
Mountain*
Kingsway Publications Limited: page 181, Bilquis Sheikh,
I Dared to Call Him Father
Marshall Pickering: page 36, Stuart Henderson, 'Messianic
Blues', *Assembled in Britain*; Blyth and Jasper, 'A World
Without Tears', *At All Times and in All Places*
Renewal magazine: page 81, South African church
advertisement; quotations on pages 203–204
Today newspaper (22 August 1989 issue): page 161, Emma
Lee-Potter, 'Our Phoney Wedding'
21st Century Christian magazine: pages 219–220, Kriss Akabusi
(September 1988 issue); Simon Mayo (December 1988 issue)

Photographs
Asian Outreach International, page 218 (below); Associated
Press, page 216; Howard Barlow, pages 91, 115 (left), 146,
149, 186, 197; Barnaby's/Gerald Clyde, page 141 /G.A.
Duncan, page 191 (below) /Colin Horsman, pages 193, 194
(left) /David Kirby, page 103 (above) /Bill Meadows, page 159
/C. Money, page 95 /Herbertus Kanus, page 191 (above)
/Mustograph, pages 100, 163 /E. Preston, page 143 /Sports
Picture Agency, page 72 (above) /Graham Tatlock, page 145

/Sarah Thorley, pages 123, 156 (below), 184; /John
Woodhouse, page 96; Benedettine di Priscilla, page 91;
Trustees of the British Museum, page 108; CAFOD/Andes
Press Agency, pages 140, 209 (above), 212; Campus Crusade
for Christ, pages 43, 47, 54, 63; Cephas/Mick Rock, page 203;
Chatham, Rochester & Gillingham News, page 174; Christian
Aid, page 206; Christian Weekly Newspapers, pages 124, 211;
Columbia Pictures, page 35; EMI Records (UK) Ltd/Paul
Cox, page 60; Mary Evans Picture Library, pages 110 (except
centre left), 115 (right), 121 (left); Chris Fairclough Colour
Library, page 147 (below); Sonia Halliday Photographs,
page 190; International Defence & Aid Fund, page 217;
Margaret Johnson, pages 118 (all), 120 (all), 147 (above and
centre), 156 (all except below), 183 (both), 185, 202; Lion
Publishing/David Alexander, pages 41, 77 /Jenny Karrach,
page 136 /David Townsend, page 75 /Jon Willcocks, page 171;
Liverpool Catholic Cathedral, page 121 (right); Mansell
Collection, pages 110 (centre left), 114, 130, 187; Medical
Mission Sisters, page 194 (right); Middle East Archive/Alistair
Duncan, pages 51, 80; North News & Pictures, page 219;
Oxford Mail & Times, page 172; Michael Page, page 57;
National Monuments Record of Great Britain, pages 119 (all);
Luis Palau Association, page 103 (below); Popperfoto, pages 72
(below), 138, 176, 218 (above); Clifford Shirley, pages 157,
162, 199, 214; The Salvation Army, page 116; Alan Stephen,
page 188; Times Newspapers Ltd, page 168; Traidcraft, page
209 (below); World Council of Churches/Johann Gürer, page
206; Wycliffe Bible Translators, page 180

Illustrations, maps and graphics
Simon Jenkins, pages 12, 14, 16, 17 (top), 37, 41, 50, 58, 67,
79, 88, 90, 98, 106, 128, 152, 153, 161, 164, 179, 195, 215
Lion Publishing, pages 24, 167, 169
All others, Lion Publishing/Tony Cantale Graphics

Design by Tony Cantale Graphics

British Library Cataloguing in Publication Data

Courtie, Brenda
  Christianity explored.
  1. Christianity
  I. Title II. Johnson, Margaret
  200

  ISBN 0-7459-1800-X

Printed in Malta

Contents

Introduction

Does your town or village have a 'church'? A special building used on Sundays for special meetings?

Imagine some tourists, perhaps foreign students, visiting this building during one of these meetings. They have never been to a church before and many things catch their attention and arouse their curiosity.

There's quite a lot of singing, which they enjoy, and extracts from a special book are read out from the front. The songs and the extracts all mention someone called 'Jesus'. The person in charge of the meeting gives a kind of lecture about this Jesus; it seems that he died in Jerusalem nearly 2,000 years ago. But after the lecture, the leader and some other people appear to be talking to Jesus as if he were there at the meeting with them!

There's a kind of table at the front, and now this is used for the sharing out of small portions of bread and wine. As the visitors watch, they are impressed by the reverence the people have for this part of the proceedings.

They have also noticed a particular shape which is used in lots of different ways. It is a simple right-angled cross with a lengthened stem. There's a silver cross ornament on the table and carved crosses on the ends of the people's wooden benches. Even the building itself seems to have been designed on a cross-shaped ground-plan.

The last song is a stirring march:

At the name of Jesus every knee shall bow,
Every tongue confess Him King of glory now;
'Tis the Father's pleasure we should call Him Lord
Who from the beginning was the mighty Word.

The visitors are now bursting with questions. They can hardly wait for the meeting to finish so that they can start finding out the answers.

● Who was Jesus?
● Why do people still talk to him, if he died so long ago?
● Why is he remembered here, so far from Jerusalem?
● What is the special book?
● Why did the people share bread and wine?
● Why is the cross-shape such a prominent feature?
● And that last song – if Jesus is dead, how can he be King now?
● Who is the Father who wants people to call Jesus 'Lord'?
● What does it mean – Jesus was the 'mighty Word', 'from the beginning'?

In asking such questions, the visitors are not merely exploring a building. They are – like you – exploring Christianity.

The Bible and How to Use It

Christianity is a world-wide religion which has its origins in the life and teaching of Jesus of Nazareth, a Jew born in Israel nearly 2,000 years ago.

Within his own lifetime, Jesus came to be seen by some Jews as the special 'anointed one' from God, as promised by their prophets. In the Jewish language (Hebrew), the word for 'anointed one' is *Messiah*; in Greek – the language of the civilized world at that time – it is *Christ*.

So Jesus eventually became known as 'the Christ' and his followers as 'Christians'.

Today's Christians look to their ancient sacred writings for details about the life and teaching of Jesus, and the beliefs and lifestyle of his earliest followers. These writings are a collection of short books which together are known as the 'New Testament'. They form part of the 'Bible', which also contains many older Jewish sacred writings under the title 'Old Testament'.

Check *your* Bible's 'contents' page to find all the 'books' of the Old Testament and the New Testament. It's like a library catalogue – a list of all the many different books available to readers.

Even when you know which book you want to look at, it's useful to be able to go straight to a particular place within that book. Fortunately, there's a **code** for finding your place in any book of the Bible – here's how it works:

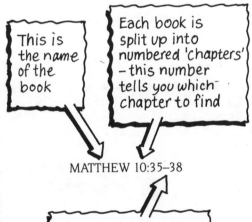

This is the name of the book

Each book is split up into numbered 'chapters' – this number tells you which chapter to find

MATTHEW 10:35–38

Each chapter is split up into numbered 'verses' – two numbers with a dash between means you have to read all the verses from the first number to the second

FACT·FILE

- It was at Antioch in Syria in about AD43 that Jesus' followers were first given the nickname 'Christians' by local people. This soon became the most popular name for believers. The Jewish name for Jesus' followers was 'Nazarenes'. In AD85 this prayer was introduced into Jewish synagogue services: 'May the Nazarenes and the heretics be suddenly destroyed, and removed from the Book of Life.'

- The early Christians themselves sometimes referred to their faith as 'the Way' (see Acts 24:14), and so they were 'followers of the Way'.

Sometimes you're given a reminder of which section of the Bible a book is in, Old Testament or New Testament. For example:

(OT) ISAIAH 9:6–7

Find Isaiah 9:6–7 for a short description of the 'Messiah' or 'Christ' whom the Jews expected to come from God.

Sometimes there is more than one book with the same name. These are identified by the order in which they come – first, second or third – like this:

2 PETER 1:5–7

Find 2 Peter 1:5–7 for a short description of a Christian's character.

So that's *where* it is!

HOLY BIBLE

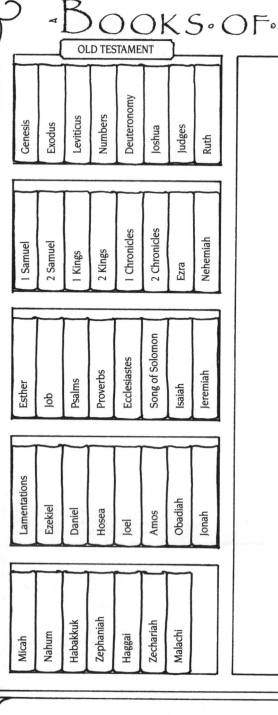

ᴬ BOOKS·OF·

OLD TESTAMENT

Genesis · Exodus · Leviticus · Numbers · Deuteronomy · Joshua · Judges · Ruth

1 Samuel · 2 Samuel · 1 Kings · 2 Kings · 1 Chronicles · 2 Chronicles · Ezra · Nehemiah

Esther · Job · Psalms · Proverbs · Ecclesiastes · Song of Solomon · Isaiah · Jeremiah

Lamentations · Ezekiel · Daniel · Hosea · Joel · Amos · Obadiah · Jonah

Micah · Nahum · Habakkuk · Zephaniah · Haggai · Zechariah · Malachi

THE·BIBLE·

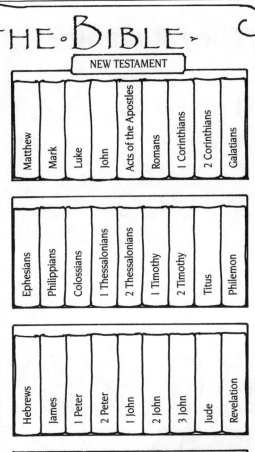

NEW TESTAMENT

Matthew | Mark | Luke | John | Acts of the Apostles | Romans | 1 Corinthians | 2 Corinthians | Galatians

Ephesians | Philippians | Colossians | 1 Thessalonians | 2 Thessalonians | 1 Timothy | 2 Timothy | Titus | Philemon

Hebrews | James | 1 Peter | 2 Peter | 1 John | 2 John | 3 John | Jude | Revelation

Because the beliefs of Christianity are based on what is written in the 'New Testament' books of the Bible, any study of Christianity has to consider three important questions:

● **Are the printed Bibles of today reliable records of what was originally written down?**

● **Were the original writers telling the truth?**

● **Why are there four different versions of the life of Jesus (the Gospels)?**

We shall look at each of these questions in turn in Units 2, 3 and 4.

◆FOLLOW UP◆

1. A quick check on your knowledge! What do you now know about the background to Jesus and Christianity?

Do you know:
● the Hebrew word for 'the Anointed One'?
● the Greek equivalent of this word?
● where the followers of Jesus were first called Christians?
● why Christians were sometimes known as the 'followers of the Way'?
● what the two parts of the Bible are called?

2. As you work through this book it will be useful if you are able to look up Bible references easily and quickly. This activity will help you to find your way around the Bible.
  You will each need a Bible to play this game.

● Find the index in your Bible.
● Write down a list of five references using the 'code' explained in this unit. For example: James 3:14; Zephaniah 2:14.
● Check that your references exist!
● Choose someone to start. They read out their first reference and give the rest of you a 'ready . . ., steady . . ., go!' routine.
● The rest of the group have to race to find the reference – using the index to help.
● The first person to find the reference stands up and reads it out.
● If they are correct it is then their turn to read out a reference.
● Keep a score!

The Gospels: Are They Reliable?

None of the original books of the New Testament is still in existence. Today's printed Bibles are based on *copies* of the originals. So are the Bibles of today reliable? Is the account we have of the life and teaching of Jesus in modern Bibles an accurate record of what actually happened 2,000 years ago?

Knowing whether documents *are* reliable records of historical events is a problem faced by historians all the time. But there is a 'test', and that is to ask these two questions:

- **How many copies are still in existence?**

- **What is the time-gap between the original manuscript and the oldest copy?**

This is how it works . . .

How many copies?

Say you have lots of *copies* of an ancient manuscript which has been lost way back . . . If these copies have turned up in all sorts of different places, and *if* these scattered copies all contain matching material, then it does look as if they all have some sort of 'common ancestor' in their history which contained the original material from which the copies were made.

Choose any two 'copies' from this tree. How far back down the branches do you have to go to find the one 'common ancestor' they were both copied from?

So when there is matching material in a great many copies that is a fair indication that those copies are accurate reproductions of some lost original.

What is the time-gap?

Say you have one copy that is very old, a copy which was made soon after the original manuscript was written. Even though the original is lost *now*, it's quite likely that it wasn't lost when the copy was made.

This means that yours is probably an accurate copy of the original. And even if your very old copy was done *after* the original was lost, there were probably other accurate copies around at the time to copy.

That's how the two-question-test works.

● The more copies you have – even if the original writing is lost – the more likely it is that any matching versions of events recorded in a variety of different copies are all *accurate* copies based on the one original manuscript.
● And the closer your oldest copy is to the date of the lost original, the more likely it is that the events recorded in that copy are the same as those recorded in the lost original.

You've probably heard of Julius Caesar. Most of the 'facts' known about him come from his own writings – war diaries, for example. But *did* he really exist? And *did* he conquer Britain? Look at how flimsy the historical evidence is, compared with the New Testament records of Jesus.

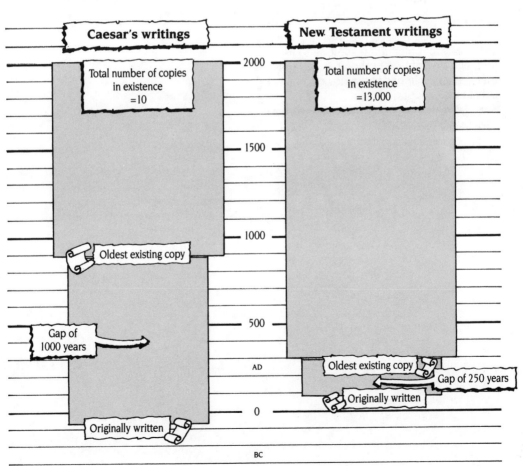

Caesar's writings

Total number of copies in existence =10

Oldest existing copy

Gap of 1000 years

Originally written

New Testament writings

Total number of copies in existence =13,000

Oldest existing copy

Gap of 250 years

Originally written

2000

1500

1000

500

AD

0

BC

Manuscript evidence for the existence of Jesus Christ

Manuscript evidence for the existence of Julius Caesar

FOLLOW UP

What would you say to the character in the first cartoon in this unit who thinks that you can't believe the Bible?
    Work in pairs:
● one of you play the role of the cartoon character,
● the other one explain why you can believe the text of the Gospels
Use the reasons given in this unit.

Now swap roles, so that you can gain confidence in the arguments you are using. Do you think your arguments could convince someone you met at a party?

What do you think? Here's what an eminent historian has said:

'No other ancient book has anything like such early and plentiful testimony to its text, and no unbiased scholar would deny that the text that has come down to us is substantially sound.'

Sir Frederic Kenyon
former Director of the British Museum

The Gospels: Are They True?

It's like that with the Gospels – each one has its own particular 'view' of Jesus, but they all agree on the vital facts.

Honest reporting

You might think the Gospels are bound to be inaccurate because the authors were biased. They were supporters or followers of Jesus, and they wanted others to become followers too. The interesting thing is that they did not 'launder' their writing to get rid of embarrassing bits that show some early followers in a bad light.

There are some examples of this kind of honest reporting in Mark's Gospel 9:33– 34; 10:13–16; 10:35–41; 14:66–72

Were the Bible's original writers telling the truth when they wrote?

The details about Jesus and his teaching are mostly found in the first four books of the New Testament, the Gospels. 'Gospel' is from two old English words *God spel* meaning 'Good News'.

The four Gospels are named after four different authors – Matthew, Mark, Luke and John – and they seem to tell four different versions of the life of Jesus. Can they *all* be telling the truth?

That depends, of course, on what you mean by truth.

Today, if you have four separate newspaper reports of a sports event, the chances are that each will be different. Reporters concentrate on different things – the form of the players, or how the result affects the league table, or the influence of a new coach or manager. But on the *vital* facts, such as who was playing and what the result was, they all have to report the same information.

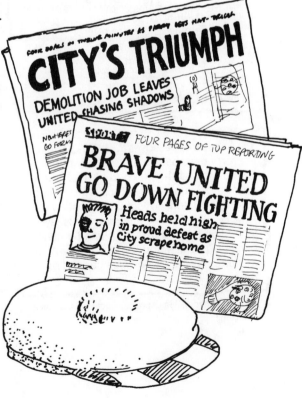

Outside evidence

But the *obvious* thing to do to check whether the Gospels were reporting truthfully, is to look for references to Jesus in other places, outside the Christian documents. This is called 'corroborating evidence'.

For example, the Gospels say that Jesus came into conflict with the Jewish leaders of his day, and with the Roman rulers. Wouldn't you expect *their* writings to mention him? And if Jesus had made such an impact on ordinary people that they thought he was the Messiah/Christ, wouldn't there be evidence of that impact somewhere?

Well . . . yes. So let's look for that evidence, in those three specific areas.

● **Jewish leaders.** First of all, there's a collection of very important Jewish religious writings dating from just after the death of Jesus. It's called the Talmud, and it *does* contain references to Jesus, recording his death on the eve of the Jewish Passover Festival, which ties up exactly with the Gospel accounts.

In the Talmud, there are references to 'Yeshu', the name 'Jesus' as Jews of his own day would have known it:

'Yeshu had five disciples.'

'On the eve of Passover Yeshu was hanged. For forty days before the execution the herald went forth and cried, "He is going forth to be stoned since he has practised sorcery and enticed Israel to apostasy. Anyone who can say anything in his favour, let him come forward and plead on his behalf.' But since nothing was brought forward in his favour he was hanged on the eve of Passover.'

Tractate Sanhedrin 43a ('Apostasy' means abandoning their faith.)

● **Roman rulers.** Then there was a Jew called Josephus who was employed by the Romans to write up a kind of 'diary of events'. He also mentions Jesus 'the Christ' who rose from death.

In writing his *Jewish War* (AD75–79) and *Antiquities of the Jews* (AD90), Josephus wanted to re-establish Jewish credit with the Romans. He obviously felt the need to make some reference to Jesus' place in Jewish affairs, for he includes quite a long paragraph about him:

'And there arose about this time Jesus, a wise man, if it is right to call him a man, for he was a doer of marvellous deeds, a teacher of men who receive the truth with pleasure. He won over many Jews and also many Greeks. He was the Christ. And when Pilate had condemned him to the cross at the instigation of our own leaders, those who had loved him from the first did not forsake him. For he appeared to them alive again on the third day, as the holy prophets had foretold, and said many other wonderful things about him. And the race of Christians, so named from him, has not died out at this day.'

Antiquities 18.3.3

This corroborating evidence in reports from the 'opposition' seems to prove at least that Jesus *existed*, and that he was involved in some sort of religious movement that attracted followers.

● **Ordinary people.** But what about the claim that Jesus' life and teaching was 'Good News', that his coming marked the arrival of the Messiah/Christ? The impact that Jesus had on ordinary people – not just the Gospel-writers and not just the opposition – can clearly be seen in *exactly* the same way that the views of ordinary people are seen today . . . in their

GRAFFITI!

When you were little, did you write 'secret signs' that only your 'gang' could understand?

Archaeologists have found two secret signs from the early days of Christianity, when to be a believer could cost you your life.

This one is a combination of two Greek letters, CHI and RHO.

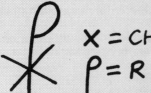

X = CH
P = R

CHR . . . short for 'Christ'

Do you know what an acrostic is? Here is a modern acrostic poem – the first letter of each line spells a word, and that's the title of the poem.

S *now melts, to reveal*
P *rimroses like lights in the hedgerows.*
R *iotous bulbs follow*
I *n a blaze of paint-box colours.*
N *o more drab days of black and white;*
G *one is the monochrome of winter.*

Here's an acrostic secret sign used by the early Christians.

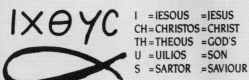

I = IESOUS   = JESUS
CH = CHRISTOS = CHRIST
TH = THEOUS   = GOD'S
U = UILIOS   = SON
S = SARTOR   = SAVIOUR

It's the Greek word for fish and, if you write it downwards, the letters stand for other (secret) words. But, to be really subtle, the Christians would often just draw the fish and leave it at that. Other Christians would know the hidden meaning.

Do you like word puzzles? The first Christians certainly did, and there was one particularly clever one that has been spotted in lots of places.

R O T A S
O P E R A
T E N E T
A R E P O
S A T O R

Do you see how the words repeat across the square in a pattern? It looks clever enough, but it doesn't mean anything wonderful. It's in Latin, and it seems to say 'Arepo the Sower holds the wheels with care.' But on closer investigation, it turns out to be an anagram of two Latin words and two Greek letters:

'Pater Noster' is the Latin for 'Our Father', the opening of a very famous prayer first used and taught by Jesus. A and O are the first and last letters of the Greek alphabet, symbols of Jesus as the beginning and end of everything.

One place where this puzzle was found was Pompeii, the Italian city destroyed under tons of volcanic lava in AD79. The impact of Jesus had obviously reached there *before* the disaster.

So it seems that the 'biased' Gospel-writers wrote the 'truth', in that Jesus was a real person known to the Jews and the Romans, a person whose life and teaching influenced ordinary people who didn't write Gospels but who did write on walls!

▲FOLLOW UP▲

1. Can you complete the following words to make a list of the sources of information which we have about Jesus?

G _ _ _ _ _ : one of the four accounts of the good news of Jesus.

_ _ _ M _ _ : Jewish religious writings.

_ _ _ _ P _ _ _ : a Jewish historian employed by the Romans.

I _ _ _ _ _ _ : the secret sign of the early Christians.

2. You can work through this exercise in groups of four.

Buy a copy of four different newspapers which all contain the same story. Cut out the accounts of that story and paste them onto a large sheet of paper, so that you can work easily.

Work through each account and list:
● the main facts each newspaper includes
● the main difference in each account from the others
● what has been added by each journalist to make a particular point
● how you can tell which newspaper each account comes from (what are the characteristics of that newspaper?).

Now complete the same exercise using the four passages from the Gospels below:
● Matthew 3:13–17.
● Mark 1:9–11.
● Luke 3:21–22.
● John 1:32–34.

The Gospels: Why Are There Four?

Why are there four different versions of the life of Jesus? The four Gospels are not 'life-stories' in the way that we have biographies of famous or interesting people today. In fact, the main bulk of the material in the Gospels is about the last three years of Jesus' life.

Two Gospels – Matthew and Luke – have some information about Jesus' birth, and Luke also includes an incident about Jesus as a twelve-year-old, but there's no information anywhere about the rest of his childhood or his years as a carpenter.

The Gospels are mainly about Jesus' time as a travelling preacher. Much of the material is about his arrest, trials and execution.

Because the Gospel-writers were so concerned with the teaching and death of Jesus, it seems that they weren't writing 'life-story' books, but books which would present a special 'view' of Jesus:
● a view which sees his years of teaching and his death as more significant than the details of his life in general;
● a view which portrays the 'Good News' that these writers believed Jesus brought.

Sometimes, the Gospels seem to contradict each other. This is because the writers weren't writing strict biographies, so they selected appropriate stories from those that had been remembered, then each writer arranged them in what *he* thought was a good order. The order wasn't always in time sequence like a diary. Sometimes, the stories were linked together by a 'theme' – like when you and your friends talk about all the different incidents you can remember that have something to do with, say, holidays or sports events.

Three that are alike

Sometimes, the Gospels are *so* alike, it seems that someone was copying someone else's work. (Sounds familiar?) This is particularly the case with Matthew, Mark and Luke. In fact, if you put these three Gospels through a computer, their contents look like this:

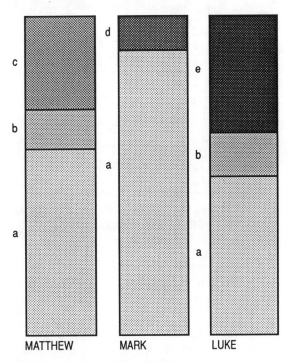

Have a close look at the similarities in the three documents.

● They all have a *lot* of identical material (a).

● Matthew and Luke both have some 'shared' material that's not in Mark (b).
● And then each of them has some material which is not found in the other Gospels at all (c), (d), (e).

If three friends handed in homework with this much 'copying', there'd be trouble!

Matthew Smith 4C
I liked the poem because it was about happy times.
The poet uses a lot of figurative language to get his point across, particularly when he talks about how the butterfly actually looks to him –

Mark Taylor 4C
This poem is very effective.
The poet uses a lot of figurative language to get his message across, particularly when he talks about how the butterfly actually looks to him

Luke Jones 4C
I thought this poem was easy to understand. The poet uses a lot of figurative language to get his message across, particularly when he talks about how the butterfly actually looks to him

But 2,000 years ago, copying, editing and using other people's work was normal practice.

Bible experts believe that Mark's Gospel was written first, then Matthew and Luke each used bits of it (a) when they came to write theirs. They must have used bits of something else, too (b), that Mark hadn't used earlier. It looks as if they had access to some source that has disappeared over the years – often referred to as 'Q' (Quelle = 'source' in German).

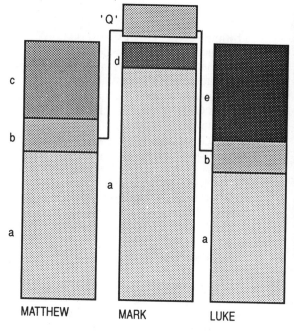

MATTHEW   MARK   LUKE

Because you can see all these shared similarities in Matthew, Mark and Luke, they are called the 'Synoptic' Gospels ('synoptic' = 'seen together').

MATTHEW 16:24–26
Then Jesus said to his disciples, 'If anyone wants to come with me, he must forget self, carry his cross, and follow me. For whoever wants to save his own life will lose it; but whoever loses his life for my sake will find it. Will a person gain anything if he wins the whole world but loses his life? Of course not! There is nothing he can give to regain his life.'

MARK 8:34–36
Then Jesus called the crowd and his disciples to him. 'If anyone wants to come with he,' he told them, 'he must forget self, carry his cross, and follow me. For whoever wants to save his own life will lose it; but whoever loses his life for me and for the gospel will save it. Does a person gain anything if he wins the whole world but loses his life? Of course not!'

LUKE 9:23–25
And he said to them all, 'If anyone wants to come with me, he must forget self, take up his cross every day, and follow me. For whoever wants to save his own life will lose it, but whoever loses his life for my sake will save it. Will a person gain anything if he wins the whole world but is himself lost or defeated? Of course not!'

The problem of explaining how they come to have so much matching material is usually called the 'Synoptic Problem'.

One that is different

John's Gospel is different from the Synoptic Gospels. He does not have any 'copied' material from Mark or from Q, and he leaves out many of the stories found in the Synoptics.

This is because John was not concerned just with recording selected events and sayings from the life of Jesus. John has arranged his chosen events and sayings to show that they revealed some deeper 'truth' about who Jesus really was.

For example, John includes the miracle of a blind man receiving his sight, to show how Christians came to understand the deeper 'truth' that Jesus was the 'light of the world'.

Because of this deep-thinking approach, Bible experts think that John's Gospel may well have been written many years after the Synoptics.

◤FOLLOW☝UP◥

1. Here is a quick revision exercise. You may need to look back at Units 1–4 for one or two of these words.
Write clues for each of the words in this crossword:

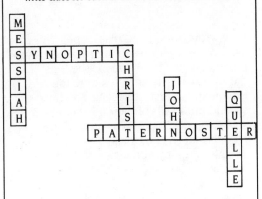

2. Why do Bible experts believe that Mark's Gospel was the first one to be written?

3. Why isn't John's Gospel thought of as one of the Synoptic Gospels?

4.

> I THINK THE GOSPELS WERE WRITTEN BY A GROUP OF PEOPLE WHO MADE UP A FAIRY STORY ABOUT A CHARACTER CALLED JESUS
>
> Susan White

In pairs discuss what you would say to convince Susan that she is wrong.

Other Christian Writings

– AND A SUGGESTED ORDER OF EVENTS

Luke wrote a sequel to his Gospel. The story of Jesus carries on after he died and rose again, in a book called 'The Acts of the Apostles'. The apostles were the leaders of the first Christians, and Luke's second book tells of their adventures in spreading the Good News around the Mediterranean countries.

Acts is mostly about two of these apostles – Peter and Paul. Peter was one of Jesus' original followers, but Paul was an important Jew who opposed the Christians. He was converted to Christianity after a dramatic encounter with Jesus on the road between Jerusalem and Damascus, some time after Jesus' death and resurrection. (See Unit 18.)

Paul may have used a pen and inkpot like this Roman one, when he wrote his letters to churches.

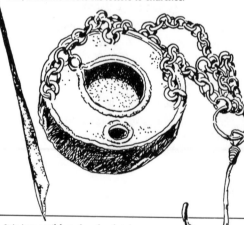

Paul spent most of the rest of his life travelling widely, preaching the Good News about Jesus and setting up groups of new believers in each town he visited, until he was put under house arrest by the Romans. While he was travelling, he kept in touch with these groups, or 'churches', by writing them letters, and it is Paul's letters which make up most of the rest of the New Testament after the Gospels and Acts.

There are other letters, too. Peter wrote two (although some experts think the second might have been written by one of his followers, rather than by the apostle himself), and the apostles James, John and Jude wrote the others. There is a letter to some Jews or 'Hebrews', which doesn't have the author's name.

At the end of the New Testament is 'The Revelation'. It describes a series of strange and wonderful visions experienced by John (the apostle or another John, as many scholars believe) and shows God as Lord of history, picturing his final judgment and the new heaven and earth.

The four Gospels and Acts, the twenty-one letters and Revelation, were collected together and officially listed as 'Scripture' (i.e. holy writings) in the fourth century AD. Some rather fanciful 'gospels' were left off the list because they seemed to contain unlikely legends about Jesus, and some letters had been lost, so they couldn't be included.

It is impossible to be absolutely specific about the timing of New Testament events and the dates of the writings. In particular, Bible experts differ in their opinions about the dating of the Synoptic Gospels. Some would date Mark near AD65, Luke at AD80–85 and Matthew at AD85–90. But others go for earlier dates all round – Mark just after AD60, Luke AD60–70 and Matthew just after AD70. This earlier dating is based on the relationship between the Gospels and the fall of Jerusalem in AD70. Some scholars believe that Mark and Luke were written before the actual event, and any apparent reference to Jerusalem's destruction by these writers is therefore to be seen as a prophetic foretelling of a future event (see Mark 13:14; Luke 21:20).

The Christian Documents – a suggested chronology

When various documents were written	Year	When various events took place
	5	Birth of Jesus of Nazareth (Matthew 1:18, etc., Luke 2:1, etc.)
	4BC	Death of Herod the Great (Matthew 2:19)
	7AD	Jesus talks with the teachers in the Jerusalem Temple (Luke 2:41–51)
	27	Jesus begins his travelling ministry – preaching, teaching, healing, miracles (Matthew 4:12; Mark 1:14; Luke 4:14; John 1:35)
	30	Death, resurrection and ascension of Jesus (Matthew 26:47–28:10; Mark 14:43–16:8; Luke 22:47–24:51; John 18:12–21:25; Acts 1:6–9)
		Holy Spirit comes to the disciples during the Jewish Feast of Pentecost (Acts 2:1–42)
	33	Conversion of Paul (formerly Saul of Tarsus) (Acts 9:1–19)
	44	Death of Herod Agrippa I (Acts 12:20–23)
	47–48	Paul's 1st missionary journey (Acts 13, 14)
Paul writes to the Galatians	48–49	
	49	Council of Jerusalem meets (Acts 15)
	49–52	Paul's 2nd missionary journey (Acts 16:11–18:22)
Paul writes to the Thessalonians (1 & 2)	50–51	
	52–56	Paul's 3rd missionary journey (Acts 18:23–21:17)
Paul writes to the Corinthians (1 & 2)	54–55	
Paul writes to the Romans	56	
	57	Paul is arrested in Jerusalem (Acts 21:27–23:30)
	57–59	Paul is imprisoned at Caesarea (Acts 23:31–26:32)
	60–61	Paul is kept under house-arrest in Rome (Acts 28:14–31)
Letter to the Hebrews (author unknown)	60–63	
Paul writes to the Ephesians, Philippians, Colossians & Philemon	61–63	
James writes a general letter	PRE 62	
	62–64	Paul is free from imprisonment
Peter writes a letter (1) to the Christians in Rome	64	The fire of Rome – Nero blames the Christians and persecutes them
Paul writes letters to Timothy (1 & 2) and to Titus	65	Death of Paul
Mark writes his Gospel	70	Jerusalem destroyed by the Romans
Jude writes a general letter	70–80	
	81–96	Widespread persecution under the Roman Emperor Domitian
Matthew writes his Gospel	85	
Luke writes his two-part book, Gospel-plus-Acts		
John writes his Gospel and three general letters (1, 2 & 3)	90	
John sees and records his 'Revelation' visions	96	
	100	Death of the apostle John
An unknown author writes a letter which is given the name of Peter (2)	150	

The order of the books within the New Testament collection – Gospels, Acts, Paul's letters, other letters, Revelation – is useful in a way. But it hides the fact that many of the letters were written before the Gospels, and that Mark's Gospel was probably written before the other three.

It isn't always possible to be precise about the actual dates when the New Testament documents were written, or about the actual dates of the various events mentioned in the documents.

However, *some* dates are known, and where Bible experts are uncertain about dates, they only differ from one another by a year or two.

FACT·FILE

The 'Canon'

The 'New Testament Canon' is the list of 27 Christian books which came to be accepted as authoritative in matters of Christian faith and life. 'Canon' comes from an old word for 'reed' or 'cane', meaning measuring-rod.

The process of selection was largely informal and took place over many years. Sayings of Jesus and stories about him were treasured, copied and circulated from earliest times, as were letters written by the first apostles/church leaders. It was not until AD367 that, out of all the many documents in circulation, the present 27 books of the New Testament were defined as authoritative. The 'canon' or 'rule' of measurement was made on the basis

- that a book was regularly read in church
- and that a book was believed to have had its origins in apostolic circles.

The 27 books of today's New Testament are those which, by the fourth century, had been identified as measuring up to these criteria and therefore could be taken as 'inspired' scriptures.

FOLLOW UP

We have mentioned briefly several books of the Bible in this unit. You probably have not enough time to read all of them now – but you could read the following selected passages:

- Acts 2:42–3:10. The early church in action!
- 1 Corinthians 16:5–24. The end of Paul's first letter to the Corinthian church.
- Hebrews chapter 11. An account of the faith of some of the characters in the Old Testament.
- James 3:1–12. Some practical instructions from James about taming the tongue . . .
- 3 John (all of it). A letter to Gaius.
- Jude 24, 25. You may have heard these verses being used as a benediction in a church service.
- Revelation chapter 21. A description of the writer's vision of heaven.

As you find each reference, check when the book was written and what was happening at that time. For example, AD70 is a very important date – Jerusalem was destroyed by the Romans and both Jews and Christians had to spread out across the Roman Empire.

Jesus: His Life and Teaching

The man known today as Jesus of Nazareth, or Jesus (the) Christ, made such a mark on history that the modern western calendar is calculated from the time of his birth.

1992 = One thousand, nine hundred and ninety-two years after the birth of Jesus. Traditionally, dates have been written as so many years before the birth of Christ – 'BC' – or so many years after the birth of Christ – 'AD' (Anno Domini = 'in the year of our Lord' in Latin).

The calculation of the date of Jesus' birth was made by a Christian monk called Dionysius about 500 years after Jesus died. Modern scholars believe he was about five or six years out, and they prefer to date the birth of Jesus at about 5BC.

Jesus' life

Details of Jesus' life are recorded or can be deduced from the four Gospels written about him. Here is a brief summary:

● Jesus' (assumed) father Joseph (a carpenter) and his mother Mary were devout Jews who, after a series of visions and dreams, were convinced that God had told them Mary would have a son (not Joseph's, but God's) who would be the Jews' expected Messiah and Saviour. (Matthew 1:18–25; Luke 1:26–38.)

● Joseph and Mary lived in Nazareth, in the north of the country known today as Israel, but at the time the baby was born they were in the family's ancestral home-town of Bethlehem, where they had gone to register during a Roman census. Because of the influx of visitors for this census, there was no room for them at the inn and the baby was born in a cave or building shared with the animals. (Luke 2:1–17.)

● Some time after the birth, the family fled to Egypt to save the baby's life. Herod, king of the Jews, had heard of this infant 'king' and was bent on murder. (Matthew 2:1–7.)

● After returning to Nazareth, it is assumed they lived a normal Jewish family life. The only incident recorded is the family visit to Jerusalem when Jesus was twelve – possibly on the occasion of his 'bar mitzvah' (growing-up ceremony). The account shows that he was already aware of his special relationship with God. (Luke 2:41–50.)

● Jesus had a cousin called John who was just six months older than himself. Like Jesus, John was marked out from birth as a man with a mission. In about AD27 John became a preacher. He warned people to repent and renew their commitment to God because his Messiah was coming soon. John baptized people ▶▶

▶▶ in the River Jordan as a sign that they were made clean, ready to start a new way of life – so he was known as 'the Baptist'. (Mark 1:1–8.)

Jesus went to be baptized by John, although he had no need to 'repent'. At his baptism the voice of God was heard calling Jesus 'my own dear Son'. Jesus spent the next six weeks in the desert facing a series of temptations to disobey God and abuse the special powers he had been given. (Matthew 3:13–17; Mark 1:9–11; Luke 3:21–22; Matthew 4:1– 11; Mark 1:12–13; Luke 4:1–13.)

● Jesus came out of the desert filled with the power of God's Holy Spirit and he began a three-year ministry of teaching, healing and working miracles. From the many followers he attracted, he chose twelve close 'disciples' who went with him on his journeys. (Luke 4:14–15; Matthew 10:1–4; Mark 3:13–19; Luke 6:12– 16.)

● Much of what Jesus said and did challenged the accepted Jewish teaching of his day, and he frequently found himself at odds with the Jewish authorities in Jerusalem. This conflict led to his arrest, trials and execution by Roman crucifixion in about AD30. (Matthew 27; Mark 15; Luke23; John 18:28–19.42.)

● His body was placed in a cave-tomb which was sealed with a large stone. Three days later, the stone was found to have been rolled back from the entrance and the body was missing. That day and during the

next six weeks, his disciples and many followers claimed that Jesus was alive – they had seen him, talked to him and even shared meals with him. (Mark 16:9; Luke 24:13–49; John 21:1–24.)

● Jesus told his disciples that they would soon receive God's power for themselves by being baptized with the Holy Spirit. After making this promise, he 'was taken up to heaven as they watched him, and a cloud hid him from their sight'. A few days later, at the start of the Jewish festival of Pentecost, the disciples and many of their friends were filled with the Holy Spirit and began preaching with great boldness and also healing and working miracles, just as Jesus had done. (Acts 1:6–11; 2:1–4; 3:1–10.)

Jesus' teaching

The teaching of Jesus can be summarized under five main headings:
● teaching about the Fatherhood of God
● teaching about the Kingdom of God
● teaching on living according to God's standards
● teaching about his own true identity
● teaching about his mission

● **The Fatherhood of God.** In Jesus' day, Jews would refer to God as 'Father' meaning 'father of the Jewish nation'. But an individual Jew would not call God *his* 'Father': this would be regarded as over-familiar, possibly even blasphemous.

Jesus, however, stressed the idea of God being each person's loving Father. He referred to God as his own Father (Matthew

11:25–27; Mark 14:36; Luke 22:29; John 5:17–19). He also encouraged others to think of God as their 'Father in heaven' (Matthew 6:26; Mark 11:25; Luke 11:2; John 14:21).

● **The Kingdom of God.** In Jesus' day, many Jews were expecting God to send his Messiah to make the Jewish nation into a great kingdom, just as it had been under King David way back in their history.

When Jesus began preaching, he claimed: 'The right time has come, and the Kingdom of God is near!' (Mark 1:15). When Jesus spoke of the Kingdom of God, he meant the rule of God in human lives, not a political kingdom (Matthew 6:33; Mark 10:15; Luke 17:20–21; John 18:36).

Jesus also taught that although the Kingdom had arrived in one sense when his own public work began, the Kingdom was also to come in a more complete sense with his return to earth as King. (Matthew 25:31–34).

● **Living according to God's standards.** Perhaps the best-known teaching of Jesus is his instructions for living – his 'ethical' teaching. Much of this is contained in a collection of sayings usually called the Sermon on the Mount (Matthew 5–7). It is often summarized as 'do unto others as you would have them do to you' – because many of the sayings are about personal relationships and our behaviour to one another. Here are two examples:

The Sermon on the Mount

After announcing the arrival of the Kingdom and calling people to repent of their bad old ways in order to enter the Kingdom, Jesus went on to teach about how life was to be lived in the Kingdom. The summary of this teaching – which was probably given on a number of occasions and in a number of places – is recorded in Matthew chapters 5–7 as the Sermon on the Mount.

● People living in the Kingdom have distinctive attitudes and ways of behaving which make them different from people in the world outside. Because they live under God's fatherly rule, they are truly happy – as described in the 'beatitudes' of Matthew 5:3–12 (from the Latin beati = happy), and their influence is felt (like light and salt) in the world around them (5:13–16).

● The new way of living in the Kingdom does not do away with the old Law of Moses, but concentrates on the inner truth behind the original commandments (5:17–20).

● The new way of living in the Kingdom is seen in people's thoughts as well as their actions (5:21–48), in their religious activities (6:1–18), in their trusting dependence on God the Father (6:19–34), and in their relationships with others (7:1–12).

● The new way of living in the Kingdom challenges people to build their lives on doing God's will rather than travelling the way of the world (7:13–27).

But there's more to Jesus' ethic than a mutual back-scratching kind of morality. Jesus stressed that people's attitude to others is bound up with their attitude to God:

'When someone asks you for something, give it to him; when someone wants to borrow something, lend it to him.'
Matthew 5:42.

'Do not judge others, so that God will not judge you.'
Matthew 7:1

'Love the Lord your God with all your heart, with all your soul, and with all your mind.' This is the greatest and most important commandment. The second is important commandment. The second is like it: 'Love your neighbour as you love yourself.' The whole Law of Moses and the teachings of the prophets depend on these two commandments.
Matthew 22:37–40. (See also Mark 12:29–31; Luke 10:27; OT Deuteronomy 6:4–5.)

Jesus taught that people's behaviour should be governed by their whole-hearted concentration on doing what God wants them to do (Matthew 7:21). And much of the Sermon on the Mount teaching is about the importance of motives rather than actions.

Jesus does not merely provide a code of good behaviour. His teaching about how to live is an integral part of his proclamation that 'the Kingdom of God is near!' (Matthew 4:17; Mark 1:15). Those people who *want* to welcome the rule of God over every aspect of their life *will* turn from their bad old ways (i.e. repent) and centre their efforts on God and loving other people. This is how God's Kingdom comes.

● **Jesus' true identity.** Even at the age of twelve, Jesus was aware of a special Father/Son relationship between himself and God (Luke 2:42–52). When people were speculating about his true identity, he made the fact of his 'sonship' plain by accepting with approval Peter's response: 'You are the Messiah, the Son of the living God!' (Matthew 16:16).

But Jesus went further than this. When arguing with his opponents he claimed that he had had his special relationship with God from before the time of Abraham, the originator of the Jewish race (John 8:42 and 58).

And when some of his followers worshipped him as if he were God, Jesus accepted it (John 9:35–38; 20:28–29).

In reinterpreting the Jewish law (Matthew 5:21–22) and claiming to have the right to forgive sins (Mark 2:9–11), Jesus was assuming for himself the authority of God.

● **Jesus' mission.** It is clear from many things that Jesus said that he had a purpose in all he did – but this was not simply to promote a moral code.
– Jesus said he came to preach 'the Good News of the Kingdom' (Luke 4:43).
– Jesus said he came to call outcasts, not respectable people (Matthew 9:13).
– Jesus said he came 'to seek and to save the lost' (Luke 19:10).
– Jesus said he came to serve others and to give his life 'to redeem many people' (Mark 10:45).
– Jesus said he was sent by 'the Father' (John 20:21).
– Praying to God, shortly before his death, Jesus said that he had finished the work God gave him to do (John 17:3– 4).
– Jesus predicted that he would die and rise from death 'so that everyone who believes in him may have eternal life' (Matthew 16:21; Mark 10:33–34; John 2:19–22).
– Jesus said he would return as Judge of the world (Matthew 25:31–46).

To look at the Jesus of the Gospels and see only a teacher whose purpose on earth was to promote a moral code is to disregard what Jesus said himself about who he was and why he came.

In the units that follow we shall look at Jesus as the Messiah, at one of his teaching methods, the conflict with the authorities – and his trials, death and resurrection.

Mad, bad – or God!

The well-known Christian writer C.S. Lewis said this:

'A man who was merely a man and said the sort of things Jesus said would not be a great moral teacher. He would either be a lunatic – on a level with the man who says he is a poached egg – or else he would be the Devil of Hell. You must make your choice. Either this man was, and is, the Son of God: or else a madman or something worse. You can shut Him up for a fool, you can spit at Him and kill Him as a demon; or you can fall at His feet and call Him Lord and God. But let us not come with any patronising nonsense about His being a great human teacher. He has not left that open to us. He did not intend to.'
Mere Christianity

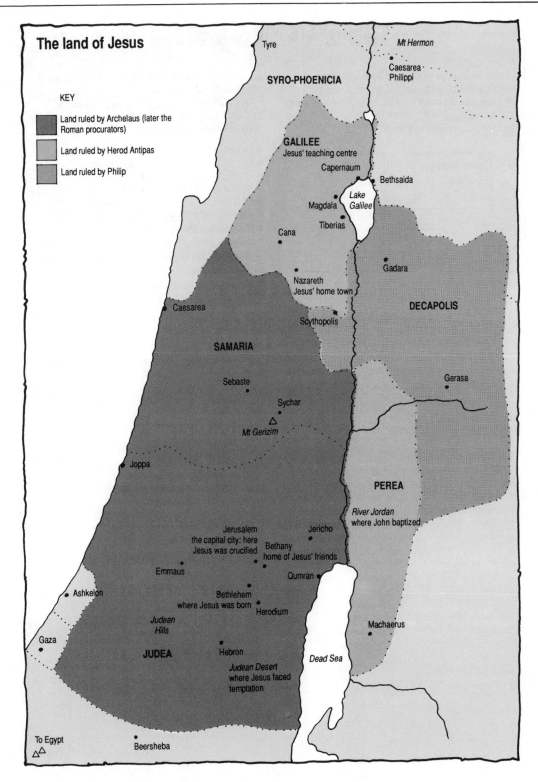

The land of Jesus

KEY

- Land ruled by Archelaus (later the Roman procurators)
- Land ruled by Herod Antipas
- Land ruled by Philip

Tyre

Mt Hermon

SYRO-PHOENICIA

Caesarea Philippi

GALILEE
Jesus' teaching centre

Capernaum

Bethsaida

Magdala

Lake Galilee

Tiberias

Cana

Gadara

Nazareth
Jesus' home town

DECAPOLIS

Caesarea

Scythopolis

SAMARIA

Sebaste

Gerasa

Sychar

Mt Gerizim

Joppa

PEREA

River Jordan
where John baptized

Jerusalem
the capital city: here
Jesus was crucified

Jericho

Bethany
home of Jesus' friends

Emmaus

Qumran

Ashkelon

Bethlehem
where Jesus was born

Herodium

Judean Hills

Machaerus

Gaza

Hebron

Dead Sea

JUDEA

Judean Desert
where Jesus faced
temptation

To Egypt

Beersheba

▲FOLLOW✦UP▲

1. Look back at the teaching of Jesus in this unit. Complete the following chart by writing a summary of not more than 20 words for each circle. (You may want to write individual words rather than sentences – these can then act as a reminder for you.)

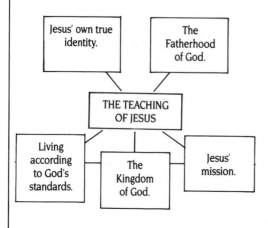

Jesus' own true identity.

The Fatherhood of God.

THE TEACHING OF JESUS

Living according to God's standards.

The Kingdom of God.

Jesus' mission.

2. Do you know what connection the following words have with the life of Jesus?

For each word write a simple sentence which explains its significance in the life of Jesus. For example: 'MARY was the mother of Jesus.'

- Dionysius.
- Mary.
- Joseph.
- Bethlehem.
- Nazareth.
- Bar mitzvah.
- John the Baptist.

- Baptism.
- Temptations.
- Conflict.
- Crucifixion.
- Cave-tomb.
- Pentecost.
- Miracles.

3. Read through the section in this Unit called 'Mad, bad – or God!'

Conduct a group survey to find out which of those three descriptions most people think fit Jesus.

Try to get the people you ask to give you reasons for that answer.

4. Look back at the Unit. Are there any reasons there which support the belief of Jesus himself – that he was God?

The Messiah

CLUES IN MARK'S GOSPEL – 1

Mark's plan

How do you write an essay? Do you always have a beginning, a middle and an end? Do you start by saying what you are going to say, then say it and then conclude by going over what you have said? Perhaps your teachers insist that you have a plan so you can tick everything off as you write and then make sure you don't miss anything out. If you have a lot to write (and that doesn't happen very often!) you can get so carried away that you miss out something very important.

Here is a plan for an English essay about the novel *Kes* by Barry Hines:

> KES
>
> BEGINNING
> • Who or what is this book about?
> • Where is the story set?
>
> MIDDLE
> • Explain how the story is told and explain why it is told from that particular point of view.
> • Describe some of the areas of conflict in the story.
> • Say which part made you feel the most angry, or sad.
> • Say which part made you feel the most satisfied, or happy.
>
> END
> • Say whether or not you think KES is a story with a 'lesson' to it, and give your reasons.
> • Did you enjoy the book?

Mark had a plan when he started writing an account of the life of Jesus. He had a beginning, a middle and an end. Surprisingly, his beginning isn't the birth of Jesus but the arrival of a wild character called John the Baptist. This is the plan he used:

> MARK'S GOSPEL
>
> BEGINNING
> • The story begins: Jesus' baptism.
> • The action continues: Jesus' miracles in Galilee.
>
> MIDDLE
> • The great truth revealed (Jesus' transfiguration).
> • The true meaning of Messiahship (Jesus' teaching to his disciples on the way to Jerusalem).
>
> END
> • The great grief (Jesus' crucifixion).
> • The great victory (Jesus' resurrection).

Let's look at Mark's introduction – how he begins his Gospel.

> 'This is the Good News about Jesus Christ, the Son of God. It began as the prophet Isaiah had written:
> 'God said, "I will send my messenger ahead of you to clear the way for you."
> Someone is shouting in the desert,
> "Get the road ready for the Lord;
> make a straight path for him to travel."'
> So John appeared in the desert, baptizing and preaching. 'Turn away from your sins and be baptized,' he told the people, 'and God will forgive your sins.'
> Mark 1:1–4

It seems an odd way to start a book about Jesus – there's no mention of him until verse 9. But what we do find in those first four verses are some very important clues to the kind of person this Jesus is going to be. Here they are:

Jesus is called the 'Christ' – which is a title not a surname like Johnson or Courtie (verse 1).

He is also called the 'Son of God' – not what ordinary people were called (verse 1)!

The bit from Isaiah is like a piece of recurring theme music for a character called the Messiah – a sort of biblical equivalent of the theme for the Pink Panther! This Messiah theme crops up in many Old Testament prophecies (verses 2 and 3).

This Messiah will have a messenger to tell people he is coming (verse 4).

So what do these clues tell us? Who was this Messiah?

Let's sort out the easy bits first. The second point is OK – the writer tells us straight away that Jesus is the Son of God – not an ordinary person.

The first point is easy too – as we've seen in Unit 1, the title 'Christ' is the English equivalent of the Greek word *Christos*, meaning the same as the Hebrew word 'Messiah'. (Now you know some Greek and some Hebrew!)

What we have is a character usually called the Messiah, who was known about in advance by Old Testament prophets like Isaiah, and whose arrival was to be announced by a messenger.

The word 'Messiah' means 'the anointed one'. In Old Testament times, kings and high priests were anointed with oil to show that they were chosen by God for their jobs. This is the account of the anointing of King David:

'Samuel took the olive oil and anointed David in front of his brothers. Immediately the Spirit of the Lord took control of David and was with him from that day on.'
I Samuel 16:13

When David was king everything went very well for the Jews. They seemed to be the most important nation in the world! But by the time Jesus was born they were just a part of the Roman Empire – and not even a very important part at that. So they tended to look back to the days of King David as a golden age when everything was wonderful (in much the same way as grandparents tend to talk about their childhood – they leave out all the bad bits!). If only they could have another king like David everything would be wonderful again – particularly if this time the king, the anointed one, could get rid of the Romans!

In the Jewish scriptures there were lots of descriptions of what the anointed one, the Messiah, would be like. So when Mark began his Gospel with one of these well-known Messiah 'tunes', any Jewish readers would realize that Mark is saying: 'Jesus is the promised Messiah' – especially as John the Baptist acts as the messenger preparing the way for Jesus. Mark's readers would now be looking for more clues – and some evidence – that Jesus really *is* the Messiah.

Jesus' baptism

Mark's next clues come in chapter 1, verses 9–11. This is an account of the baptism of Jesus. There are two clues here.

'Jesus saw heaven opening and the Spirit coming down on him like a dove.'

Think back to the anointing of David. When Samuel poured oil on him the Spirit of the Lord took control of him. Mark is showing again that Jesus is the Messiah – the anointed one who, like David, has received the power of the Holy Spirit for his work.

'... a voice came from heaven, "You are my own dear Son, I am pleased with you."'

This is not quite such an easy clue. Obviously, to be called the 'Son of God' was very special but it had a particular meaning which the Jewish readers would have spotted. It was actually a quotation from Psalm 2 – a worship song which may have been used when kings were anointed at their coronation:

'He said to me: "You are my son; today I have become your father . . ."'
Psalm 2:7

Keep your Bible open at that psalm.

When the Jews heard these words at the baptism of Jesus some of them would have become very excited, because in Psalm 2 God promises to help the king:

'Ask, and I will give you all the nations . . .'
verse 8

Ruler of all the nations! Maybe Jesus, who appeared to be the Anointed One, would actually get rid of the Romans!

Miracles in Galilee

We've seen that Mark presents the main character of his story as 'Son of God' and 'anointed' by the Spirit of God.

So what would the Jews be looking for next? Certainly someone who would set them free from the Romans. But also someone who could do special things. One of the prophecies about the Messiah says this:

'The Sovereign Lord has filled me with his spirit.
He has chosen me and sent me to bring good news to the poor,
To heal the broken-hearted,
To announce release to captives
And freedom to those in prison.'
Isaiah 61:1

They would be looking for someone who was kind and good to everyone and who could also do magic. And of course the bit they'd really be interested in would be the 'magic' – or miracles.

In the musical *Jesus Christ Superstar* Jesus is sent to Herod. Herod is very excited to meet Jesus because he wants to see the miracles – to see exactly what this Messiah, or Christ, can do: 'Prove to me that you're divine – change this water into wine.'

In *Jesus Christ Superstar* King Herod challenges Jesus to prove his claims: 'Walk across my swimming-pool.'

And yes – Mark's account shows Jesus doing lots of miracles.

Have your Bible open at Mark chapter 1 and check the following events:
● After his baptism Jesus goes away into the desert where he is tempted to do the kind of things that Herod asks him to do in that song (verses 12, 13).
● Next he starts to gather a group of people who become known as his disciples (verses 16–20).

Then he starts to do miracles:
● He heals a man possessed by an evil spirit (verses 21–28).
● He heals Peter's mother-in-law (verses 30, 31).
● He heals many people (verses 32–34).
● He heals a man with a terrible skin disease (verses 40–45).

And that is only in chapter 1!

If you look at the section headings in the next few chapters of the Gospel you will see that Mark records many more miracles which Jesus performed.

Wherever Jesus went, the crowds who followed him were amazed by what he did.

'. . . everywhere Jesus went, to villages, towns, or farms, people would take those who were ill to the market-places and beg him to let them at least touch the edge of his cloak; and all who touched it were made well.'

Mark 6:56

In the song from *Jesus Christ Superstar* Herod challenges Jesus to:
● change his water into wine
● walk across his swimming-pool

In his poem 'Messianic Blues' Stuart Henderson says that people seem to want:

'What kind of Saviour . . . .
a cure your back ache
wrapped in soap flakes
exploded from huge birthday cakes Saviour . . .'

Conduct a survey among your friends:
Imagine Jesus is coming to Wembley Arena. Ask your friends what they will expect him to do to prove that he is the Son of God.
On the basis of your findings write a letter to Jesus explaining what you think he will need to do if he wants to attract followers.

The Messiah

CLUES IN MARK'S GOSPEL – 2

Even if people did not know the details of Jesus' baptism, the miracles must have alerted them to the possibility that the Messiah had arrived. And Mark's readers would also be thinking along the same lines. So in chapter 8 Mark reaches the point in the story where Jesus asks his disciples who they think he is, as they are walking around the villages near Caesarea Philippi.

Caesarea Philippi

READ MARK 8:27–30

You can see from this account that some people are not sure if Jesus is John the Baptist or the prophet Elijah reborn. But Peter is *very* sure – that Jesus is the Christ.

Jesus does not deny it, but he warns his disciples not to tell anyone. (This is one of a number of occasions in Mark's Gospel when Jesus tries to keep his identity as Messiah 'under wraps': it is called the 'Messianic secret.')

For all that, they must have been excited about being with the Messiah, and probably ready to make their own plans for storming Jerusalem and overcoming the Roman Occupation Army. But Jesus soon crushes that excitement!

READ MARK 8:31–33

Jesus tells his disciples that he will be killed by the Jewish authorities – but that he will rise again from the dead. Peter only seems to hear the first part of this and tells Jesus off for talking rubbish. How can the Messiah be put to death by the authorities? Surely he has the power to avoid death.

Six days later we find that the disciples' faith in Jesus seems to have been justified.

The transfiguration

READ MARK 9:1–10

By now you should be getting good at spotting the clues!

Clue 1. There is a repeat of what was said to Jesus at his baptism.

Clue 2. Elijah and Moses appear with Jesus.

Clue 3. Jesus appears to be dazzling white.

What do these clues mean? Let's examine them one by one.

Clue 1. Remember this is confirming Jesus as the anointed one. (See Unit 7.)

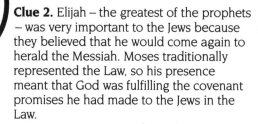

Clue 2. Elijah – the greatest of the prophets – was very important to the Jews because they believed that he would come again to herald the Messiah. Moses traditionally represented the Law, so his presence meant that God was fulfilling the covenant promises he had made to the Jews in the Law.

Clue 3. This not only symbolizes the holiness and purity of Jesus, it emphasizes that he is no ordinary man. His glory as the Son of God shines through his human form (his divinity is revealed in his humanity).

The disciples are stunned by what has happened and Jesus has to warn them that they must not tell anyone about his transfiguration until he has risen again from the dead. He also reminds them that he will have to suffer and die.

For the rest of Mark's Gospel his suffering and death is the main theme of Jesus' conversation with his disciples.

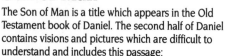

READ MARK 10:32–34

Here for the third time, Jesus predicts his own death as they travel to Jerusalem.

Finally Jesus and his disciples reach Jerusalem, where – despite the expectations of the disciples and other Jewish followers – he is tried and executed like a common criminal. (See Units 11, 12, 13.)

Son of Man

We have seen that at Caesarea Philippi, and after his transfiguration, Jesus is very concerned not to let people know that he is the Messiah. Each time something out of the ordinary happens he tries to stop people talking about it. And when Peter calls him 'the Christ ', Jesus doesn't actually say, 'Yes – I *am* the Messiah.'

Instead, Jesus prefers to call himself 'Son of Man'.

In a number of other places Jesus connects the title with his suffering and death.

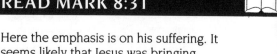

READ MARK 8:31

Here the emphasis is on his suffering. It seems likely that Jesus was bringing together two different ideas – the idea of *suffering* with the idea of being a *king*. We shall see how those two ideas reach a climax in his death and resurrection. (See Units 12, 13, 14.)

Son of Man

The Son of Man is a title which appears in the Old Testament book of Daniel. The second half of Daniel contains visions and pictures which are difficult to understand and includes this passage:

I saw in the night visions,
and behold, with the clouds of heaven
there came one like a son of man
and he came to the Ancient of Days
and was presented before him.
And to him was given dominion
and glory and kingdom,
that all peoples, nations, and languages
should serve him;
his dominion is an everlasting dominion,
which shall not pass away,
and his kingdom one
that shall not be destroyed.

Daniel 7:13–14, Revised Standard Version

We don't know exactly why Jesus chose to use this title, but it was a title which was occasionally used for the Messiah. The main idea in Daniel seems to be that the Son of Man will receive a kingdom from God – the 'Ancient of Days'. Maybe Jesus is looking beyond his death to his resurrection and glory. When he is on trial this conversation takes place:

Again the high priest questioned him, 'Are you the Messiah, the Son of the Blessed God?' 'I am', answered Jesus. 'And you will see the Son of Man seated on the right of the Almighty One and coming with the clouds of heaven!'
Mark 14:61–62

From the idea of sonship in Jewish thought, the title Son of Man may also indicate that Jesus showed all that God intended humankind to be.

Titles of Jesus

In the Gospels many titles are used to describe Jesus. Three very significant religious titles are **'Christ/Messiah'**, **'Son of Man'** and **'Son of God'**.

Christ, from the Greek *Christos*, means 'anointed one' – as does the Hebrew word 'Messiah'. The expected Messiah-figure found in Jewish prophecy had given rise by Jesus' day to a variety of ideas about who this promised, chosen, anointed deliverer could be, when he might come and what he would do for God's people. But common to all expectations were the twin notions that

● the Messiah was God's chosen Leader, bringing God's victory to the Jews;

● the Messiah was God's chosen Messenger, bringing God's rule to mankind.

Although his disciples came to believe very firmly that Jesus was the expected Messiah (see Mark 8:29 and Acts 5:42), Jesus refused to proclaim himself as Messiah during his ministry, preferring to use the title **Son of Man**.

But there is no sense of contradiction here, for the origins of 'Son of Man' in the Jewish scriptures show this to be the title of a future Messianic figure who will receive a kingdom/rule from God and mediate it to others (Daniel 7:13). Jesus' teaching that the Son of Man must suffer and die (Mark 8:31) links the title to another picture of the Messiah in Jewish prophecy – that of the Suffering Servant in Isaiah 52 and 53.

Son of God, although not a prophetic title for the Messiah, is used as a title for Jesus in John's Gospel, sometimes appearing as 'the Son', with 'of God' implied. This is an indication of the belief that Jesus' Messiahship was part of unique relationship with God, of Father-Son closeness (see John 1:18, 3:16, 10:36, 20:31). The Synoptic Gospels also contain indications of the same belief, without actually using the title 'Son of God' (see Matthew 11:25–27 and Mark 12:1–12).

▲FOLLOW▼UP▲

1. Read through Mark chapters 8, 9 and 10 and complete the following chart. In the 'meaning' column write a sentence (or a few words) which explains what you think the title tells us about Jesus.

TITLE	MEANING	REFERENCE
Messiah		Mark 8:29

2. Here is a hymn written by Isaac Watts which contains some more titles for Jesus.
There are 8 titles here.
Can you make a list of them?
What do you think each one means?

Join all the glorious names
Of wisdom, love, and power,
That ever mortals knew,
That angels ever bore:
All are too mean to speak His worth,
Too mean to set my Saviour forth.

Great Prophet of my God,
My tongue would bless Thy name:
By Thee the joyful news

Of our salvation came:
The joyful news of sins forgiven,
Of hell subdued and peace with heaven.

Jesus, my great High Priest,
Offered His blood, and died;
My guilty conscience seeks
No sacrifice beside:
His powerful blood did once atone,
And now it pleads before the throne.

My Saviour and my Lord,
My Conqueror and my King,
Thy sceptre and Thy sword,
Thy reigning grace I sing:
Thine is the power; behold, I sit
In willing bonds beneath Thy feet.

Now let my soul arise,
And tread the tempter down:
My Captain leads me forth
To conquest and a crown.
March on, nor fear to win the day,
Though death and hell obstruct the way.

3. Draw a 'wanted' poster for Jesus which uses the ideas behind some of the titles from either Mark's Gospel or this hymn.

Jesus' Teaching in Parables

In Mark's Gospel, there are fourteen references to Jesus teaching the crowds or teaching his disciples. Teaching was a vital part of Jesus' work. In John chapter 17 he describes his work as 'making God known', giving to people the message that God had given him. There were no books, no videos, no ring-files, no worksheets in Jesus' day! Yet he got his message across so well that many years later his followers were able to recall his words and write them down for others.

(Could you write down today the words your teacher used yesterday? Last week? Last year?)

There were several teaching methods used by Jewish teachers in Jesus' day, and the Gospels contain evidence that Jesus used all of them. For example:

- **question-and-answer**
Matthew 9:5; Matthew 16:26
- **contradictory-seeming statement**
Matthew 5:3–12; Matthew 10:39
- **object lesson**
Matthew 18:1–6; Luke 21:1–4
- **logical argument**
Matthew 22:15–45

But Jesus is best known for his use of the 'parable' method of teaching.

A parable is a description of some common object or incident which illustrates a spiritual truth. The description can sometimes take the form of a story. As a teaching method, story-telling (and re-telling) was both entertaining and effective, which is one obvious reason why Jesus used parables to get his message across.

Another reason is perhaps less obvious, but it is just as important. The spiritual truth within a parable was not always easily understood, even if the setting was familiar. Jesus' parables often 'hid' their message within an entertaining story, unless the hearers really thought hard about it. Jesus was not concerned to gather a popular following of supporters or fans; his

teaching presented people with the challenge to take seriously God's message to them.

There are about fifty different parables in the Gospels, some of them only one sentence long. Many of them are 'parables of the Kingdom', beginning 'the Kingdom of heaven is like . . .' In these short parables Jesus uses situations from everyday life to illustrate something important about 'God's Kingdom'.

You can find five short 'parables of the Kingdom' in Matthew 13:

● **the parable of the mustard seed**
Matthew 13:31–32
● **the parable of the yeast**
Matthew 13:33

● **the parable of the hidden treasure**
Matthew 13:44
● **the parable of the pearl**
Matthew 13:45–46
● **the parable of the net**
Matthew 13:47–49

One of Jesus' most famous parables is the parable of the good Samaritan (Luke 10:25–37). This is the dramatic tale of a near-fatal mugging and a generous rescuer, told to illustrate the importance of people caring for each other even if they are traditional enemies (as the Jews and the Samaritans were in Jesus' day).

In Luke 15, there are three story-parables illustrating the truth that God cares about people who are cut off from him – 'sinners':

● **the parable of the lost sheep**
Luke 15:1–7

● **the parable of the lost coin**
Luke 15:8–10

● **the parable of the lost son**
Luke 15:11–32

The parable of the lost son is often called the parable of the 'prodigal son' because the son in the story was very 'prodigal' (= wasteful) with his money while he had it. But the point of the story is at the end – the son 'was lost but now he has been found'.

One of Jesus' best-known parables is the story of the lost sheep. He paints a vivid picture of how God cares for people.

Jesus' does not ask his Jewish listeners to be kind to the despised Samaritans – which would have been hard enough to stomach. By making his victim a Jew and the rescuer a Samaritan, he's asking his Jewish hearers to consider a situation in which one of the hated Samaritans is kinder to the injured man than his fellow Jews. They are to imitate the kindness of the Samaritan in the story. It's a powerful lesson against racial prejudice, at the same time as demonstrating that the 'neighbour' whom God requires people to love is *anyone* in need.

Parables like this were an effective teaching method because they took everyday situations, were relevant to the listener's needs, and were easy to remember.

▲ FOLLOW UP ▲

1. Which of the following statements best describes a parable?
A parable is:
- a sermon
- a series of questions and answers
- a description of a common object or incident which illustrates a spiritual truth
- an object lesson which makes something easier to understand.

2. Look again at the five parables of the Kingdom in Matthew chapter 13. For each of the parables complete the following fact file:

FACT FILE			PARABLES
Title of parable	Reference	Brief description	Meaning

3. Now look at the parable of the good Samaritan in Luke 10:25–37. There is a famous modern version of this parable called 'The Good Punk Rocker' – the Samaritan has become a Punk Rocker and the religious people a Vicar and a Social Worker.
In groups of four write your own version of the parable – and then act it out to the rest of your group. Try to get a balance between the story and the meaning. Don't let your characters hide the meaning!

Conflict with the Authorities

During the three years Jesus spent as a travelling teacher, there was a mixed reaction to the things he said, the stories he told and the miracles he performed.

He was very popular in the north – the area called Galilee, where the people gathered round him in great crowds, amazed at the power and authority of the local carpenter from Nazareth.

But some of the Jewish religious teachers (Pharisees) were very critical of Jesus. They constantly tried to catch him breaking their rules. For example:

● They accused Jesus of blasphemy when he forgave people's sins – only God could do that.
● They accused Jesus of mixing with 'unclean' people when he had meals with non-Jews and other outcasts – good Jews kept themselves separate as 'God's chosen people'.
● They accused Jesus of breaking the Sabbath laws when they found him picking

In this scene from the film *Jesus*, Jesus is surrounded by a hostile crowd. His teaching won him many friends – but made enemies too.

corn during a walk through a cornfield on a Saturday – work was forbidden on the Sabbath.

Jesus' response to these criticisms was even more infuriating to the Pharisees:

● He reckoned to have the right to forgive people their sins.
● He said that his mission was to the outcasts.
● He claimed that he was Lord of the Sabbath.

And in addition to all this, Jesus attacked the Pharisees themselves, calling them hypocrites who had added their own petty rules to God's Law and made rule-keeping a substitute 'god'.

It was inevitable that ultimately there would be an enormous clash between Jesus and the Jewish leaders.

The show-down came when Jesus went to Jerusalem for the annual religious festival called Passover. Each year Jews flocked to the Temple in the capital to thank God for miraculously rescuing them from slavery in Egypt centuries earlier, a key event in their history as 'God's chosen people'.

The Gospel-writers present this final show-down in the framework of one action-packed week, but some people think that things have been condensed simply to show just how dramatic the conflict was between Jesus and the authorities.

The day-by-day pattern which emerges from a study of all four Gospels looks something like this:

SUNDAY
Jesus arrives in Jerusalem from Bethany, riding on a donkey, to be welcomed by cheering crowds waving palm branches and shouting 'Hosanna to the Son of David!'

MONDAY
Jesus goes to the Temple and denounces the traders and money-changers (profiteers who had the monopoly on providing the 'right' money for Temple collections and the 'right' animals for Temple sacrifices). Jesus overturns their stools and tables and drives them out of the Temple.

TUESDAY
Jesus teaches in the Temple and is asked some leading questions intended to trap him:
■ by the Pharisees (about his authority and about his views on Roman taxation)
■ by another Jewish group called the Sadducees (about his views on the possibility of resurrection after death, which they did not believe in).

WEDNESDAY
Judas Iscariot, one of Jesus' close followers (the twelve disciples), goes to the Jewish authorities with an offer to betray Jesus so that he can be arrested on the quiet. The price is thirty pieces of silver.

THURSDAY
Jesus shares the evening Passover meal with his disciples. Judas leaves early. Later, in the Garden (olive orchard) of Gethsemane, Judas arrives with the Temple police who arrest Jesus. Judas identifies him for them in the dark by greeting Jesus with a kiss on the cheek, in the eastern manner.

FRIDAY
During the early hours, Jesus faces the first of several trials, starting at the home of an influential former High Priest, and ending at the Roman fortress – the official residence of the Roman Governor, Pontius Pilate. Jesus is condemned to death by crucifixion, i.e. normal Roman criminal execution – being nailed to a large upright wooden cross, and left to die.

Jerusalem at the time of Jesus

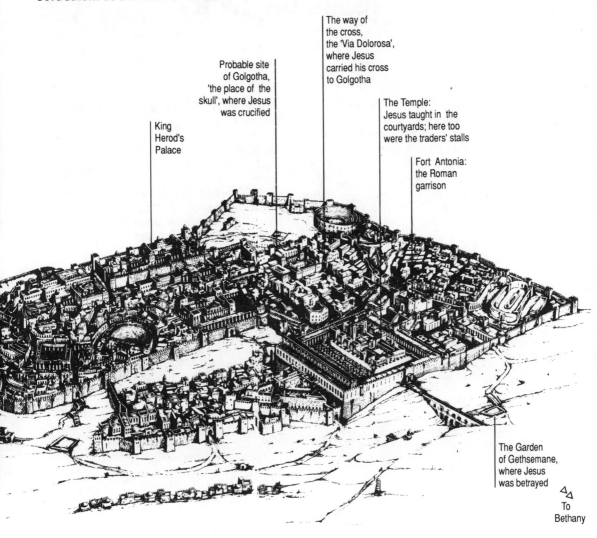

The way of the cross, the 'Via Dolorosa', where Jesus carried his cross to Golgotha

Probable site of Golgotha, 'the place of the skull', where Jesus was crucified

The Temple: Jesus taught in the courtyards; here too were the traders' stalls

King Herod's Palace

Fort Antonia: the Roman garrison

The Garden of Gethsemane, where Jesus was betrayed

To Bethany

FOLLOW UP

1. This unit has looked at the conflicts between Jesus and the religious authorities.
● Why did the Scribes and the Pharisees object to Jesus so strongly?
● What did they think he ought to be like?

2. Here are some modern situations about which Christians have different opinions. What do you think Jesus might do in these situations?

● Shopping on a Sunday – you have run out of milk.
● Going into a red light district to talk to prostitutes.
● Going into a bar which is known to be used by drug pushers.

Do you think there might be reasons to go into some of these situations and other times when it might not be the right thing to do? What are those reasons?

UNIT 11

Jesus on Trial

After his arrest, Jesus went through a series of trials and questionings. From the details given in the four Gospels there may have been as many as six.

1

HEARING BEFORE THE FORMER HIGH PRIEST, ANNAS

Jesus is questioned about his disciples and about his teaching.
John 18:12–14, 19–24

2

HEARING BEFORE THE CURRENT HIGH PRIEST, CAIAPHAS

Further preliminary questioning while the full Jewish Council assembles.
Matthew 26:57; Mark 14:53; John 18:24

3

TRIAL BEFORE THE JEWISH COUNCIL (SANHEDRIN)

The Sanhedrin has power to try only *religious* crimes. Jesus is accused and found guilty of blasphemy, partly on the spurious evidence of unreliable witnesses, but mostly because he answers 'I am' to the question 'Are you the Messiah/Christ?' The Jewish Council cannot carry out the death sentence. Jesus must be found guilty by a Roman court if he is to die, and a charge of blasphemy will not do – so this is changed to treason.
Matthew 26:59–66; Mark 14:55–64; Luke 22:66–71

4

TRIAL BEFORE THE ROMAN GOVERNOR, PONTIUS PILATE (PART 1)

Pilate is not convinced that Jesus has committed treason against Rome by claiming to be the king of the Jews. Hearing that Jesus is from Galilee, Pilate sends him to Herod Antipas, the ruler of that area,
who happens to be in Jerusalem for the Passover.
Matthew 27:1–2 and 11–14; Mark 15:2–5; Luke 23:1–4; John 18:28–38

5

HEARING BEFORE HEROD ANTIPAS

Herod, like Pilate, can find nothing to charge Jesus with. He and his men see Jesus as a figure of fun and treat him to some cruel horse-play.
Luke 23:6–12

6

TRIAL BEFORE PILATE (PART 2)

Pilate wants to release Jesus – it had become a tradition to release a Jewish prisoner during Passover – but the crowds have been persuaded to shout for the release of a murderer called Barabbas. Pilate agrees to execute Jesus.
Matthew 27:15–26; Mark 15:6–15; Luke 23:13–25; John 18:39–19:16

Of all these trials and hearings it was two that brought about Jesus' death. The Sanhedrin found him guilty of blasphemy, and Pilate finally accepted their charge of treason against Rome.

It is easy to understand how Jesus' conflict with the Jewish authorities would eventually lead to serious charges before the Sanhedrin. But it is not so easy to understand how a Roman governor could have been persuaded to execute him.

In all his teaching Jesus never spoke out against the Romans. This was probably one more reason why some Jews resented him. Many Jews wanted someone to lead an armed revolt against the occupying forces. Some people think that Judas may have betrayed Jesus out of disappointment, when he realized that Jesus was not that

Jesus stands trial. This picture of the hearing before Herod is from the film, *Jesus*.

kind of leader. Or he may possibly have been trying to make Jesus *do* something.

When Jesus rode into Jerusalem on a *donkey* (a symbol of peaceful intentions), it was perhaps meant to counter these wrong expectations.

But Jesus did still pose a threat to the Roman authorities. Just because he was so popular, he *could* have led an uprising. However, Pilate seemed satisfied that Jesus was not a trouble-maker. So why did he sentence him to death?

There seem to be two reasons:

• The crowds were demanding the release of Barabbas – bribed to do so by some Jewish leaders – and Pilate feared they would riot if he refused their request. Unless he took firm control his position would be at risk.

FACT·FILE

The Sanhedrin

The Sanhedrin was the Jewish High Court, composed of seventy-one Scribes, Pharisees, Sadducees and Elders. It was presided over by the High Priest. Sanhedrin procedures changed over the years, but it is thought that the regulations for the conduct of trials at the time of Jesus may have included the following:

• Decisions were valid only if taken within the Temple precincts.
• A quorum of twenty-three members was required.
• Criminal cases had to be heard only during daytime.
• No criminal cases were to be heard during Passover season.
• Evidence for the innocence of the accused had to be heard first.
• Evidence had to be guaranteed by two independent witnesses.
• Perjury was punishable by death.
• Only 'Not Guilty' cases could be completed within one day.

● Ruling the Jews was no easy task, and Pilate may have hoped for better co-operation from the Jewish leaders in the future if he did them this favour now.

In agreeing to the execution, Pilate was publicly accepting the Jewish leaders' charge – that when Jesus claimed to be the Messiah/Christ, this meant he was setting himself up against the Romans as a king.

At the same time Pilate also publicly washed his hands (Matthew 27:24). This was a dramatic way of saying that if there was any trouble over this execution, *he* was not to blame.

FOLLOW UP

1. In pairs read through the accounts of the trials of Jesus and then complete this table:

Reference	
Trial before	
Accusation	
Jesus' reply	
Response to his reply	

2. Look at:
● the section about the Sanhedrin
● the references to the trial before the Sanhedrin.
– Why would that trial have been illegal?
– What two charges brought against Jesus finally brought about his death?
– Why was the Roman governor persuaded to execute Jesus?

3. By now you should be becoming familiar with the accounts of the trials.

Make a brief list of what each Gospel writer chooses to include.

What do you think each Gospel writer is trying to emphasize by the selection of events he has chosen?

4. In the section on the Messiah we saw that Jesus knew before he arrived in Jerusalem that he would be put to death, and in fact saw *that* death as part of his role as the Messiah. Look back at the accounts of the trials of Jesus.
● Can you see any points at which Jesus could have convinced the authorities of his innocence?
● Can you see any evidence to support the idea that Jesus *chose* to be put to death?
● Why do you think that Jesus didn't use his miraculous power to free himself, either at his trials or when he was going to be crucified?

To help you with this you might like to look back at some of the key points in the ministry of Jesus:
– Luke 2:22–38. Jesus is presented at the Temple.
– Matthew 4:1–11. Jesus' temptations.
– Mark 9:2–13. The transfiguration.
– John 14: 27–31. Jesus' farewell speech to the disciples before he is arrested.

The Crucifixion – Why Did Jesus Die?

All four Gospels describe Jesus' death by crucifixion: Matthew 27, Mark 15, Luke 23, John 18:28–19:42.

There were other death penalties in use at that time, including stoning, execution by the sword, and fighting wild animals in an arena in front of an enthusiastic audience. But crucifixion was devised by the Romans to punish the lowest of the low – criminals who were slaves or members of conquered races. A Roman citizen could not be crucified. The victim was nailed to an upright pillar of wood (sometimes with a cross-beam) and left to die in agony.

Far from attempting to hide the fact that Jesus died such an undignified death, Christians have always focussed on it. Paul and all the apostles proclaimed 'the crucified Christ'.

Such a humiliating execution seems an embarrassing and unnecessary end for someone whose teaching could reform the worst character (Luke 19:1–9), whose touch could heal the sick (Luke 5:12– 13), and whose command could change the weather (Luke 8:22–25).

The apostles obviously believed that the crucifixion was no accident of fate, no tragedy which could have been avoided. Even Jesus himself taught that his death was an inevitable and necessary part of his mission (Mark 9:30–32; 10:45; John 10:11–18).

So, if the crucifixion was not a dreadful mistake, exactly why did Jesus die? The Bible gives three clear reasons:
● Jesus died in order to bring people to God (1 Peter 3:18).
● Jesus died to purify people from their wrongdoing and make forgiveness possible (1 John 1:5–2:2).
● Jesus died as a substitute for others (Romans 5:6–10).

These reasons for Jesus' death reflect the fact that Jesus and his first followers were Jews. The Jews of the Old Testament days before Jesus were extremely conscious of three things:
● their unique close relationship to God;
● the way this relationship was spoiled by their wrongdoing;
● the constant need for a 'clean sheet' that would restore the close relationship.

To understand why the apostles focussed on the importance of Jesus' death, we need to understand something of the background to these three key ideas.

The Jews believe that the most important fact in their history is that they were chosen by God to be his special people and that what *we* would call 'history' is actually an account of how God looked after them.

Covenant (Genesis 17:1–8)

The Old Testament records that nearly 2,000 years before the time of Jesus, God promised a man called Abraham two things:
● he would become the Father (or 'Patriarch') of a very important nation who were going to be God's own people;
● this nation would be given the land of Canaan to live in.

God made these promises in the form of a covenant or special contract with Abraham, both sides entering into a solemn commitment – very similar to a modern marriage contract. God would make Abraham's descendants (the Jews) into his special people; Abraham and his descendants would be faithful to God and obey him.

However, although Abraham's descendants increased in number, they were forced by famine to move away from Canaan, settling in Egypt where they eventually became slaves of the Egyptians.

Redemption (Exodus 3–14)

Many years later, God rescued the Jews from Egypt under the leadership of Moses. It was a very dramatic escape. Each Jewish household had to kill a lamb for their final meal before the journey. They put its blood on the doorposts and above the doors of their home, to protect them from the Angel of Death who would see the blood and 'pass over' as he brought death to the eldest son of every unprotected family (the Egyptians). In the ensuing chaos, the Jews fled across the Red Sea, where the waters miraculously parted for them, and into the desert which would bring them eventually back to Canaan.

The night of the escape came to be remembered annually at the time of the Passover Festival, but the escape itself is usually called the 'Exodus', which means 'getting out', and it is very important to Jews right up to today. When they look back to the Exodus, it reminds them of how God rescued them from slavery and took them back to their own country. They call it being 'redeemed' – 'bought back', rather

like a treasured object being reclaimed from a moneylender. The Jews' escape from Egypt was their 'redemption'.

Law (Exodus 19:1–8; 20:1–17)

While the Jews were still living as nomads in the desert, before they re-entered Canaan, God laid down a set of ground rules to help them keep their side of the covenant contract, in being faithful and obedient once they were in their 'promised land'.

This set of rules – the 'Law' – was based on ten very important instructions called the Ten Commandments, which were given to Moses after God had reminded him of the special covenant relationship: 'If you will obey me and keep my covenant, you will be my own people' (Exodus 19:3–8). The Ten Commandments also begin with a reminder of the covenant relationship: 'I am the Lord your God who brought you out of Egypt . . .'

Sin

The Jews found that they were simply not able to keep the Ten Commandments or any of the covenant laws which God gave

Why did Jesus die? To make a new contract (covenant) between God and humankind. To pay the 'ransom' which would buy freedom from sin for people everywhere. These are just two of the pictures used in the New Testament to explain the mystery of his death.

What is sin?

The Bible describes sin in at least three different ways:

• The story of Adam and Eve's rebellion in Genesis 3 presents the idea that the whole of mankind exists in a state of prideful revolt against God. The label 'original sin' is sometimes given to this aspect of sin – the idea that all people are born in a state of sin; sinfulness is part of what it is to be human.

Because of mankind's in-born state of sin, every person is by nature a sinner and the Bible further describes how people therefore 'commit sins', either

• by falling short of God's standard of perfection;
or
• by acting in a law-breaking way.

them. The Bible calls that inability 'sin'. If they were to remain the covenant people of God, the Jews had to say and to show that they were sorry for their sin.

Sacrifice (Leviticus 6 and 7)

God set up a system to help the Jews to say sorry for their sins. To show that they were sorry for the times when they had sinned (accidentally or deliberately) the people had to kill – make a 'sacrifice' of – a perfectly unblemished bird or animal as a gift or offering to God. At first this was done in a special worship tent called the tabernacle, but later a special temple was built.

Specially appointed priests were in charge of the sacrifice rituals. There were many ways of offering the different sacrifices for accidental or deliberate wrongdoing (for individuals or for the whole nation), but four factors were important:

● the transferring of the sins from the person/people to the animal substitute, by touching its head before it was killed;
● the sprinkling of the animal's blood (life-source) as a sign of new cleanness, new life;
● the burning up of a whole animal (or cereal-grain offering) as a sign of giving the person's whole life back to God;
● the eating of the burned animal flesh as a fellowship meal shared between the newly-cleansed people and their God.

Atonement (Leviticus 16)

The sacrificed animal renewed the contract, the covenant, which had been broken by disobedience or unfaithfulness. Now, God

Under Jewish Old Testament Law animals were offered in sacrifice, to put people right with God. The New Testament sees the death of Jesus as the final once-for-all sacrifice in atonement for sin. The picture shows a Passover lamb being sacrificed in Israel.

and the Jew were in a close relationship again. The technical word for being joined together again like that is 'atonement' (at one·ment).

Once a year, there was a special Day of Atonement for the whole nation, when the priest took two goats but killed only one of them, taking an offering of the blood behind the Temple curtain and into the 'Most Holy Place', where no one could normally go because it was the place where God was thought to be especially present. The blood stood for a life given in place of the life of each person who had sinned. Then the priest would lay his hands on the head of the second goat, transferring the sins of the people to the animal, and send it off into the desert so that their sins were taken away.

● Read again 1 Peter 3:18; 1 John 1:5–2:2; Romans 5:6–10. This time, look out for all the reminders of the Jews' special relationship with God.

● Now read Matthew 27:45–54; Hebrews 9:11–14; 9:24–26; 10:11–12.

 Christians believe that when Jesus died he became a sacrifice for the sins of the whole world so that everyone can be at one with God. Those people who accept this for themselves are God's new covenant people, because they have been rescued from their sins and have dedicated their lives to faithfulness to him.

Here is a verse from a hymn by Charles Wesley which brings together the Jewish and Christian ideas behind the crucifixion.

> 'Tis finished! The Messiah dies:
> Cut off for sins, but not his own:
> Accomplished is the sacrifice,
> The great redeeming work is done.'

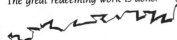

FOLLOW UP

1. Here is a hymn which explains the meaning of the death of Jesus.

1 Not all the blood of beasts,
　　On Jewish altars slain,
Could give the guilty conscience peace,
　　Or wash away the stain.

2 But Christ the heavenly Lamb,
　　Takes all our sins away:
A sacrifice of nobler name
　　And richer blood than they.

3 My faith would lay her hand
　　On that dear head of Thine,
While like a penitent I stand,
　　And there confess my sin.

4 My soul looks back to see
　　The burdens Thou didst bear,
When hanging on the cursèd tree,
　　And knows her guilt was there.

5 Believing, we rejoice
　　To see the curse remove:
We bless the Lamb with cheerful voice
　　And sing His bleeding love!

In pairs look back at the unit and then write an explanation of the following lines:

. . . all the blood of beasts,
On Jewish altars slain (verse 1)

Christ the heavenly Lamb . . . (verse 2)

My faith would lay her hand
On that dear head of Thine (verse 3)

. . . the burdens Thou didst bear (verse 4)

. . . we rejoice
To see the curse remove (verse 5)

2. Try to write a one-sentence definition of each of the following words:
● covenant
● redemption
● Law
● sin
● sacrifice
● atonement

3. Can you list three of the reasons that Christians use to explain why Jesus had to die on the cross?

4. What are the strengths and weaknesses of one of the reasons you have listed?

The Crucifixion –
Historical Details

One of the strongest arguments for Jesus' existence as a real person in history is the factual evidence of his execution.

Even before the Gospels were written, Paul and Peter wrote in their letters about Jesus' death 'on the cross' (1 Corinthians 1:17; Philippians 2:8; 1 Peter 2:24).

Later, when Luke wrote the Acts of the Apostles, he included details of some of the very first sermons preached about Jesus, and these also mentioned the crucifixion (Acts 2:22–33; 13:26–29).

Even Josephus, the Jewish writer, recorded in his reports about Jesus that 'Pilate condemned him to be crucified and to die'.

When was Jesus crucified?

Knowing that Jesus was sentenced by Pilate gives us some idea when the crucifixion took place – Pilate was Governor of Judea from AD26 to AD36. But we can pin the date down more accurately than that . . .

● Luke's Gospel gives us a date for the ministry of John the Baptist – the fifteenth year of the Emperor Tiberius – and we know Jesus was baptized at this time, at the beginning of his own ministry. The fifteenth year of Tiberius was AD27.
Luke 3:1–3

● John's Gospel mentions three annual Passovers during Jesus' ministry, so it must have lasted three years, until AD30.
John 2:13; 6:4; 13:1

● All the Gospels (and the Jewish Talmud) record Jesus' death taking place at the time of the Jewish Passover Festival – March/April on a modern calendar.
Matthew 26:17–19; Mark 14:12–16; Luke 22:7–13; John 13:1

● Luke tells us the execution took place on the sixth day of the Jewish week, a Friday. Mark tells us that Jesus was nailed to the cross at nine o'clock in the morning and that he died at about 3 p.m.
Luke 23:50–54; Mark 15:25, 34–37

Although all four Gospels record the crucifixion taking place on a Friday, there is a discrepancy between John and the Synoptics over the date. John says it is 14 Nisan, the day on which the evening meal was the special Passover meal. The Synoptics date it as 15 Nisan, the day *following* the evening of the special Passover meal. Some Bible scholars say that there is no difference between John and the Synoptics, because the Greek in John 13.1 can mean both 'the day before' and 'the day of' the festival.

(NB: the Jewish day runs from sunset to sunset, so the Sabbath, and the first day of a festival, would cross two calendar 'days' by our reckoning).

Where was Jesus crucified?

Roman crucifixions always took place in a specially designated area, outside the city or town. In Jerusalem, this place was called 'Golgotha' (Latin name, 'Calvary').

Jerusalem today is vastly bigger than it was then, but the ancient Church of the Holy Sepulchre is said to have been built on the place where Jesus died. The site of this church can be traced back to a fifth-century map; it may well have been outside the city walls in AD30.

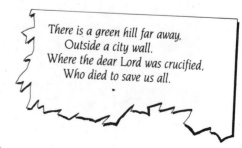

There is a green hill far away,
Outside a city wall.
Where the dear Lord was crucified,
Who died to save us all.

How was Jesus crucified?

Historians and archaeologists provide us with information about execution by crucifixion.

The Gospels describe the crucifixion of Jesus. Dying with him, on either side, were two thieves.

The scourge, a whip with pieces of metal attached, inflicted terrible injury.

● The prisoner was beaten with a vicious 'cat-o'-nine-tails' whip, which had small metal weights attached to the ends of the thongs.

● Then he was made to walk through the streets to the crucifixion site, carrying the cross-beam which would later be fixed to a wooden upright set in the ground.

● At the site, the prisoner was stripped and fixed to the cross – his arms were lashed to the beam with ropes, often with nails hammered through the wrists, and his feet were nailed to the upright.

● The prisoner was allowed drugged wine, as a kind of anaesthetic against the pain.

● Fixed to the cross was a notice informing onlookers of the crime for which the prisoner had been sentenced to death.

● Death was usually by suffocation, because the full weight of the prisoner's body pulling down from his arms made it difficult to breathe, and he would gradually become too weak to push his body weight up from his nailed feet.

● Death often took several days, but the centurion in command could speed things up by breaking the prisoner's legs with a hammer (to stop him pushing up for breath), or by piercing his side with a sword.

All the details of Jesus' crucifixion in the Gospels are consistent with these historical findings.

(See Matthew 27:26, 32–50; Mark 15:15, 21–37; Luke 23:36, 33–46; John 19:1–34.)

The interesting thing is that the Gospel writers don't dwell on the agony of Jesus' death when they describe the crucifixion. They give Jesus' words and the comment of the army officer on duty, and they tell us of the torn curtain in the Temple.

It is this last fact which gives a clue to the great significance of Jesus' death. What is achieved by this atoning sacrifice (see Unit 12) completely overrides the shame, as Paul stresses in his portrayal of Jesus in his letters (see Unit 18).

The Church of the Holy Sepulchre

People have regarded the site where the Church of the Holy Sepulchre stands as the place where Jesus was buried for nearly as long as Christianity has been in existence. In AD135 the Emperor Hadrian built a temple to the Roman goddess Venus there, hiding any evidence of a tomb of Jesus.

But, nearly 200 years later, Christians remained certain that this was the place. St Helena, the mother of the Emperor Constantine, persuaded him to build a shrine and a church on the site. These were completed in AD335. At one side, a rocky outcrop was kept as the site of Calvary.

Constantine's buildings were largely destroyed by invaders. Most of the present single building is the work of Crusaders.

Today, 1600 years later, pilgrims still flock to the site, convinced that this was the tomb the disciples found empty on the first Easter Sunday.

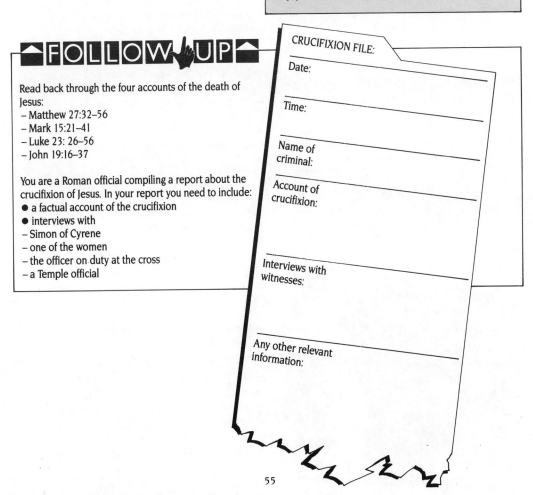

FOLLOW UP

Read back through the four accounts of the death of Jesus:
– Matthew 27:32–56
– Mark 15:21–41
– Luke 23: 26–56
– John 19:16–37

You are a Roman official compiling a report about the crucifixion of Jesus. In your report you need to include:
● a factual account of the crucifixion
● interviews with
– Simon of Cyrene
– one of the women
– the officer on duty at the cross
– a Temple official

CRUCIFIXION FILE:

Date:

Time:

Name of criminal:

Account of crucifixion:

Interviews with witnesses:

Any other relevant information:

Jesus' Resurrection and Ascension

Perhaps it seems strange that Jesus' followers did not try to cover up the fact that he died a criminal's death by Roman crucifixion.

If you look at the way they wrote about the crucifixion you can see something even stranger. They have a reason *not* to hide the facts.

Read: Matthew 28:5–6; Mark 16:6; Luke 24:2–9; Acts 2:22–24; Acts 5:29–30; Acts 10:39–40; Acts 13:28–31; Romans 4:24–26; 1 Peter 1:3.

Jesus' followers were convinced of two things:
● Jesus died on a cross.
● God restored him to life three days later. (The usual word for this is 'resurrection'.)

Jesus was buried in a rock-cut tomb like this one, with a circle of stone to seal the entrance.

What had happened to make them believe that God had raised Jesus from the dead? Two things:
● First of all, on the Sunday morning Jesus' body was missing from its tomb.
● And then, people started *seeing* him – *alive!*

You can read the Gospel accounts of the empty tomb and people meeting the risen Jesus in Matthew 28; Mark 16; Luke 24, and John 20:1 – 21:22.

These appearances of the risen Jesus continued for nearly six weeks. They are summarized in 1 Corinthians 15:3–6.

Believing that someone came back to life three days after a Roman crucifixion is a pretty tall order – and plenty of theories have been put forward to explain that empty tomb . . .

● *Perhaps Jesus wasn't really dead. Perhaps he was only unconscious when they took him down from the cross.*

But the soldiers would certainly have made sure their prisoner was dead. There's some evidence that the officer in charge of a crucifixion risked being sentenced to death himself if the job wasn't done properly. Jesus died fairly quickly, which is why the soldiers didn't break his legs. But they thrust a spear into his side to make sure.

● *Perhaps the disciples had made a mistake and looked inside the wrong tomb.*

Unlikely: Jesus' closest friends would certainly have known exactly which tomb they laid him in. And although they did not find a body in it, it wasn't *entirely* empty – there were undisturbed grave clothes where a body had been. It was these, lying in place but collapsed, which convinced

John that Jesus had simply passed through them, just as he later came through a locked door (John 20:6–8, 19).

The resurrection of Jesus brought great joy to his followers. It still does, today.

● *Perhaps someone stole the body and the disciples pretended or thought he'd been raised.*

Within weeks of Jesus' death his previously timid followers were risking death themselves by preaching openly about his resurrection. Those first Christians would hardly have staked their lives on a lie based on their own theft. If the authorities had removed the body, they would have produced it as evidence once the disciples started preaching about the resurrection. But they never did.

● *Perhaps the disciples were so upset that they began seeing things, and imagining they could see Jesus alive again.*

The disciples would certainly try to account for the undisturbed grave clothes, and they might have innocently 'imagined' a non-dead Jesus.

This theory might have been believable if there had been only one or two claims to have seen Jesus. But on one occasion Jesus appeared to 500 people at once. They couldn't *all* have been hallucinating.

What IS a Christian?

'If you confess that Jesus is Lord and believe that God raised him from death, you will be saved.'
Romans 10:9.

● **A Christian is** – someone who believes that Jesus was more than a remarkable teacher. The word 'Lord' in the Bible stands for God. Christians believe that Jesus is 'God made human'.

● **A Christian is** – someone who believes that God proved that Jesus was all he claimed to be, by *raising him from death.*

● **A Christian is** – someone who is prepared to proclaim these beliefs to others.

● **A Christian is** – someone who believes that he/she has been set free from death (which is the result of sin) and given new (eternal) life.

The teaching of the New Testament is that Jesus died in order to set people free from sin and death: 'Because of our sins he was handed over to die, and he was raised to life in order to put us right with God' (Romans 4:25). The resurrection proves Jesus' claim to be the Messiah/Christ and shows his victory over death. His followers can be confident of life after death.

Of course, there's no scientific *proof* for the resurrection. But none of these other 'explanations' is more convincing than the disciples' claim that God raised Jesus from the dead. One thing *is* clear – those first Christians were suddenly transformed from disappointed and bewildered mourners into joyful, powerful preachers whose message spread like wildfire throughout the Roman Empire. Something had obviously happened to convince them that Jesus was still present with them. And Christians today share that same belief.

The despair Jesus' disciples felt at the time of the crucifixion turned to joy at the realization that Jesus had risen from the dead. Their hopes were rekindled – surely Jesus *would* now accomplish all the things Jews expected of their promised Messiah-King.

Jesus' ascension

READ ACTS 1:1–14

'They asked him, "Lord, will you at this time give the kingdom back to Israel?"'

Would Jesus, using the same power that had raised him from the dead, now get rid of the Roman occupying forces and give Jerusalem and the Promised Land back to the Jews?

In his reply Jesus did speak of 'power'. But he said that this power would be given to his disciples:
● not military power to overthrow the Romans, but God's inner power for telling people about Jesus;
● not just telling people in Jerusalem and the surrounding area of Judea but telling them in the areas around (Samaria) and right across the world.

Once and for all Jesus here finally dismisses the old idea of a 'military Messiah', coming to make Jerusalem a political king-pin among the nations. His Kingdom is a spiritual kingdom empowered by the Holy Spirit (the Spirit of God, whom Jesus promised his followers as a permanent Helper, once he himself had gone).

There will be a revolution, but a spiritual revolution, which will start in Jerusalem when the disciples receive the power of the Holy Spirit. That experience will be like a stone thrown into a pond – the ripples will spread, from Jerusalem out to Judea, then out to the wider regions like Samaria, then out to the whole world.

Spreading the Kingdom is not going to be a spectator sport, with supporters watching Jesus use God's power to establish God's reign in the world. God's power is to be given to the supporters themselves, so that *they* can play their part in establishing God's reign.

Once the disciples' expectations had been re-programmed and they were prepared for things to happen to them and through them by the power of the Holy Spirit, Jesus withdrew from them. This moment has become known as the 'ascension' because of the simple 'upward' description given by Luke.

'After saying this, he was taken up to heaven as they watched him, and a cloud hid him from their sight.'
Acts 1:9.

Although this simple description seems to be based on a primitive view of the universe (heaven above the earth and hell below it), it is really saying something much more profound.

READ PHILIPPIANS 2:6–11

In Units 17 and 18 we shall consider further this New Testament belief that Jesus existed before the universe was created and came from that existence to live and die as a human being.

The simple description of the ascension is emphasizing the belief that after Jesus' mission on earth was accomplished, he was 'raised to the highest place' by God. This is a picture-language phrase which gives the idea of a supreme champion, an unbeaten winner, being awarded his rightful place 'at the top' – not just placed on the winner's podium ('raised to the highest place' physically), but ranked the highest of all ('raised to the highest place' compared to the achievements of others).

◆FOLLOW UP◆

1. Jerusalem TV is preparing an in-depth report on the rumours about the resurrection of Jesus. As a reporter you have to:
● give a brief introduction about Jesus;
● interview two people who claim to have seen Jesus after his death (there are four questions you can ask them about the resurrection of Jesus in the section you have just read);
● interview an official spokesperson for the:
– Sanhedrin
– Roman Governor
– King
to find out their reactions to the rumours;
● try to draw some conclusions for your viewers based on the evidence and comments you have received.
(Perhaps you could borrow a Camcorder and record your programme?!)

2. Why do you think that the early Christians made no attempt to hide the fact that Jesus died like a common criminal? Give reasons for your answers.

3. Why do you think the resurrection of Jesus is so important to Christians? Do *you* think it is important? Why?

4. Look at the four statements 'A Christian is . . .', given in this unit. Conduct a survey among your friends to see what they think.

A CHRISTIAN IS . . .

The Picture of Jesus in Matthew, Mark and Luke

> Who is this?
> What sort of person is he?

> He's a singer – I've got every one of his records since 'Move It'.

> He's a kind man – he came to my village with a team of relief workers.

> He's my record-producer – it's great for a Christian artist like me to have the help of someone so experienced in the music business.

Can you guess who's giving these answers? Why are all the answers different? Is one answer 'untrue' if it doesn't include all the information from the other answers? Does having three answers give you a better 'picture' of this person than if you had only one answer?

Each of the three Synoptic Gospels gives us a slightly different answer to the questions: '*Who is Jesus? What sort of person is he?*' Matthew, Mark and Luke give different 'pictures' of Jesus because each has a particular readership in mind and a particular purpose in writing.

None of them actually wrote a day-by-day diary called *My Travels With Jesus*. In fact, they didn't start writing their Gospels until some years after Jesus died.

Up till then, the various sayings and stories connected with Jesus had been carefully passed on by word of mouth. This was quite normal in the days when few

people could read or write. People then had much better-trained memories, and quite detailed information could be accurately preserved and handed on, until someone finally wrote it down.

This method would not be as reliable today. We are all so dependent on easy access to books, videos, computer disks and so on, that any attempt to pass on important information by word of mouth would be like the kids' party game of Chinese Whispers!

In The Acts of the Apostles (the sequel to Luke's Gospel), you can find some places where Luke describes people telling others what they knew about Jesus, long before there were any Gospels for them to read. The words these people used would have been remembered accurately and passed on to Luke by word of mouth – the 'oral tradition'.

We can see fragments of the oral tradition written down in Acts in a series of speeches:
– chapter 2, verses 14–39
– chapter 3, verses 12–26
– chapter 4, verses 8–12
– chapter 5, verses 29–32
– chapter 10, verses 34–43

Bible experts who have sorted out all the different 'facts' contained within these fragments have worked out a standard 'proclamation' about Jesus. They call it the *kerygma* – the Greek word for 'proclamation'.

The kerygma

The proclamation known as the *kerygma* goes like this:

● The man Jesus (Acts 2:22), who was known personally to many early believers (2:22; 10:39), was no less than God's Chosen One, the Christ, the Messiah (2:31–32; 2:36; 3:20; 4:10).

● The proof that Jesus is God's Christ is that, three days after he was put to death by crucifixion, God raised him to life again (2:32; 3:15; 4:10; 5:30; 10:40), and many early believers were witnesses of this (2:32; 3:15; 5:32; 10:41).

● If Jesus is God's Christ, this means that he is also judge of the world (10:42) and exalted in heaven (2:33; 3:13; 5:31; 10:36).

● The Good News is that if people will turn away from their bad old ways (2:38; 3:19) and accept God's forgiveness through Jesus (4:12; 5:31; 10:43), then God will give them his Holy Spirit (2:38), to transform them from within – in the all-powerful name of Jesus (2:38; 3:6; 3:16; 4:10; 10:43).

These basic *kerygma* facts of the earliest proclamation of the Christian message, which were passed down by oral tradition, can also be traced in the letters written by the apostle Paul some years before the Gospels.

This *kerygma* framework was probably filled out with well-known stories and sayings of Jesus, some of which are thought to have been circulating in written form by the time the Synoptic Gospels appeared.

In the Gospels of Matthew, Mark and Luke we have three different 'angles' on Jesus, all based on the *kerygma* framework but written for different readers and with different aims in view.

All the Synoptic Gospels include some basic biographical details about Jesus of Nazareth, although there are no birth stories in Mark's Gospel, only in Matthew and Luke.

However, *all* the Synoptic writers include accounts of the crucifixion and resurrection, because these events were at the heart of early Christian teaching, proving that Jesus was not *just* a compassionate man or a miracle-worker – but God's Messiah, the Son of God, foretold and expected by the Jews.

There is nothing in the Synoptic Gospels to suggest that the writers played down any of the basic teachings because they didn't believe them. Rather, each concentrated on the particular aspect of Jesus that meant most to themselves and to their particular readers.

Matthew's Gospel

The first Gospel in the New Testament has Matthew's name attached to it, because from earliest times it was associated with the disciple of that name.

Matthew (also known as Levi) was a Jew who was a tax collector for the Romans before he decided to follow Jesus (Matthew 9:9–13). Matthew's *kerygma*-based picture of Jesus is clearly aimed at Jewish readers. He concentrates on Jesus as God's 'Chosen One' (Messiah or Christ), foretold in the old Jewish prophecies. He makes dozens of references to these prophecies which would really only be appreciated by Jews.

The Jewish scriptures contain several descriptions of the expected Messiah, but the one Matthew emphasizes in his portrait of Jesus is the *kingly* Messiah. He calls Jesus 'king' eight times and 'Son of David' (i.e. descendant of the greatest Jewish king) nine times. The new life or new age which begins with Jesus coming to earth is called 'the Kingdom of heaven'.

Jews expected all their old Messianic prophecies to be fulfilled one day, and Matthew's Gospel claims that they have been fulfilled in the person of Jesus. Matthew's special emphasis is that Jesus of Nazareth is the kingly Messiah of Jewish prophecy.

Mark's Gospel

Mark's Gospel is thought to have been written by John Mark (Acts 12:12 and 25), a young friend of Simon Peter, the fisherman-turned-disciple. It is thought that Peter's preaching provided Mark with much of his material.

There are only a few references to Jewish prophecies in Mark, and any Jewish words or customs that are used are explained. Mark was clearly taking care that non-Jewish (Gentile) readers, as well as Jews, would understand why Jesus was so special.

Although Mark's is the shortest Gospel, his *kerygma*-based picture of Jesus is packed full of incidents which show Jesus as a man of action, the unflagging helper of the needy. The phrase 'at once' is used frequently.

Mark records nineteen miracles – eight show Jesus' power over disease, five show his power over nature, four show his power over demons and two show his power over death. Mark's special emphasis is that Jesus is a compassionate wonder-working Messiah whose miracles reveal God to the world.

Luke's Gospel

The author of Luke-Acts was a Gentile doctor (Colossians 4:14), a close friend of the apostle Paul. Not being a Jew himself, Luke obviously wrote a Gospel for Gentile readers. Or rather, *one* Gentile reader in particular, because Luke's two-part book is actually addressed to someone called Theophilus (Luke 1:1; Acts 1:1). Luke's *kerygma*-based picture of Jesus reflects his own position as a Gentile 'outcast' and also Paul's distinctive teaching – that you don't have to become a Jew first in order to become a Christian. Luke's Gospel shows the humanity of Jesus – the 'Son of Man' who befriends all outcasts and underdogs, including Gentiles and women.

Luke fills out the *kerygma* framework with his own special material, including the parable of the good Samaritan (chapter 10), and the parables of the lost coin, lost sheep and lost ('prodigal') son (chapter 15). It is only Luke who tells us about Elizabeth (mother of John the Baptist), Mary (mother of Jesus), and the sisters Mary and Martha. Several widows are also mentioned, and women Jesus healed.

Luke's special emphasis is on Jesus as the friend of outcasts and sinners – anyone at all who chooses to come to him.

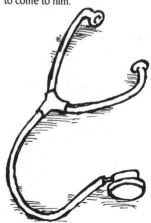

Who is this?
What sort of person is he?

He's the Messiah – the King foretold in our scriptures. God raised him from the dead – that proves it.

He's the man who did great miracles by the power of God, the Messiah. God raised him from the dead – that proves it.

He's the one who came to be a friend to the friendless, to bring them to God. God raised him from the dead – that proves it.

We have no actual pictures of Jesus – not even a description of what he looked like. This is a picture from the film, *Jesus*.

FOLLOW UP

1. In your book write a heading 'Matthew's Gospel'. Now look at the three descriptions of Jesus at the end of the unit and copy under that heading the one which you think best sums up Matthew's Gospel – and explain why.

Now do the same for Mark and Luke.

2. Design clues for each of the words in this 'crossword'.

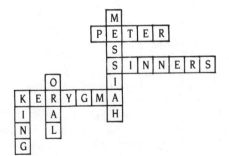

3. You are a well-known television chat show host! Your guest next week will be Jesus Christ. You have to prepare an introduction of him for your show – and find out enough to interview him properly at the same time.

The research department has provided you with the outline of the *kerygma* from this unit. When you have read through this information you will have to write (in your own inimitable style) a description of Jesus based on the *kerygma* which could be used as an introduction to Jesus for your show.

4. Go back to the outline of the *kerygma* in this unit. Which particular parts of that *kerygma* do you think are specially emphasized by which of the Gospel writers? For example:

Luke emphasizes the part about . . . because his Gospel was written to . . .

John's Reflective Picture of Jesus – 1

Signs and sayings

John's Gospel, written by one of Jesus' closest friends, is noticeably different from the three other Gospels. It omits some events recorded by the Synoptic writers and includes others which they left out.

Many Bible experts think that John wrote his Gospel in his old age, after a lifetime of pondering on the years he spent with Jesus, and the things Jesus said and did. Certainly, John seems to have an entirely different approach to his 'life of Jesus' from the other Gospel writers.

He actually *explains* his approach, in his Gospel:

> 'In his disciples' presence Jesus performed many other miracles which are not written down in this book. But these have been written in order that you may believe that Jesus is the Messiah, the Son of God, and that through your faith in him you may have life.'
> John 20:30–31

John apparently selected and arranged his material carefully in the hope that people reading his Gospel would come to believe in Jesus.

Today, a booklet written specially to convince people about a particular product would probably be called a 'promotional brochure'. You've probably seen quite a few of these, perhaps trying to convince you about a postal compact disc club or a new local leisure centre! But there are 'promos' about serious issues, too – political, social and ecological issues.

You may even have read one or two religious leaflets promoting Christianity; sometimes these are still called by a rather old-fashioned name – 'tracts'. Well, John's Gospel seems to be something like this.

Because John was writing a kind of promotional booklet, he used only selected events from the life of Jesus – those events which he thought would show more precisely who Jesus really was. For example, in John's Gospel Jesus feeds 5,000 people, just as in the Synoptic Gospels, but

SIGNS OF JESUS

REFERENCE	SIGN	MEANING OF SIGN	WHO JESUS IS
Chapter 2, verses 1–11	Water turned into wine	(acted out)	Jesus replaces the 'water' of the old Jewish Law with the 'wine' of the new order
2:13–25		Cleansing the Temple	
4:46–54	Healing the official's son	You must be born again	Jesus the 'Word', Creator of life, gives new life
3:1–21			
5:1–18	Healing the paralyzed man	Jesus and the Father	Jesus claims to be equal with God the Father
5:19–47			
6:1–15	Feeding the 5,000	I am the bread of life	Jesus is the new manna – the 'life-sustainer' from heaven
6:22–59			
6:16–21	Walking on the water	(none given)	Jesus the Creator rules creation
9:1–41	Healing the blind man	I am the light of the world	Jesus gives spiritual inner sight
8:12			
11:1–44	Raising Lazarus from death	I am the resurrection and the life	Jesus gives life that conquers death
11:25			

SAYINGS OF JESUS

REFERENCE	SAYING	WHO JESUS IS
Chapter 8, verses 48–59	'Before Abraham was born, I AM'	Jesus is the one who has been alive since before the world began
10:1–21	'I am the gate' and 'I am the good shepherd'	Jesus provides the way in to eternal life
15:1–8	'I am the real vine'	Jesus is the source of spiritual life

here we find Jesus also declaring the deeper meaning of the miracle – 'I *am the bread of life*.'

John records just seven of Jesus' miracles in his Gospel, and he calls them 'signs'. He has selected them because they are indicators, pointing out that Jesus is God's chosen representative ('the Christ') and that with his arrival a new order has begun. Some of these signs are placed alongside passages which explain the deeper meaning of the miracle.

Apart from the signs, John includes other sayings of Jesus which also point to his supernatural personality and his special mission.

Jews reading John's Gospel would be particularly struck by Jesus' repetition of the words 'I am'. This was the phrase used by Jews from earliest times as a title for God.

▲FOLLOW UP▲

1. Choose a topic you feel strongly about (something like animal welfare or students' rights).

Design a leaflet to promote your views.

Your leaflet must:
● be bright and attractive
● put your views across clearly and simply
● include an explanation of why you think this issue is important.

2. Now look back through the unit. Design a leaflet which could have been written by John to promote Jesus as the Christ.

As well as making your leaflet bright and attractive you must include:
● features that show Jesus as the Christ (John calls them signs)
● statements made by Jesus which support his claim to be the Christ
● an explanation of the meaning of 'the Christ'.

John's Reflective Picture of Jesus – 2

The Prologue

The first thing that strikes the reader of John's Gospel is the introduction, or 'Prologue'.

READ JOHN 1:1–18

This Prologue is a bit like the 'blurb' on the outside of a modern novel – it gives you a taste of what the book is about.

It is also like the Introduction which comes at the beginning of many non-fiction books.

John's Prologue introduces the readers to topics they will find in the book proper: life, light, grace, truth, glory. And all these key themes have something to do with the person John calls 'the Word'.

Although the Prologue to John's Gospel is not identical to a modern cover 'blurb', John's original readers would be quite familiar with his style of introduction.

There are two devices used by modern writers which are very obvious in John's Prologue. They are:

● Know your reader/audience.
● Catch the reader's attention with your opening.

> The market for which you are writing will not only influence your choice of subject but also have a considerable effect on the style of any particular piece. If it is intended for the popular Press, you will have to use brief, simple sentences . . .
>
> The first words of anything you write are of vital importance, and especially so with an article. Look for an 'eye-opener' at the very beginning, something which will really grab your reader's attention and make him want to read more.
>
> From *Writing for Pleasure and Profit* by Michael Legat

John used both of these devices to make sure his Gospel would appeal to the audience it was aimed at. His opening, '*Before the world was created, the Word already existed . . .*' might seem to modern readers nothing more than a pleasantly poetic statement. But to John's original readers, that opening phrase was loaded with popular ideas that people would find instantly fascinating. And by the time readers got as far as ' . . . *the Word became a human being and . . . lived among us*' they would be reeling from the impact of what was, for them, a mind-blowing concept.

The Word/Logos

Who were John's original readers?

John was a Jew living in a Greek culture

This is a book which is hard to put down. In fact, it'll stay with you for life.

The History of BUBBLE GUM

in the city of Ephesus, so he wrote with Jews and Greeks in mind.

Because Jews had a great reverence for God, they avoided giving him a name, as this would make him seem human. Instead, a tradition arose whereby Jews in their writings used the phrase 'the Word of God' to mean God himself.

Other Jewish writings described God's great wisdom as a person, and spoke of 'Wisdom' to mean God himself.

The Greeks thought of a great Mind responsible for the created world. They spoke of the 'reason' of God.

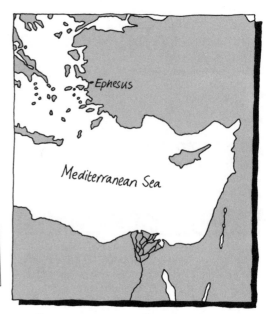

Word
Wisdom } =*logos*=mind/character of God
Reason

The Greeks of John's time worshipped many gods, but one Greek philosopher, Heroclitus, had looked at the created world and decided that there had to be one great, orderly, reasoning 'Mind' behind it all. This 'Mind' became known to Greeks as the 'Reason' of God.

The Greek word for 'reason' is *logos*.

The Greek word for 'word' is also 'logos'.

By the time John was writing his Gospel (in Greek), a Jewish philosopher called Philo had brought three ideas together – the Jewish 'Word of God' and 'Wisdom of God' and the Greek 'Reason of God' – into one word conveying the mind and character of God. That word was *logos*.

When John opened his Gospel with 'Before the world was created, the Word (logos) already existed . . .', Jews would hear the reference to the activity of their God in the creation of the world, and Greeks would hear the reference to the 'reason' of God existing before the world itself.

Both Jews and Greeks would read on to discover John's amazing statement that this *logos* God behind creation *became a human being and . . . lived among us*. The *logos* became a human being.

According to John, Jesus' ministry didn't begin with his baptism (where Mark begins); Jesus' ministry didn't even begin with his birth (where Matthew and Luke begin). John's claim is that the man Jesus was the human form taken by the mind and character of God – *logos*/Word – who existed before the creation of the world.

A modern cover 'blurb' for John's Gospel might read:

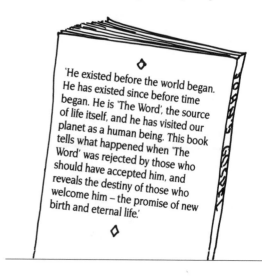

'He existed before the world began. He has existed since before time began. He is 'The Word', the source of life itself, and he has visited our planet as a human being. This book tells what happened when 'The Word' was rejected by those who should have accepted him, and reveals the destiny of those who welcome him – the promise of new birth and eternal life.'

In many Christian churches the beginning of John's Gospel is read at Christmas and people's minds and hearts are stirred by the traditional version of his words: 'In *the beginning was the* Word, *and the* Word *was with God, and the* Word *was God . . . And the* Word *became flesh and dwelt among us, full of grace and truth.'*

These words would certainly have stirred the minds and hearts of the people of Ephesus in the first century. It was John's intention that after this 'taster', they would read on, be persuaded by his presentation of Jesus, and become believers like himself.

FOLLOW UP

1. Read through John's Prologue and in your own words write down what he is telling his audience about Jesus under these headings:
– life
– light
– grace
– truth
– glory.

2. In groups of four, design a series of posters which 'advertise' Jesus as each of the words above. (Don't forget you can use examples from the chart in Unit 16.) You may want to link these posters with the promotional leaflets you designed at the end of Unit 16.

Paul's 'Cosmic' Picture of Jesus

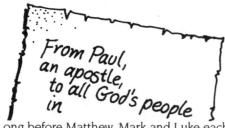

From Paul, an apostle, to all God's people in

Long before Matthew, Mark and Luke each wrote about Jesus' life, and long before John wrote about Jesus' true identity, Paul was already writing about Jesus, not in a Gospel or any kind of book, but in his many letters.

Paul's letters were mostly written to groups of new believers, to encourage them in their Christian living or to correct them if they were getting hold of wrong ideas about Jesus and the Christian life.

Paul's knowledge of Jesus was partly based on the word-of-mouth information he received from Jesus' original companions. But it was Paul's firm conviction that Jesus was alive and could be known personally by anyone. He had become a believer himself after he met Jesus on the road between Jerusalem and Damascus some time after the resurrection. It was a very dramatic conversion because Paul, a devout and respected Jew, was actually on his way to arrest the Damascus Christians for what he saw as their 'heretical' beliefs about Jesus of Nazareth.

This personal encounter with Jesus convinced Paul that Jesus, the crucified criminal, was indeed everything the 'heretical' Christians were claiming him to be – the risen Son of God, the Messiah.

And the better Paul got to know Jesus, by serving him and doing whatever he could to please him, the more Paul understood who Jesus really was, why he came to earth to die, why he rose from death and why people everywhere had to be told about Jesus – Jews *and* Gentiles.

If you look at Paul's letters to new believers, you get a clear impression of Paul's view of Jesus, as he passes on his own understanding to others.

God's secret plan... by means of Christ... to bring all creation together...
(Ephesians 1:9–10)

● Paul sees Jesus as the focal point in God's ancient **plan** to bring people close to him again.

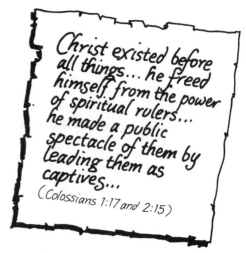

Christ existed before all things... he freed himself from the power of spiritual rulers... he made a public spectacle of them by leading them as captives...
(Colossians 1:17 and 2:15)

● Paul sees Jesus as the unbeatable **victor** over all the powers of darkness that try to keep people separated from God.

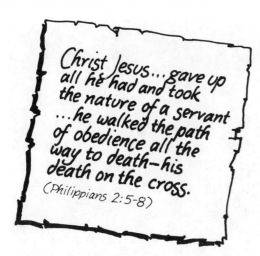

Christ Jesus... gave up all he had and took the nature of a servant ... he walked the path of obedience all the way to death—his death on the cross.

(Philippians 2:5-8)

● Paul sees Jesus' mission of rescue as the supreme **example** of selfless service and self-giving sacrifice.

A closer look at these beliefs will show that Paul's view of Jesus is wider in scope than the views of the Synoptic writers and John. Paul expands and fills out the view of Jesus as the expected Messiah-king (Synoptics). He explores more fully the idea of Jesus as the power and personality of God expressed in human form (John).

Paul (like John) sees Jesus as the Son of God who existed with God before the world was created. He presents Jesus as the one who always was and always will be superior over any other power that has ever existed or will exist, natural or supernatural, but who gave up his privileged position at God's right hand to come to earth to die on behalf of others.

These beliefs about Jesus are threaded all through Paul's letters, but it is possible to see each of them particularly clearly in his letters to the Ephesians, the Colossians and the Philippians.

The agent in God's plan

● **Jesus in God's plan of reconciliation**
(seen, for example, in Ephesians 1:3–14).

Paul says that God planned from the beginning of the world that he would have a close, loving relationship with the people he created.

But people chose to turn their backs on their life-source and so humanity brought upon itself the penalty for this – inevitable death and separation from God for ever.

God's plan – to have a close loving relationship with humanity – *has* been accomplished however, by the creation of a *new* humanity, made up of those people who have been reconciled to God through the death of Jesus.

These are the people who are 'saved' from separation because they believe that by his death Jesus paid the penalty for their own selfish independence (sin).

God's wants *all* people to be re-united with him and with each other. In the meantime, Paul urges Jesus' followers to live as those who are at one with Jesus and with one another, through their family and church life.

The victor

● **Jesus as the unbeatable victor**
(seen, for example, in Colossians 1:15–20).

Paul says that Jesus has always been pre-eminent (i.e. supreme above all things), since before the world was created. In fact, it was through Jesus that other things came into existence.

In the person of Jesus on earth God was showing himself to the world he created.

Jesus on the cross was God's way of bringing his creation back into a loving relationship with himself, by providing someone to take the punishment for the sins of the world.

So, although the crucifixion looked like the worst kind of *defeat* at the hand of powers and authorities opposed to God, the fact that it brought peace and reconciliation between God and humanity meant it was actually the supreme *victory* for Jesus.

Victory! The New Testament proclaims Jesus as the supreme victor, winning the battle against sin and death.

ROLE 3

The example

● Jesus as the supreme example

(seen, for example, in Philippians 2:6–11).

Paul quotes an early Christian hymn to remind his readers that although Jesus shared God's nature from before the beginning of time, he did not insist on his rightful supremacy. Instead, he 'gave up all he had' and came to earth – not as a great king, but as a servant, humble about himself and obedient to God.

Jesus' selflessness went as far as giving up his life and dying a criminal's death, a sacrifice which God rewarded by exalting him above everything in heaven and on earth.

In leaving his rightful place with God in order to die on the cross, Jesus gives an example to believers. Those who follow his example of humble obedience will also know God's reward.

US President Reagan shakes hands with Soviet leader Mikhail Gorbachev in 1988: a token of reconciliation between hostile nations. The New Testament describes Jesus as God's agent in his plan for reconciliation with humankind.

According to Paul, Jesus belongs to an environment which is outside the dimensions of time and space, beyond earth's limitations, beyond the reach of any challenging power. Paul's 'cosmic' view of Jesus shows him stepping into human existence for one very special reason – to do what was necessary to 'save' or rescue humanity from eternal separation from God – and then taking up his exalted position once again.

This is why Paul in his many letters frequently refers to Jesus as the Rescuer or **Saviour**, because in Paul's view that was Jesus' vital role in God's plan to bring people back to himself.

►FOLLOW UP►

1. Here is quick check on this unit.
Are these statements true or false? For each one write out a correct statement.
● Paul wrote many Gospels to new Christians.
● Paul met Jesus on the road to Damascus.
● This meeting resulted in Paul being converted to Christianity.
● Paul's conversion meant that he no longer believed that Jesus was the Messiah.

Now some more difficult questions:
● What does Paul see to be God's *plan* for the world?
● Why does Paul use the title of *Victor* for Jesus?
● What is the *example* which Jesus gives to Christian believers?

2. We have looked at Paul's use of plan, Victor and example. These titles can all be brought together in the ideas behind the title 'Saviour'.
Here is a hymn which contains all four titles. Can you identify them?

At the name of Jesus
Every knee shall bow,
Every tongue confess Him
King of glory now;
'Tis the Father's pleasure
We should call Him Lord,
Who from the beginning
Was the mighty Word.

Humbled for a season,
To receive a name
From the lips of sinners
Unto whom He came;
Faithfully He bore it
Spotless to the last,
Brought it back victorious,
When from death He passed.

Bore it up triumphant
With its human light,
Through all ranks of creatures
To the central height,
To the throne of Godhead,
To the Father's breast,
Filled it with the glory
Of that perfect rest.

In your hearts enthrone Him;
There let Him subdue
All that is not holy,
All that is not true;
Crown Him as your captain
In temptation's hour,
Let his will enfold you
In its light and power.

Brothers, this Lord Jesus
Shall return again,
With His Father's glory,
With His angel-train;
For all wreaths of empire
Meet upon His brow,
And our hearts confess Him
King of glory now.

When you have read through the hymn and the unit again, try to write a paragraph which explains how plan, Victor and example are all brought together in the title Saviour.

3. We have now looked at three views of Jesus – those of Paul, John and the Gospel writers.
Look back through Units 15–18, and then in pairs:
● Write a list of all the similarities in these views of Jesus (e.g. they all believe that he was the Son of God).
● Now try and work out what the main differences are. (That's hard!)

Pentecost and After:
The Ripples Spread

The expansion of the church

The book of Acts is Luke's account of what happened after the ascension, a detailed report of the Holy Spirit's power coming to the disciples and the ripples which spread from that event, taking the Good News about Jesus from Jerusalem out to Judea, to the surrounding regions and to the rest of the world.

Luke's account is titled (in Greek) 'The Acts of the Apostles'. 'Apostles' was the word used for the first Christian preachers and leaders. But, in fact, most of Acts is about the activities of just two apostles – Peter and Paul.

The book of Acts falls into two main parts:

● Chapters 1 to 12 tell of the rise of the Christian community (or 'church') in Jerusalem, and its spread from there to Judea, Samaria and Antioch. (By this time in his book, Luke has turned the spotlight from Peter to Paul.)

● Chapters 12 to 28 tell of Paul's three missionary journeys, his arrest in Jerusalem, his imprisonment in Caesarea and finally his journey to Rome.

Paul was a dedicated and effective pioneer, preaching about Jesus and founding new Christian communities (churches) wherever he went. It was through Paul that the ripples spread across Asia and into Europe. The vast Roman Empire, which had seemed initially to have a stranglehold on the disciples, now became the means by which the Good News travelled throughout the then-known world. Roman law and order, Roman roads and trade-routes, with Greek as an international language, made the rapid spread of Christianity possible.

What happened on the Day of Pentecost

Jesus was crucified in Jerusalem at the time of the Jewish Passover Festival. The next festival on the Jewish calendar began on the fiftieth day (in Greek, *pentecost*) after the Passover Sabbath.

It was this Jewish festival that marked the beginning of the Spirit-powered movement which became known as the Christian church.

> ## Jewish festivals
> The Jewish festival which began on the the the Day of Pentecost was the Harvest Festival (OT Exodus 23:16; Deuteronomy 16:9–10), also called Feast of Weeks, referring to the seven weeks since Passover. It celebrated the end of the grain harvest and, because it fell at a time of year that was good for travelling by mule or on foot, Jerusalem was normally crowded with Jews from outlying districts coming in for the festival.

READ ACTS 2:1–14

Jesus' followers were in Jerusalem, waiting for the spiritual power they needed before they could start their work of spreading the Good News of the Kingdom. Jesus had promised 'when the Holy Spirit comes upon you, you will be filled with power' (Acts 1:8).

They were indeed 'filled with the Holy Spirit', a dramatic experience involving wind and fire – two Old Testament pictures of the power and presence of God. The promised result – 'you will be witnesses for me' – was underlined by the fact that the Holy Spirit miraculously enhanced the disciples' speaking ability. Filled with God's Spirit, humble fishermen could communicate powerfully, even to foreign-born Jews.

📖 READ ACTS 2:14–42

Any sermon that results in 3,000 conversions has to be something special! But when you consider that it was Peter the uneducated fisherman's very first sermon which had that result, it bears looking at closely, to see exactly what 'got' to those listeners.

After reminding the Jewish crowd what their prophet Joel had foretold – that a new age would dawn, a day when God's Spirit would be poured out and all who called on God for help would be saved – Peter goes

on to make four points about Jesus:

● Jesus, a man many people in Jerusalem knew, or knew about (verse 22), was in fact the Messiah (verse 36).
● When Jesus had been crucified, God raised him from death – proof that Jesus was God's Messiah (verses 24, 32, 36).
● Although he died a criminal's death by crucifixion, God has given him the greatest possible honour, raising him to 'the right-hand side of God' (verse 33).
● Jesus offers forgiveness of sins and the gift of the Holy Spirit to all who repent of their old lives and start a new life by being symbolically washed clean in the waters of baptism (verse 38).

This proclamation (in Greek, *kerygma*) occurs again and again with slight

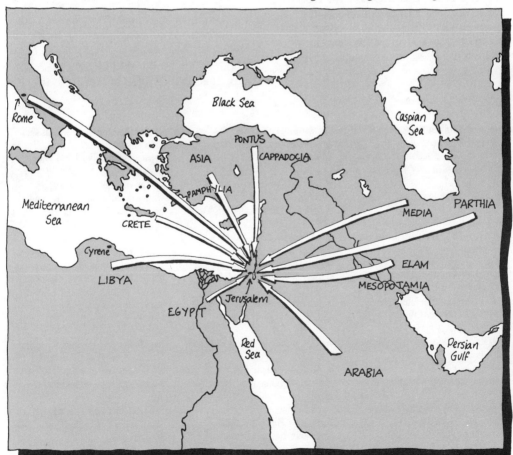

variations in Luke's account of the spreading of the ripples of the gospel. It is the kind of effective preaching which could only be accomplished with the power of the Holy Spirit.

The power of the Holy Spirit

At his final meeting with his disciples before his ascension (see Unit 14), Jesus promised that they would receive the power of the Holy Spirit to enable them to carry out the task of extending God's Kingdom.

The people's response: conversions

The first converts to Christianity were Jews, assembled in Jerusalem for a Jewish festival.

But as the ripples spread, the Good News was heard by non-Jews who had not been expecting a Messiah to come and bring them into God's Kingdom, but who still felt the need to be brought close to God.

Cornelius. One such person was Cornelius, a Roman centurion based in the coastal town of Caesarea (not the inland town of Caesarea Philippi mentioned in Unit 6).

READ ACTS 10:1–23

Because Jesus was a Jew, and all his first followers were Jews, the idea that the Good News was also for non-Jews might easily have been overlooked – despite Peter's Pentecost sermon, where he claimed that God's promise of forgiveness and the gift of the Holy Spirit was made 'to you (the Jews in Jerusalem), and your children and to all who are far away – all whom the Lord our God calls to himself' (Acts 2:39).

When Peter was actually put on the spot by the call to preach in the home of a Gentile (non-Jew), any misgivings he might have felt were dispelled in advance by the vision he had on the roof of his friend Simon's house. Although this seemed to be about eating food forbidden by Jewish law, it opened Peter's mind and heart to the

---

The term 'Holy Spirit' (or 'Spirit') is used in the Bible to mean 'the power of God in action'. The Spirit of God is seen in the Old Testament

● creating the universe (Genesis 1:2)
● giving super-human power to chosen individuals, such as Samson (Judges 13–16)
● speaking through the prophets, such as Ezekiel (Ezekiel 1:26 – 2:5)
● promised by the prophets to all God's people in the future (Ezekiel 36:25–27; Joel 2:28–29).

The Spirit of God is seen in the New Testament

● in the ministry of Jesus (Luke 4:16–21)
● promised by Jesus to his followers (John 16:7–15; Acts 1:6–8)
● coming to the disciples on the

Day of Pentecost (Acts 2:1–4)
● guiding the apostles (Acts 9:10–11; 10:9–22; 13:1–3 and 8–11; 16:6–10)
● promised to other believers (Acts 2:38–39)
● coming to other believers (Acts 8:14–17; 10:44–48; 19:1–6)
● living in believers (Romans 8:9–10)
● changing people's personalilities to make them more like Jesus (Galatians 5:16–26)
● assuring believers that they are part of God's family (Romans 8:14–17)
● helping people to pray (Romans 8:26–27)
● giving special abilities to help the Christian community in its spiritual growth (1 Corinthians 12).

Christians today continue to experience the power of the Holy

Spirit in just the same way as the early Christians did, both in preaching the gospel and living as Christians.

The evangelist Billy Graham, whose preaching regularly results in hundreds and thousands of converts, says:

'Evangelists cannot bring conviction of sin, righteousness, or judgement; that is the Spirit's work. They cannot convert anyone; that is the Spirit's work. The evangelist can invite men to receive Christ, and exhort them. But the effectual work is done by the Spirit as He works on the minds, hearts, and wills of the unsaved. We are to take care of the possible and trust God for the impossible.'

See Unit 53 for other accounts of how people experience God's Holy Spirit today.

idea that God might be challenging him to put away his Jewish preconceptions in order to spread the Good News.

The Bible describes the Spirit of God (the Holy Spirit) as being like a strong wind. We cannot see it, but every sailor knows its driving force.

READ ACTS 10.24–48

While Peter was still preaching, his listeners were convinced and became believers. But before they had even had a chance to ask about baptism, they experienced a dramatic outpouring of God's Holy Spirit, very like what happened to disciples on the Day of Pentecost. They found themselves speaking strange languages, and could not contain their praise for God.

Later, Peter had to explain his actions to the other apostles, and they all concluded that God meant to include repentant Gentiles as well as Jews in his new order (Acts 11:1–18).

This was a necessary process if the ripples were to spread 'to the ends of the earth' as Jesus had promised.

Saul of Tarsus. The most significant Jewish convert to Christianity in the early days was undoubtedly Saul of Tarsus, an extremely religious Pharisee.

Saul was an unlikely candidate for conversion. His devotion to the Jewish law and traditions made him hostile to any influence that might 'water down' the true Jewish religion as he saw it. So, when a young Jewish Christian called Stephen was stoned to death for trying to explain to the Jewish authorities just how Jesus *was* the expected Messiah, Saul was an approving spectator (Acts 7:54–8:1).

Stephen's death led to fresh moves to stamp out this new 'heresy' (false teaching), and the believers fled from Jerusalem to the outlying towns and cities of Judea and Samaria (fulfilling Jesus' words).

Before long, Saul had tracked down a group of believers in Damascus, and got permission from the Jewish authorites to go and arrest them.

READ ACTS 9:1–9

Saul was literally stopped in his tracks by an encounter with Jesus himself – Jesus who had been crucified, but who was being proclaimed by his followers as raised by God from the dead. All Saul's ideas about Jesus were suddenly and dramatically changed.

Many Christians today come to understand who Jesus is in a gradual way, through the teaching in their family and their church. But there are thousands of Christians who have had such a sudden and dramatic conversion experience that they call it a 'Damascus road experience'.

READ ACTS 9:10–31

Imagine how you would feel today, if you were under threat of real persecution and death (not at all unusual in many parts of the world). Imagine how you'd feel if you were asked to meet and befriend the Chief Persecutor!

No wonder the local believers were wary of Saul, until they saw and heard for themselves that he too was now boldly preaching the Good News about Jesus.

Saul eventually became the great missionary to the Gentiles, and so became known by his Roman name, Paul.

Paul spent the rest of his life preaching the gospel and setting up churches all over Asia Minor (Turkey) and the countries of southern Europe around the Mediterranean.

▲FOLLOW✺UP▲

1. Read through Acts chapter 3.

Look closely at verses 11–26. Can you see each of the four points of the *kerygma*?

Write out the reference for each point and mention what the references are about.

2. Imagine that you are one of the Sanhedrin who interrogated Peter and John (chapter 4). Write a letter to a friend which includes the following:
● the reason why Peter and John were arrested
● your interview with them
● your interview with the man who has been healed
● an explanation of what Peter and John believe about Jesus
● why, as a good Jew, you don't believe that Jesus is the Messiah (you will have to look back at units 7 and 8 to help with this)
● some other news that your friend will be interested in!

3. Now read Acts chapter 9.

Write another letter to your friend explaining what has happened to Saul. Make sure you are suitably horrified by his conversion, and not pleased!

4. Come back to being yourself now . . . You have been asked to give a talk about the power of the Holy Spirit in the Bible. Your talk is to last for no more than three minutes . . .

Make sure you include:
● who the Holy Spirit is
● what his work was in the Bible
● some examples of people in the Bible (Old Testament or New Testament) whose lives were changed by the Holy Spirit.
● the effect of the Holy Spirit on the early church
● what happened on the Day of Pentecost.

You will need to write your speech out and probably edit it down to three minutes.

Imagine that your audience don't know anything (!) and you want to interest them in your subject.

When your speech is complete try it out on your group, with a stop watch . . .

The New Community and its Leaders

After Peter had preached his very first sermon on the Day of Pentecost, 3,000 people were so convinced by his words that their lives were completely changed. As a sign of the start of this 'new life', they were baptized. But that wasn't the end of the matter. Far from it – their conversion and baptism were only the beginning of a whole new way of living.

A new community

READ ACTS 2:42–47; 4:32–37

The new believers began to form themselves into a loving and sharing community. The sharing of money and belongings was very important. But so were other things in their new life:

- learning (2:42)
- worship and prayer (2:42 and 47)
- living and eating together (2:42, 44 and 46)
- establishing a good reputation with people (2:47)
- telling people about Jesus (4:33).

The importance of this new lifestyle to these new converts can be seen by the fact that they were prepared to sell all their possessions, even land and houses, so that no one in the group was in need (4:34–35).

Leaders of the church

READ ACTS 6:1–7

Obviously, with converts coming in to the new faith by their hundreds and thousands,

some organization was needed in the new Christian community or 'church'. In this particular incident, there seems to have been some suspicion that native Jewish widows were getting more than Greek-speaking Jewish widows when it came to sharing out goods and food.

The twelve apostles decided to hand over this aspect of the work to an authorized team of seven helpers (the Greek word is *diakonos*=deacon).

The problem of selecting suitable leaders was also important when new churches were set up in other towns and cities, away from the main church in Jerusalem.

We get some idea of how the selection was made, in the details of a letter sent by Paul to a disciple called Timothy, who was responsible for choosing and training leaders for some of these new churches.

The first Christian community emerged from the response to Peter's sermon in Jerusalem on the Day of Pentecost. Jerusalem was also the location for the first Church Council.

Apostles and deacons

The twelve disciples called by Jesus to be his closest followers are listed by name in Matthew 10:2–4; Mark 3:16–19 and Luke 6:14–16. They are **Simon** (=**Peter**), **Andrew**, **James**, **John**, **Philip**, **Bartholemew** (=**Nathaniel**), **Thomas**, **Matthew** (=**Levi**), **James** (son of Alphaeus), **Thaddaeus**, **Simon** (the Patriot/Zealot) and **Judas Iscariot**. (NB: Luke has 'Judas, son of James' in place of the 'Thaddaeus' in Matthew's and Mark's lists).

After the suicide of Judas Iscariot, a meeting was held to discover God's choice for a replacement. They prayed and used a special two-sided dice to choose between the two men proposed. And **Matthias** became one of 'the Twelve' (Acts 1:15–26), also known as 'the twelve apostles'.

The word 'apostle' means a messenger or ambassador. The original twelve apostles were personally chosen by Jesus to witness the events of his life, death and resurrection. The eleven who remained, with Matthias, became the acknowledged leaders of the early church.

Paul also counted himself an apostle (see 1 Corinthians 15:3–11) – although 'the least of all' because he had persecuted God's church. He uses the title at the opening of most of his letters.

The seven men selected to take over the practical administration in the Jerusalem church (Acts 6:1–6) were chosen by the whole group, guided by the Holy Spirit. They are usually described as 'deacons', a word used elsewhere in the New Testament but only implied here by their function. The word 'deacon' means servant or helper. Although their work was practical, their qualifications were spiritual. These seven men were all Greek-speaking Jews – **Stephen**, **Philip**, **Prochorus**, **Nicanor**, **Timon**, **Parmenas** and **Nicolaus**. The basic qualifications for deacons are listed in 1 Timothy 3:8–13, and a deaconess named Phoebe is mentioned in Romans 16:1–2.

Other people who it is assumed gave close support to the apostles include **Joseph Barsabbas** (Acts 1:21–23), **Barnabas** (Acts 11:19–26), **Silas/Silvanus** (Acts 16), **Timothy** (1 Corinthians 4:17), **Titus** (2 Corinthians 8:23), **Apollos** (1 Corinthinans 1:12), **Priscilla** and **Aquila** (Romans 16:3).

In these early days there was no formal hierarchy. The leaders were chosen for a specific work.

 READ 1 TIMOTHY 3:1–13

Leadership in the early church was not just a matter of business management or good example. All the leaders profiled in the New Testament are men and women of faith. They exercised a ministry which depended wholly on the power of God, and their unity with him through Christ.

READ ACTS 3:1–10; 5:1–11; 9:32–43

These leaders were able to perform miracles of healing, mind-reading, prophesying future events, even raising the dead – not by means of magic or personal ability, but through the power of God's Holy Spirit.

Decision-making

Advice and teaching could be sent to individual groups of Christians by letter, but when it came to really important matters affecting all Christians everywhere, decisions were made after much prayer by the whole group, with the apostles taking the lead.

 READ ACTS 15:1–35

Christianity developed out of Judaism, with the arrival of Jesus as the expected Messiah and the establishing of God's new 'Kingdom' empowered by the Holy Spirit.

So it is not too surprising that the first major issue which could have split the whole church concerned the relationship between Christianity and the old Jewish religion. Questions raised were:

● Should we preach the Good News about Jesus being the Christ/Messiah to Jews only, or also to Gentiles?
● If Gentiles accept that Jesus is the Christ/Messiah and want to come to him for forgiveness and the gift of the Holy Spirit, do they have to become Jews first by being circumcised?

The Council of Jerusalem, made up of all the most senior church leaders gathered together, heard the different views, and made the vitally important decision that Gentiles could become Christians *without* having to keep the Jewish Law. But Gentiles should take care that their lifestyle did not cause offence to some of the more conservative Jewish Christians and so create division.

This first Council decree was of enormous significance, for it gave Paul (and others after him) freedom to preach to all nations, ensuring that Christianity would spread, not just to the regions around Judea or wherever Jewish influence was strong, but throughout the Gentile world. The Council's decision confirmed Paul's stand. From that time, the Christian message has been that men and women, Jews and non-Jews, are saved as they respond in faith to God's free gift – not by keeping rules and regulations.

▲FOLLOW UP▲

1. Look again at Acts chapter 15.
Design a letter to be read out in every church, explaining very simply:
● who Paul, Silas, Judas and Barnabas (the men who have brought the letter to you) are
● why it was necessary to hold the Council of Jerusalem
● the discussion that took place at the Council
● the main decisions the Council reached
● the other decisions that were reached by the Council.

2. Read through the Bible references to church leadership in this unit. Now draw up a job description for a deacon at the church in Jerusalem. (Make sure you include the selection process of prayer in your description.) Here is a modern job description for an Anglican priest to give you an idea of format:

> **Anglican Church – South Africa**
> A large established church in Cape Town is looking for a priest in charge. The church is evangelical, charismatic and is involved in evangelism and social outreach. We require an outgoing positive person who is a teacher of the word of God. The ideal man will be a facilitator able to guide our leadership team. Reply Selection Committee.
>
> **PO Box 59**
> **KENILWORTH**
> **7745**
> **Republic of South Africa**

Worship

SUNDAY MEETINGS, THE LORD'S SUPPER AND BAPTISM

After the first conversions at Pentecost, the new believers began meeting together daily for fellowship, teaching and worship (Acts 2:42 and 46–47). Later, Christians met regularly on the first day of the week, Sunday (1 Corinthians 16:2). (In Unit 43, we shall consider the reasons for meeting on a Sunday).

Sunday meetings

The first Christians met in each other's homes (1 Corinthians 16:19; Colossians 4.15) and their worship included

● prayer (1 Timothy 2:1)
● praise and thanksgiving (Ephesians 5:19–20; Colossians 3.16)
● reading from the (OT) scriptures (1 Timothy 4:13; 2 Timothy 3:16)
● preaching (1 Timothy 4:13)
● teaching (1 Timothy 4:13)
● singing hymns and psalms (Ephesians 5:19; Colossians 3:16)
● collection of money to help those in need (1 Corinthians 16:2).

Meeting together for worship was an important part of Christian community life. Praying, praising and learning together provided Christians with opportunities for mutual encouragement (Hebrews 10:25).

The Christian community had two religious rites based on specific commands given by Jesus – the Lord's Supper (Luke 22:19–20) and baptism (Matthew 28:18–20).

The Lord's Supper

The most important feature in Christian worship, right from the time of the first converts on the Day of Pentecost, was a shared meal during which they re-enacted Jesus' Last Supper with his disciples, the night before he was crucified, when he took bread as a token of his broken body and wine as a symbol of God's new covenant with mankind.

On the walls of the catacombs, deep beneath the city of Rome, is this picture of the celebration meal associated with the Lord's Supper – painted by the early Christians.

On that occasion, it had been a Jewish Passover meal. For the new converts, it became a symbolic drama, proclaiming the meaning of Jesus' death as a sacrifice for the sins of the world (see Unit 12).

But in Corinth some Christians had a feast while others went hungry and Paul had to write and put them straight:

READ 1 CORINTHIANS 11:17–34

Paul's teaching about the Lord's Supper gives us an insight into
● how the early Christians sometimes gathered to share a meal together
● how the early Christians were supposed to celebrate the Lord's Supper.

Christians began meeting to share meals together soon after the first conversions in Jerusalem (Acts 2:46). Because of the emphasis on love and fellowship expressed through eating together, the community meal became known later as the *agape* feast, from one of the Greek words for 'love'.

When sharing bread and wine with his disciples at the Last Supper, Jesus had specifically commanded them to

'do this in memory of me.'
Luke 22:19

The two strands – fellowship together and remembering Jesus' death – were part of the Corinthians' worship when they met together. But the fellowship meal was

spoiled by selfishness and because of this the Lord's Supper was also spoiled.

Paul's reminder of Jesus' words – passed on by the disciples who had been at the Last Supper – provides all Christians with a formula for the Lord's Supper. It is to be a re-enactment of Jesus' last meal with his disciples, practised as a way of remembering Jesus' death and proclaiming the benefits of his sacrifice until he comes to earth again.

Paul's condemnation of the thoughtlessness of some of the Corinthian Christians at the fellowship meal underlines the importance of the Lord's Supper. People who take the bread and wine without first examining their attitudes and relationships will come under God's judgment.

Baptism

From the Day of Pentecost onwards, anyone who joined the Christian community in response to the preaching of the gospel had to be baptized, that is, ceremonially immersed in water.

Baptism was not a new rite. Gentile converts to the Jewish religion (called

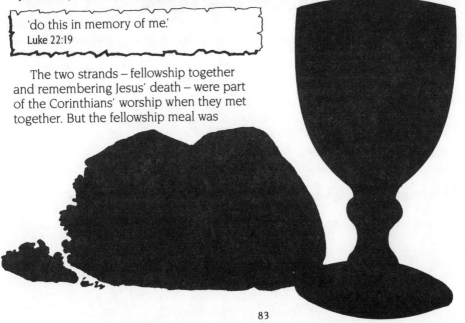

'proselytes') were baptized to symbolize that they were cleansed from their impure Gentile past.

John the Baptist thought that Jews needed cleansing every bit as much as Gentiles; he appealed to the Jewish people to repent of their old ways in preparation for the arrival of God's Messiah, and baptized those who responded.

When the apostles preached and people responded, those who were baptized in water also received the 'baptism of the Spirit' (Acts 1:4–5; 2:38–39). God's Spirit filled them with new power to live as God wanted. This empowering was associated with the baptism in water, although it sometimes happened separately either before baptism (Acts 10:44–48) or after baptism (Acts 8:14–17). Within the new community, the practice of baptism was the initiation (joining or starting) rite, symbolizing
● the new believer's desire to start a new life after repenting of his/her bad, old ways
● the new believer's willingness to be empowered by the Holy Spirit for his/her new life and responsibilities within the Christian community.

Although Christian baptism was not a particularly formal rite in the early days (Acts 8:36–37), some parts of the New Testament indicate that later it became the practice to instruct new converts about the Christian faith before they were baptized. This instruction may perhaps have been part of the teaching given at Sunday meetings.

There are traces of short statements of belief ('creeds') in 1 Timothy 2:5–6 and 3:16, and in Titus 3:4–7, which may have been part of the formal instruction for new believers and perhaps part of what was said publicly by the new believer on the occasion of his/her baptism.

Paul describes the meaning of Christian baptism in Romans 6:3–4. It is a way of identifying with Christ's death and resurrection, by being 'buried' in the water, then being raised again to 'live a new life'.

The first letter of Peter seems to be based on a sermon given at a baptism service (1 Peter 1:3 – 4:11). It assures the listeners of this new life and describes the sort of conduct expected of a baptized Christian.

▲ FOLLOW UP ▲

1. A quick check. Do you know the answers to these questions?
● What happened at the Last Supper?
● Which Jewish festival was being celebrated by Jesus and his disciples?
● What new meaning did Jesus give to the bread and the wine at that festival meal?
● What do Christians believe about the meaning of the death of Jesus?
● What problems did Paul have to sort out for the Corinthian church regarding the Lord's Supper?

2. Look back at the references for Sunday meetings in the early church.

Write a description of what you think would have been a typical Sunday meeting.

What are the similarities and differences between that meeting and a typical Sunday service at your local church? (You may need to attend a church service or interview a minister.)

3. Here are some of the key words in the belief of the early church about the meaning of baptism.
● REPENTANCE
● CLEANSING
● EMPOWERING
● JOINING
● DYING
● RESURRECTION

Write a sentence explaining the significance of each one.

Spiritual Gifts

Jesus had promised:

> **"**When the Holy Spirit comes upon you, you will be filled with power.**"**
>
> Acts 1:8

On the Day of Pentecost, the disciples were 'all filled with the Holy Spirit and began to talk in other languages, as the Spirit enabled them to speak' (Acts 2:4).

God gave them the gift they needed to make his message understood by people who came from far-off Persia and Asia Minor (Turkey) and Egypt.

That same day, Peter was given the power to preach in a way that changed people, and in his sermon he assured them that 'God's promise was made to you' (Acts 2:39).

It was true: the new converts saw 'many miracles and wonders done through the apostles' (Acts 2:43). But was there any justification for Peter's promise that *all* believers could expect to be filled with the Holy Spirit and be channels of this same supernatural power?

The evidence of the New Testament (and of the present-day – see Unit 53) is a resounding *yes*!

Spiritual gifts

READ I CORINTHIANS 12

When Paul sent this letter to the Christians in Corinth, it was written in Greek. And in order to help the Corinthians to understand just *how* the Holy Spirit's power would operate in their lives, Paul chose very particular Greek words to describe these 'spiritual gifts'.

He calls them

● 'gifts from the Holy Spirit' (verse 1)
● 'spiritual gifts' (verse 4)
● 'ways of serving' (verse 5)
● 'abilities to perform service' (verse 6)
● 'The Spirit's presence . . . shown in some way' (verse 7).

Paul's original Greek words in these verses have the following ideas behind them:

● 'filled with wind, breath or spirit' (verse 1)
● 'free gifts – not earned or deserved' (verse 4)
● 'helping others' (verse 5)
● 'bursts of dynamic energy' (verse 6)
● 'clearly seen' (verse 7).

In choosing to use these words to describe the activity of the Holy Spirit, Paul was encouraging the Corinthian Christians to expect God to give them the special gifts they needed in order to become a strong and caring community.

(verses 10 and 11). The power of God seen in the person of Jesus is the power of the Holy Spirit, given to every believer.

The effects of this 'presence of the Spirit' (verse 11) in the Christian's life are as follows:

● The penalty for living in the bad, old way is removed (verse 1).
● The Christian is no longer under the power of human nature (verses 5 and 9).
● The Christian is given a new kind of life which will not die when the body dies (verses 10 and 11).
● The Christian becomes part of God's own family (verses 14–17).
● The Christian is given a genuine hope, despite the apparent hopelessness of the world (verses 18–25 and 28).
● The Christian is helped in her/his prayers by the Holy Spirit (verses 26 and 27).
● Assurance is given that nothing will ever come between the Christian and God's love given 'through Christ Jesus our Lord' (verses 31–39).

In Paul's mind, everyone who belongs to God's family through Christ possesses the Holy Spirit and his power.

Anyone who was not aware of the Spirit's part in bringing help, hope and power into a Christian's life could have jumped to wrong conclusions about the spiritual gifts. People *could* have wondered whether the gifts were tricks that could be learned or even bought – as one quite famous magician clearly thought:

Unwrapping Paul's Greek

In verse 1, the Greek word for 'the gifts from the Holy Spirit' ' is *pneumatica*, which means 'filled with wind or spirit' (like your bike tyres!). These gifts are specially given by God – they are not human talents.

In verse 4, the Greek word for 'gifts' is *charismata* which means 'free gifts – not earned or deserved'. These gifts are not prizes awarded by God to those making good progress.

In verse 5, the Greek word for 'serving' is *diaconia* which means 'helping others'. These gifts are for the benefit of other people, not for self-gratification.

In verse 6, the Greek word for 'abilities' is *energemata*, which means 'bursts of energy or power'. These gifts are expressions of God's great power.

In verse 7, the Greek word for 'is shown' is *phanerosis*, which means 'something which makes an appearance and can be seen'. These gifts are clearly seen, not all in the mind.

Spiritual gifts are therefore special powers (*energemata*) given to people by God's Spirit (*pneumatica*), given freely without being earned (*charismata*), shown clearly (*phanerosis*) through people's ordinary faculties, and used for the benefit of others (*diaconia*).

In another letter, the one to the Christians in Rome, Paul expands on this theme of the Holy Spirit living in and working through Christians.

 READ ROMANS CHAPTER 8

It is interesting to note that Paul switches between 'Christ lives in you' and 'the Spirit of God . . . lives in you' when describing the inner power available to the Christian

READ ACTS 8:9–25

It seems that although Simon the magician was a converted and baptized believer, he was not able to be filled with the Holy Spirit. This was not just because he had offered to *buy* the Spirit's power, but because his heart was not right before God (verse 21). Peter could see that Simon was bitter and full of envy. Until these things were dealt with there was no place for the Holy Spirit in his life.

God's special gifts

What exactly *were* God's special 'spiritual gifts'? Evidence from the rest of the New Testament, and from the present-day, suggests that the gifts listed in 1 Corinthians 12:8–10 were as follows:

- **a message full of wisdom:** an appropriate piece of advice or guidance, not out of someone's intellect or human understanding, but 'given' by the Holy Spirit – a supernatural 'word'

- **a message full of knowledge:** a statement of the true facts in a situation, which the speaker could not have known about unless God had revealed them (Acts 5:1–5)

- **faith:** a confident state of certainty in God (Acts 3:1–7)

- **gifts of healing:** the power of God to restore to health of body, mind or spirit (Acts 9:32–35)

- **working of miracles:** supernatural power over natural physical laws (Acts 8:39–40)

- **speaking God's message** ('prophecy' in some versions): not so much foretelling the future as speaking God's words – making his pronouncements

- **the gift of discernment:** the ability to distinguish between what is true and what is false, even when the false claims to be from God (Acts 8:18–21)

- **speaking in strange tongues:** the God-given ability to speak in an unlearned language, usually in public or private prayer and praise, but sometimes also in present-day prophecy (Acts 10:44–47)

- **explaining what is said in tongues:** the ability to interpret what is said when unknown tongues have been used in worship or prophecy (1 Corinthians 14:5–13).

Paul makes it clear that each of these gifts is given by God to individuals in order to help and strengthen the whole church. Important as they are, the things which every Christian should strive for are the great, lasting qualities of hope, faith and, above all, love (1 Corinthians 13 and 14).

FOLLOW UP

Look back at the list of the gifts of the Spirit in 1 Corinthians chapter 12 and the descriptions of these gifts at the end of this unit.

In 1 Corinthians 14:12 Paul states:

'since you are eager to have the gifts of the Spirit, you must try above everything else to make greater use of those which help to build up the church.'

- Why do you think the Corinthian church was 'eager to have the gifts of the Spirit'?
- How do you think that the gifts of the Spirit listed in 1 Corinthians 12 would 'help to build up the church'?
- Try to write your own general description of the gifts

of the Holy Spirit. Use the key ideas from 1 Corinthians 12 in your description:
- 'filled with wind, breath or spirit'
- free gifts
- helping others
- bursts of energy and power
- something which makes an appearance and can be seen.

Start: 'The gifts of the Holy Spirit are . . .'

Now check *your* description against the one given in this unit. Could you now describe the gifts of the Spirit to a friend? Try!

Love: Jesus' Teaching

Jesus' teaching about love covers four main ideas.
- God loves every individual.
- The individual therefore should love God.
- The individual should also love other people – friends and enemies.
- Jesus' followers should have a special love for each other based on his own love for them.

God's love

The importance Jesus gave to showing how much God loves people can be seen in the three parables of Luke 15:
- The lost sheep (Luke 15:1–7)
- The lost coin (Luke 15:8–10)

- The lost ('prodigal') son (Luke 15:11–32)

Each story makes the same basic statement – God is active in seeking out his lost people; no one is too insignificant or too sinful to be loved by him.

Responding to God's love

The central part of Jesus' teaching on love is his reminder of the old covenant commandments, which required God's people to love and obey him and also to love and respect their fellow human beings:

> Jesus answered, '''Love the Lord your God with all your heart, with all your soul, and with all your mind.'' This is the greatest and the most important commandment. The second most important commandment is like it: ''Love your neighbour as you love yourself.'' The whole Law of Moses and the teachings of the prophets depend on these two commandments.'
> Matthew 22:37–40

The importance Jesus gave to the need for people to love each other can be seen in another three parables:
- The good Samaritan (Luke 10:25–37)
- The rich man and Lazarus (Luke 16:19–31)
- The sheep and the goats (Matthew 25:31–46)

Each story asks the same basic question – How much do you love your fellow human beings? The test of real love is how we treat one another, not just how we feel.

Jesus takes this obligation to love other people to its limit. Loving those who love you, he says, is easy enough (Luke 6:32). But God wants more than that; he wants us to love our enemies as well (Luke 6:35).

Love for enemies has two dimensions:
- not taking revenge for any wrongs done against you (Matthew 5:38–39)
- giving more than duty requires (Matthew 5:41).

Love one another

When speaking to his closest followers, Jesus introduced a 'new commandment' of love to stand alongside the two 'great commandments' of love for God and our neighbour.

READ JOHN 13:34–35; 14:21; 15:12–13

Jesus taught that his followers should love each other in a particular way – the way that he has loved them. The Gospels record how Jesus loved those around him, by
- caring for them
- encouraging them
- healing them
- teaching them
- providing for their needs
- setting their fears at rest.

They also record Jesus' greatest act of love, which he hints at in John 15:13, by
- dying for them

Jesus in his own life and death has given a pattern of love for his followers to imitate in their dealings with each other.

This costly self-sacrificing kind of love is not optional; those who call themselves disciples are commanded to love in this way. Loving each other this way, in obedience to the 'new commandment'
- shows everyone that they are Jesus' disciples (John 13:35)
- shows Jesus that they love him (John 14:21)
- makes them Jesus' friends (John 15:14).

The apostles went on to explore and expand Jesus' teaching on love, as we shall see in Unit 24. In 1 Corinthians 13:4–7, Paul describes the kind of love Jesus wants to see in his followers:

'Love is patient and kind; it is not jealous or conceited or proud; love is not ill-mannered or selfish or irritable; love does not keep a record of wrongs; love is not happy with evil, but is happy with the truth. Love never gives up; and its faith, hope and patience never fail.'

This description of the 'new commandment' is also a picture of the one who gave that commandment – Jesus himself.

▲ FOLLOW UP ▲

1. Either:
- draw a poster which sums up the four main ideas of Jesus' teaching about love;
or:
- write a short story which illustrates these four points. (Have a look at the parables in this unit for some ideas.)

2. Read this prayer, which was found on a piece of wrapping-paper beside the body of a dead child at Ravensbruck Concentration Camp:

"O Lord,
remember not only the men and women of good will, but those of ill will.
But do not remember all the suffering they have inflicted upon us;
remember the fruits we have bought thanks to this suffering –
our comradeship, our loyalty, our humility, our courage, our generosity, the greatness of heart which has grown out of all this;
and when they come to the judgement, let all the fruits which we have borne be their forgiveness."

Does it remind you of any words of Jesus? (Look back at Luke 23:34.)

What do you think is the value of love like this? Do you think it is senseless?

3. The Jews at the time of Jesus believed that it was their *actions* which were important. Jesus taught that *attitudes* were even more important.

In pairs discuss the following, with one person taking the Jewish side and the other agreeing with the teaching of Jesus:

Right actions are meaningless without right attitudes.

Now swap roles and try arguing the other viewpoint!

Love:
The Apostles' Teaching

Jesus' teaching about love (see Unit 23) was taken up and developed by his followers. You can see this in the things some of them wrote about love.

What John says

John, in his Gospel, recorded what he remembered Jesus saying about love to his disciples, the 'new commandment' to 'love one another' (John 13:34–35: 14:20–21; 15:12–15).

But in his letters to other Christians, John stressed the importance of love in his own words:

 READ 1 JOHN 4:7–21

John's firm belief that love and God are inseparable makes him put it *very* strongly – '*God is love*', he says. This God-love was shown beyond all doubt when he 'sent his Son to be the means by which our sins are forgiven'. John puts the two-fold teaching of Jesus in a nutshell of his own in verse 11:

> If this is how God loved us, then we should love one another.

We love because God first loved us.

What James says

It was another disciple, James, who gave some practical suggestions as to *how* Christians ought to love one another:

 READ JAMES 2:1–17

Christians, says James, are to look after the material needs of people poorer than themselves, and they are not – definitely *not* – to show preference for rich and

influential people. Genuine faith shows itself in actions.

He warns Christians of the danger of becoming hypocrites – basing their judgments on the wrong motives (verse 4). (This should remind you of something. If you're not sure what, check back to Matthew 6:1–2; 7:1–5.)

What Paul says

Paul, in his letter to the Romans, gives his own teaching on how Christians should love each other, and combines loving with serving. Love and obedience go together, as in Jesus' teaching.

READ ROMANS 12:3 – 13:10

Paul's teaching on love, like that of John and James, is very close to the teaching of Jesus. You can probably find several parallels between this section and Jesus' words in the Gospels of Matthew and John. The most obvious parallel is Paul's summary in 13:8–10:

'Be under obligation to no one – the only obligation you have is to love one another. Whoever does this has obeyed the Law. The commandments, "Do not commit adultery; do not commit murder; do not steal; do not desire what belongs to someone else" – all these, and any others besides, are summed up in the one command, "Love your neighbour as yourself". If you love someone, you will never do him wrong; to love, then, is to obey the whole Law.'

See how this echoes Jesus' words:

Jesus answered, '"Love the Lord your God with all your heart, with all your soul, and with all your mind." This is the greatest and the most important commandment. The second most important commandment is like it: "Love your neighbour as you love yourself." The whole Law of Moses and the teachings of the prophets depend on these two commandments.'
Matthew 22:37–40

'My commandment is this: love one another, just as I love you. The greatest love a person can have for his friends is to give his life for them.'
John 15:12–13

READ EPHESIANS 5:1–5

In another of his letters – to the Christians in Ephesus – Paul gives a list of things to be avoided by Christians whose lives are controlled by love. (Paul was always giving lists – it made things easier to remember.)

Love within marriage

Paul's picture of love within a Christian marriage also comes in his letter to the Ephesians:

READ EPHESIANS 5:21–33

A loving marriage provides one of the best pictures we can have of human love. The teaching of Jesus and the apostles gives the whole concept of love a new and far deeper dimension.

Paul is often thought to be down on women. But here, before he tells wives to submit to their husbands, he says, 'Submit yourselves to one another.' The keynote of Paul's view of married love is verse 25:

66 Husbands, love your wives just as Christ loved the church and gave his life for it. 99

Think of how Jesus loved those around him –
● by caring for them
● by encouraging them
● by healing them
● by teaching them
● by providing for their needs
● by setting their fears at rest
● by dying for them.

That's a pretty tall order for any husband to try to match up to!

Paul's concept of wives submitting to their husbands may reflect the social and cultural conventions of his time. But however the Christian husband and wife relate to each other, Paul's high ideal for the husband's love rules out force or domination.

Love within the church

66 I may be able to speak the languages of men and even of angels, but if I have no love, my speech is no more than a noisy gong or a clanging bell. I may have the gift of inspired preaching; I may have all knowledge and understand all secrets; I may have all the faith needed to move mountains – but if I have no love, I am nothing. I may give away everything I have, and even give up my body to be burnt – but if I have no love, this does me no good.

'Love is patient and kind; it is not jealous or conceited or proud; love is not ill-mannered or selfish or irritable; love does not keep a record of wrongs; love is not happy with evil, but is happy with the truth. Love never gives up; and its faith, hope, and patience never fail.

'Love is eternal. There are inspired messages, but they are temporary; there are gifts of speaking in strange tongues, but they will cease; there is knowledge, but it will pass. For our gifts of knowledge and of inspired messages are only partial; but when what is perfect comes, then what is partial will disappear.

'When I was a child, my speech, feelings, and thinking were all those of a child; now that I am a man, I have no more use for childish ways. What we see now is like a dim image in a mirror; then we shall see face to face. What I know now is only partial; then it will be complete – as complete as God's knowledge of me.

'Meanwhile these three remain: faith, hope, and love; and the greatest of these is love. 99
1 Corinthians 13

This is one of the most beautiful passages in the Bible, and therefore one of the most famous. But the context is also important.

In the previous chapter (12) of this letter to Corinth, Paul has been talking to the Corinthians about the special gifts from the Holy Spirit to the church. (See Unit 22.)

And in the chapter after the famous passage on love, (14) Paul teaches them more about how to organise the use of the spiritual gifts in their church meetings. (See Unit 21.)

Some of the spiritual gifts are quite spectacular – miracles, healings and speaking in strange tongues. (They tend to get more attention than gifts of helping or encouragement.) So Paul knows there will be problems in using them – arguments about whether such things are proper in church, and whether or not they're a sign of being more mature than other Christians.

So, in the middle of his teaching about spiritual gifts, Paul puts in this very firm reminder of what should motivate *all* Christian behaviour – love. In fact, the spiritual gifts are worthless if they are exercised without love, says Paul, for love will outlast them all.

He starts his teaching on the importance of love with a reminder of the emptiness of the 'speaking' gifts without it (verses 1, 2), and goes on to say that the gifts of faith and serving others are useless too, without love (verses 2, 3).

There is a summary of love in action in verses 4–7, which describes the attitude of a truly loving person.

Then comes a reminder that so much of what seems important now is in fact only temporary, whereas love is a quality which will last for ever. Paul uses picture language about a growing child and a dim mirror to point out that things will look different in eternity when everything will be seen clearly – all the more impressive spiritual gifts will have disappeared (verses 11, 12). They are no longer needed.

To keep the balance right, says Paul, it is best to concentrate on faith, hope and love – especially love (verse 13).

FOLLOW UP

Write a sermon to be preached at a Christian wedding. You must include the following points:
- the Christian meaning of love
- how a Christian husband should treat his wife
- how a Christian wife should treat her husband.

Make sure that your sermon is no more than five minutes! The congregation will stop listening after that time . . .

Life in All its Fullness

NEW TESTAMENT TEACHING ABOUT THE CHRISTIAN EXPERIENCE

Jesus promised to his followers: 'I have come in order that you might have life – life in all its fullness' (John 10:10). Sometimes, this special kind of life is called 'eternal life' (John 10:28; John 3:16).

Eternal life

All those who welcome Jesus as God's Messiah and the only perfect sacrifice for people's sins are assured of a new and undying experience of God's love (Romans 8:38–39). This new relationship, with all it means, –

● forgiveness for sins (Ephesians 1:7; Colossians 1:14)
● adoption into God's family (Romans 8:15–16)
● God's help to live a life that pleases him
● assurance of God's welcome after death (Romans 8:38–39)

– makes so much difference to their way of thinking and living that it is like being 'born again' (John 3:3). This new birth cannot be brought about by making an effort to be good (Ephesians 2:8–9). The new birth is the result of God's Holy Spirit coming to live within a person when they have acknowledged that Jesus died for their sins, and accepted God's rule over their life for the future (John 3:5–7; Romans 8:10).

A new family

Just as a new baby is part of a family, so the new Christian is part of the larger Christian family. The Father of this family is God himself (Romans 8:15) and the eldest son is Jesus (Romans 8:29). All other believers are brothers and sisters (2 Corinthians 1:1; 2:13; Romans 16:1).

The most usual name for God's family is 'the church' (1 Corinthians 1:2; 2 Corinthians 1:1; Galatians 1:2). This comes from the Greek word for 'a gathering of people', and it is used in two ways in the New Testament. It can mean the group of believers in a local situation, or it can refer to the whole company of believers everywhere (Colossians 1:18).

In the New Testament the word church is never used to refer to a building, because believers at that time met in each other's homes. But sometimes the New Testament

---

The New Testament uses many different names for God's family, each name reflecting some special truth about the family of believers. There is a list of names in 1 Peter 2:9:

● **the chosen race** – those who, like the Jews of old, have been rescued from slavery (to sin and its consequences) and brought into a new land (God's love and acceptance)
● **the King's priests** – acting as go-betweens, presenting God and his demands to people, and presenting people and their needs to God
● **the holy nation** (holy means 'kept separate for a special purpose') – people who keep separate from the world in general, in order to carry out a special mission
● **those who proclaim the wonderful acts of God** – those who tell others about God's love in sending Jesus to be the sacrifice for people's sins so that anyone can become part of God's family for ever.

Just as every new baby is born into a family, so the new Christian belongs to the family of God. Believers are brothers and sisters in Christ.

speaks of the family of God being *like* a building (Ephesians 2:19–22; 1 Peter 2:5; 1 Corinthians 3:9; 1 Timothy 3:15). This shows that Christians are those whose faith, life and future are based on a firm foundation, and that they are joined to others – like building-stones – to form part of something much bigger than each individual, where God's Spirit and God's truth reside.

Witnesses

Jesus promised his first disciples: 'you will be witnesses for me' and this is the most important part of the life of the New Testament church.

Telling others about Jesus was not a chore undertaken reluctantly. His followers were so full of joy and excitement about their new life in Jesus that they spoke about it freely and with great enthusiasm, helped by God's Holy Spirit.

Filled with the power of God's Spirit, Peter preached to the Pentecost crowds and told them that Jesus was God's Messiah, that anyone repenting of their bad, old ways and being baptized in his name would receive forgiveness and the gift of the Holy Spirit (Acts 2:38–39).

Telling others the good news about Jesus continued to be the major concern of the new church (Acts 4:33) and, wherever the new Christians went, they took this message with them (Acts 8:4), always pointing to Jesus as the only way to find acceptance with God (Acts 4:11–12).

Sometimes the message was received as

'Can you tell us what happened . . . ?' Like the man being interviewed, Christians are witnesses – telling others about Jesus.

the honesty and integrity of the believers was sufficient to prove that their message was worth hearing. Paul and Silas did not take advantage of an earthquake to escape from prison (which would have resulted in a death sentence on the jailer for his carelessness). As a result, the jailer asked about their faith and became a Christian along with the rest of his family (Acts 16:23–34).

The experience of the Philippian jailer is typical of all the New Testament Christians who had discovered the secret of new life in God's family through Jesus:

'He and his family were filled with joy, because they now believed in God.'
Acts 16:34

joyfully as it was given (Acts 8:5–8; 10:44–48; 13:47–48). At other times, there was open hostility (Acts 4:1–4; 5:17–18; 9:22–25; 14:19). But not even persecution could diminish the believers' joy; for example, Paul and Silas sang hymns in prison (Acts 16:22– 25). And persecution did not stop them witnessing (Acts 4:18–20; 5:19–21; 14:19–21).

On many occasions, it was easy to see God's power in action when the believers preached about Jesus, because there were miracles accompanying the preaching (Acts 8:4–8; 13:4–12; 14:1–3).

There was one notable occasion when

FOLLOW UP

Design a leaflet to give to people who want to join a church in your area.

Use a piece of A4 paper or card folded like this:

page 1: the cover. Think of a bright attractive design to catch people's interest.

pages 2/3: an explanation of the concept of the Family of God – maybe in diagram form? Make sure you include an explanation of the concepts discussed in this unit:

– new family
– chosen race
– kings
– priests
– holy nation
– the proclaimers
– the church
– witnesses.

page 4: an explanation of how someone can join the family of God by being 'born again' – receiving eternal life.

The Cost of Discipleship

TEACHING ABOUT DEATH AND RESURRECTION

After Peter's confession at Caesarea Philippi, that Jesus was indeed the expected Messiah, Jesus took the opportunity of explaining to his disciples that because he was the Messiah, he would have to face suffering and death.

But this was not all. His disciples must expect suffering too.

The cost of commitment

READ LUKE 9:18–26

Not only would the Messiah, Son of Man, himself suffer – Jesus spells out the implications for his followers. Anyone who wants to follow Jesus has to be prepared to adopt a life of sacrifice:

> ● **Give up** . . . Jesus' followers must 'forget self': be prepared to put aside all personal preferences, hopes and ambitions

> ● **Take up** . . . Jesus' followers must 'take up his cross every day': be prepared for pain and ridicule – even death for Jesus' sake

> ● **Shape up** . . . Jesus' followers must follow his example: be prepared to live a life modelled on Jesus himself.

This sounds very grim indeed! It was meant to make the disciple think. And it is balanced by Jesus' extraordinary promises: the promise of eternal life – life in all its fullness (John 10:10); the promise of real freedom and true happiness, of belonging for always to the 'family of God'.

Jesus assures his disciples that things are not what they seem. What looks likes personal success to the world at large is – in eternal terms – failure. And what looks like personal loss to the world at large is – in eternal terms – gain.

Suffering through persecution

READ MATTHEW 10:16–39

Here we have an example of Jesus foretelling the future. He is outlining what will happen to the disciples when they go out spreading the Good News.

Once again, these warnings sound more like *bad* news for the disciples. Jesus warns those who preach his message, 'The Kingdom of heaven is near' (Matthew 10:7), that they will have to face

> ● being arrested and flogged

> ● being brought to trial before governors and kings

> ● being hated and betrayed

– just as Jesus himself was. Servants cannot expect to be treated better than their master, the suffering Messiah.

But again, Jesus' warnings of suffering are accompanied by assurance that all *will* be well, despite appearances. For those 'who kill the body . . . cannot kill the soul' (Matthew 10:28). In God's upside-down Kingdom loss is gain and gain is loss. This

life is not all there is. No one can 'snatch (Christ's followers) from the Father's care' (John 10:29).

It is more important to please God the Father than human authorities: he is always in control. And he cares so much for Jesus' followers that he knows even how many hairs they have on their heads! (This is probably picture language, but it gets the message across – 'You are in safe hands: don't be afraid'.)

The cost of putting God first

 READ LUKE 18:18–30

Jesus does not teach that wealth is sinful in itself. Rather, it is what people *do* with their wealth that matters. (In Paul's words: 'the *love* of money is a source of all kinds of evil' – 1 Timothy 6:10.) Note how Jesus challenges this rich man. He had kept God's commands yet his riches were a stumbling block. His possessions meant too much for him to give them up and follow Jesus. God has to come first: riches may be the barrier for some; others may put a relationship or something else before God.

Giving up one's claim to material possessions may look like a painful option,

but it brings a double reward. The disciples are assured that in this life they will be given far more than they give up and, in addition, they will receive eternal life.

Here is a hint that the reward given to those who suffer for Christ's sake is not *totally* confined to spiritual benefits.

Beliefs about death and resurrection

The centre-piece of the Good News preached by the first believers was that God had raised Jesus from the dead.

Death, mankind's worst enemy, had been defeated by the resurrection of Jesus. He had certainly been killed in the most thorough and professional manner, yet Jesus had returned from death – fully alive.

Only after the resurrection could the believers begin to grasp the relevance of Jesus' teaching about life after death – that there is, for all believers, a whole new life of joy and security to be experienced beyond the grave.

Paul's suffering

Paul wrote to the Corinthians about the things he had had to suffer for the sake of the gospel. He mentions

- hard labour
- being whipped
- being put in prison
- coming near to death
- being stoned
- three shipwrecks
- twenty-four hours in the water
- danger from floods
- danger from robbers
- lack of sleep
- lack of food, shelter and clothing

(See 2 Corinthians 11:23–27.)

But in his letter to the Philippians he stresses that he has joyfully given up all claims to status and importance 'for the sake of what is much more valuable, the knowledge of Christ Jesus my Lord' (Philippians 3:7–11). (See also 2 Timothy 4:6–8.)

READ JOHN 3:14–16; JOHN 11:17–27; LUKE 23:39–43

The thrust behind all these verses is that for the believer death is not the end of existence.

READ 1 CORINTHIANS 15:1–20, 35–44, 51–58

Paul's views about death and resurrection were coloured by his Jewish background, his experience of Jesus (whom he met only some time after the resurrection and ascension – Acts 9:1–6) and his observation of Stephen at the point of death – as well as the teaching of the apostles.

Resurrection was not a new idea. Some Jews believed that there would come an 'End Time', a 'Day of the Lord', when God's Messiah would call the faithful into some new kind of existence. Within Judaism, the Pharisees believed that this would necessarily require the resurrection of those faithful Jews who had died before the 'End Time'.

Another group of Jews, the Sadducees, did not believe in any kind of resurrection. As the idea of resurrection could be gleaned only from the later parts of the Jewish Scriptures, and the Sadducees recognized only the first five books of the Old Testament (the Torah), the idea was alien to them.

In his letter to the Corinthians, Paul points out that the fact of resurrection can hardly be disputed, because the evidence for Jesus' resurrection is so strong. There are many witnesses who can be questioned.

Christ's resurrection is important, not just because it confirms the possibility of resurrection for others, but because it is only in the death and resurrection of Christ that human sin is dealt with and death – sin's penalty – conquered.

Paul's readers were concerned about what kind of bodies people will have after their own resurrection. This may seem unimportant, but behind the question were differences of opinion which Paul speaks to.

The Jews who believed in resurrection saw it in terms of the whole person, body and soul. But the Greeks had a low opinion of the body as the prison of the soul. Any resurrection which re-animated the physical

Stephen, the first martyr

Stephen was the first person to be killed because of his belief in Jesus as the Christ. The word for such a person is 'martyr' from a Greek word meaning 'a witness who speaks out'.

READ ACTS 6:8–15 AND & 7:51–60

Stephen's vision of heaven (which we only know about because he spoke out when he saw it – 7:55–56) enabled him to endure his inevitable execution without fear.

Stephen's knowledge of Jesus enabled him to follow his Lord's example in praying to God to forgive his killers.

Stephen's death was undoubtedly an object lesson for Christians who saw it or heard about it. What believers knew in theory – that Christ's resurrection had robbed death of its sting – they could now see worked out in practice. For believers, death was no longer an enemy to be feared. Rather, it was the gateway to a new life in heaven with Jesus and God the Father.

body would seem to them like the return of an unwanted burden.

Paul explains that the Christian's resurrection body will be real and recognizable, like the old physical body. But it will be completely different – as different as a plant is from the seed that was buried in the ground.

(Jesus' body, after the resurrection, was the same – even to the scars – but without the normal human limitations. He could appear and disappear. He could pass through the grave cloths and through closed doors.)

Christians believe in a new life beyond death. Something far more wonderful than the old – a change as exciting as that from caterpillar to butterfly.

There will come an End Time, signalled by the sound of a trumpet, when all believers still alive will be transformed, metamorphosed from their physical body to their spiritual body 'in the twinkling of an eye', and the dead will be raised to life.

This resurrection of believers will be the ultimate victory over death, a victory glimpsed briefly but powerfully in Stephen's vision of heaven (Acts 7:54–60 – see box).

It is a victory made available to believers through the death and resurrection of Jesus.

FOLLOW UP

1. Explain in your own words, and then make brief notes on, the meaning of the following sentences from this unit:
- 'Anyone who wants to follow Jesus has to be prepared to adopt a life of sacrifice . . .'
- 'Jesus' followers must "take up the cross every day".'
- 'what looks like personal loss to the world at large is – in eternal terms – gain.'
- 'It is more important to please God the Father than human authorities . . .'
- 'God has to come first . . .'
- ' . . .there is, for all believers, a whole new life of joy and security to be experienced beyond the grave.'
- 'Christ's resurrection is important . . .'

2. Using these notes explain the meaning of the words underlined in this hymn written by Thomas Kelly.

*The head that once was crowned with thorns
Is crowned with glory now;
A royal diadem adorns
The mighty Victor's brow.*

*The highest place that heaven affords
Is His by sovereign right,
The King of kings, the Lord of lords,
And heaven's eternal light.*

*The joy of all who dwell above,
The joy of all below,
To whom He manifests His love,
And grants His name to know.*

*To them the cross, with all its shame,
With all its grace, is given;
Their name an everlasting name,
Their joy the joy of heaven.*

*They suffer with their Lord below,
They reign with Him above;
Their profit and their joy to know
The mystery of His love.*

*The cross He bore is life and health
Though shame and death to Him;
His people's hope, His people's wealth,
Their everlasting theme.*

3. Helen Roseveare was a doctor in the Congo (Zimbabwe) during the Simba rebellion which eventually led to independence for that country. During the fighting she was ill-treated, imprisoned and raped. In her book *Give Me This Mountain* she sums up the suffering she experienced like this . . .

. . . God has no second-best. This is very often a contradiction of terms. If I am in God's will for me, it is His very best for me. God is eternal present tense. If I step out of His will, then I deliberately choose my own path and I have nothing of His best. When I confess my error, seek His loving forgiveness, and return to His will, then at once He restores me. It is always present to Him, so at the moment of restoration I am in His present will for me. Once repentance is real, and forgiveness sought, the past is past, and has no longer an interpretation in the present. The present may well be different from the 'might-have-been', it may well be affected by the consequences of previous disobedience and sin which can leave their mark on both character and circumstance, but nevertheless, it is the best in the immediate now. I have found this to be a most liberating and glorious truth. If it were not so, who among us would not live his life in an atmosphere of continual regret?

The night I was first taken captive by the rebel soldiers He worked that liberation for me in the midst of all the horror and anguish! I saw it in a verse in Peter's Epistle: 'For what glory is it, if, when ye be buffeted for your faults, ye shall take it patiently? but if, when ye do well, and suffer for it, ye take it patiently, this is acceptable with God' (I Peter 2:20). In that moment, I *knew* utterly and unquestioningly, whatever the past might have held of failures, that I was in the *second* half of the verse. God allowed the circumstances to be such that even I, so often a veritable 'doubting Thomas', could not argue. Therefore He showed me, with a gentle smile, a smile of reproof, perhaps, that I had taken so long to learn, a smile of deep love that I truly wanted to learn, that I was 'acceptable with God' – and this could only mean that I was in the centre of His will. Certainly this could be no 'second-best'.

In your group discuss what Helen has written:
- what was your first reaction to her attitude to her suffering?
- Can you match this to any statements from the unit?

The End of the World and the Last Judgment

It was part of the Jews' expectation of the Messiah that he would come finally to earth at the end of time, to gather up the faithful and establish a new heaven and a new earth.

The end of the world

Jesus' disciples, believing him to be the Messiah, questioned him about his final 'coming' at the 'end of the age':

 READ MATTHEW 24:1–14; 36–44

There are hard times to be endured before the End, Jesus tells them, with wars and great troubles. There will be confusion, too, with false prophets claiming to be the returned Messiah.

No one will know exactly when the Messiah will come. The only indications are the wars and hardships that precede his coming, and the assurance that all nations, by that time, will have heard the Good News of the Kingdom.

The way each person responds to that gospel will determine who will be taken from their workplace to be with the Messiah in the new Kingdom, and who will be left.

Because no one can be sure when all this will take place, the disciples are warned to watch and be ready.

Some of Paul's converts wondered exactly how this gathering up of believers would work out in practice – particularly as some of their number had already died.

Paul gives further teaching about the gathering up of Christians at the end of the world in his first letter to the Thessalonians:

 READ 1 THESSALONIANS 4:13 to 5:11

Paul says that when the Lord comes with the sound of God's trumpet those who have died believing in Christ will rise first. Then the living believers will be 'gathered up along with them in the clouds to meet the Lord'.

The ideas of the last judgment and God's avenging angels has often been used to frighten people, but the message is an urgent call to respond to God's offer of salvation while there is still time.

Because there is no way of knowing exactly when the Lord will come, Paul stresses the importance of readiness, just as Jesus himself had done (Matthew 24:36–44). Part of that readiness is obeying his command to share the Good News with everyone. Being ready to meet Christ at any time also has a radical effect on the Christian's priorities and way of life.

The last judgment

READ MATTHEW 25:31–46

Jesus' teaching to his disciples about the Day of Judgment is in the form of a parable. The people of the nations will be divided into two groups 'as a shepherd separates the sheep from the goats'.

But this is not *just* a picture-story containing a deeper message, like the earlier parables. It tells us a number of things about the last judgment.

● The judge will be the Son of Man, Messiah, now enthroned as King (verses 34, 40).

● People will be separated into two groups – those placed at the King's right hand, and those placed to his left.

● Those on the right are called 'blessed' and 'righteous' and they will inherit the Kingdom prepared for them (34) and eternal life (46).

● Those on the left are 'under God's curse'. They will depart to 'the eternal fire . . . prepared for the Devil and his angels' (41) – sent off to eternal punishment (46).

● The judgment is not arbitrary. It is based on people's conduct. By their loving actions, the 'righteous' have shown the family characteristics of the 'Father' and are therefore those 'blessed by my Father'. In stark contrast, those at the King's left hand are punished for the self-interest which has made them blind to the needs of others.

Jesus said that before the end of the world there would be wars and great troubles. But there will be time for all nations to hear the Good News of the Kingdom.

It is wrong to press the details of a parable, and the Gospels contain other criteria which will be used for judging a person's ultimate acceptance by God. You can find some of these in Matthew 10:22; Mark 16:16; Luke 23:39–43; John 3:16–17. Again and again it is the response made to the person of Jesus – belief or unbelief – that is the determining factor.

The particular significance of the parable of the sheep and the goats is its picture of a Day of Judgment when the people of all nations will be judged by the Son of Man/Messiah – i.e. Jesus Christ.

READ ACTS 10:38–43; 17:31

The idea of a final Day of Judgment – with Jesus as the judge – was part of the early *kerygma* proclamation about Jesus and continued to be part of the apostles' teaching.

● Judgment comes to everyone after death (Hebrews 9:27).
● Judgment will be made on the basis of conduct, good or bad (2 Corinthians 5:10).

● Judgment includes rescue for 'godly people' (2 Peter 2:9).
● Judgment will bring a 'prize of victory' for 'those who wait with love for him to appear' (2 Timothy 4:8).

But the overriding theme of the apostles' preaching was that anyone who believes in Jesus is assured of a welcome from God at the time of judgment:

> But God has shown us how much he loves us – it was while we were still sinners that Christ died for us! By his death we are now put right with God; how much more, then, will we be saved by him from God's anger! We were God's enemies, but he made us his friends through the death of his Son. Now that we are God's friends, how much more will we be saved by Christ's life! But that is not all; we rejoice because of what God has done through our Lord Jesus Christ, who has now made us God's friends.
> Romans 5:8–11

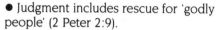

FOLLOW UP

In the Middle Ages not many people could read. They learned about the Bible from the village priest who would want to make sure that all his congregation went to heaven.

So, as well as preaching very frightening sermons about the end of the world and the last judgment many priests had pictures painted on the walls of their churches to instil the 'fear of God' into the people even more, to keep them on the straight and narrow.

You can still see a few of these wall paintings in some very old churches.

Draw your own picture (or make a written plan) entitled 'The Last Judgment', using some of the ideas in this unit.

(Remember that when you look at something left and right are reversed – make sure that you put the righteous on the proper right hand side of God.)

Write a detailed caption to explain what you have drawn.

The Church Grows and Divides

Luke's history of the very first Christians – the book of Acts – shows how rapidly Christianity spread throughout the civilized world.

The first 1,000 years

The movement started in Jerusalem, but before long the followers of Jesus were persecuted there, so they moved further afield, taking the message with them.

Antioch became an important centre: it was here that they were first called 'Christians' (a nickname given by other people). It was from Antioch that Paul set off on his missionary journeys.

Paul's letters to believers in places as far apart as Philippi, Corinth, Crete (the letter to Titus) and Colossae show that within a few years groups of Christians – churches – had been established in these places.

Less than fifty years after the death of its founder, Christianity had taken root in Syria, Asia Minor (Turkey), Greece and Rome. But this expansion took place against tremendous difficulties, for the persecution continued.

The Roman Emperor Nero blamed the Christians for the great fire of Rome in AD64. He rounded them up in their hundreds, crucified many of them, had

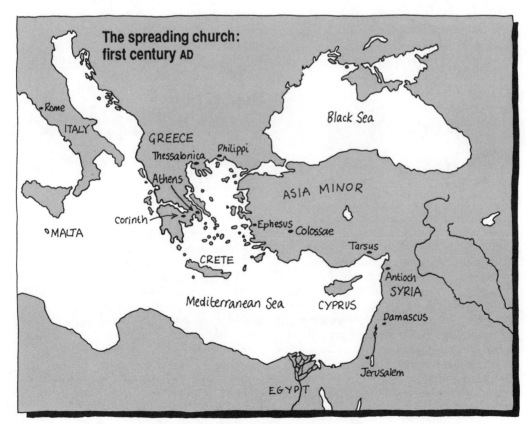

The spreading church: first century AD

Rome
ITALY
GREECE
Thessalonica
Philippi
Black Sea
Athens
ASIA MINOR
Corinth
MALTA
Ephesus
Colossae
Tarsus
CRETE
Mediterranean Sea
CYPRUS
Antioch
SYRIA
Damascus
Jerusalem
EGYPT

others torn apart by wild animals as a spectator sport in his own garden arena, and burned many Christians alive as human torches to 'floodlight' the event.

The tide turns

The persecution continued to a greater or lesser degree for more than 200 years under successive emperors, until the tide finally turned in AD312, when Constantine became emperor.

Constantine had been a sun-worshipper, but became a Christian after seeing a vision of the CHI RHO sign (see Unit 3) on the face of the sun, with the words 'Conquer by this'. Constantine did indeed conquer; he captured Rome and took control of the Empire, and in gratitude he became a follower of the Christian God who brought him to power.

Although Constantine did not make Christianity the state religion, he gave it official recognition, partly because he thought it could help to unite his large and scattered empire. Places of worship were now permitted, Christian ministers were exempted from civil duties and crucifixion was abolished.

Under these favourable circumstances, the city of Rome – centre of the Roman Empire – soon became the centre of the widespread Christian church.

However, Constantine gave his empire a *new* capital, the city of Byzantium, which, being very much further east than Rome, would make governing the eastern part of his empire easier. The city was renamed Constantinople (in 1930 it was changed again, to Istanbul), and it became the centre for Christianity in the eastern part of the Roman Empire.

But there had been a Christian presence in Rome from New Testament times, so Rome remained the more important centre. The church leader there, the bishop, was looked up to as leader of the whole church throughout the world.

After the apostle Peter's recognition of Jesus as Messiah at Caesarea Philippi, Jesus had said to him, 'Peter: you are a rock, and on this rock foundation I will build my church' (Matthew 16:13–18). Opinions vary as to whether Jesus was referring to Peter himself, or to his faith in the Messiah, as the foundation of the church. But the seniority of the Roman church was recognized generally, and bishops who succeeded Peter eventually became known by the title 'Pope', meaning 'Father'.

Separation

There were other centres of Christianity, but they were less important than Rome and Constantinople. Jerusalem was important as the place where the religion began and where James and the early leaders held Council. Antioch was important as the spring-board for Christian expansion. Alexandria in Egypt became important through its great university which attracted Christian academics.

Because of the distance between Rome and Constantinople, both in miles and in culture, the two cities nurtured two strands of Christianity which grew further and further apart – although the Bishop of Rome (the Pope) was always assumed to be senior to the Patriarch of Constantinople and therefore 'Father' of the whole church.

In AD1054, each centre accused the other's church of being in error in its beliefs. The Pope decided to excommunicate –

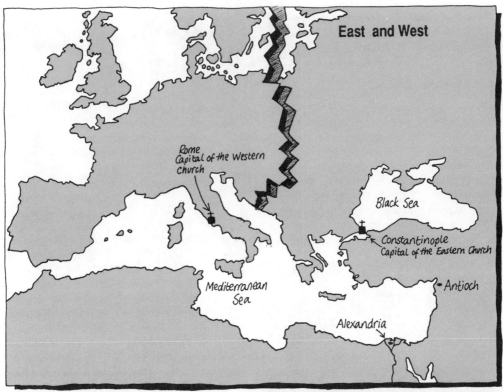

East and West

Rome
Capital of the Western Church

Black Sea

Constantinople
Capital of the Eastern Church

Antioch

Mediterranean Sea

Alexandria

exclude from membership and Holy Communion – the whole of the eastern church. (In the event, he died, so the order of excommunication was given by his representative.) However, in Constantinople, the Patriarch dismissed the Pope's claim to universal authority. He declared the eastern church completely independent of the western church, and equal to it.

So the two great churches of west and east were separated. They became known as the Roman *Catholic* (=universal/ worldwide) Church and the Eastern *Orthodox* (=correct/true) Church. They have never been reunited.

FOLLOW UP

1. Copy the chart below into your books and fill in the blanks, using the information given in this unit.

JERUSALEM	This city was the original home of the early church.
ANTIOCH	
ROME	
CONSTANTINOPLE	

2. Now test yourself! What happened on these dates?
– AD64
– AD312
– AD1054

3. And finally – what is the difference between Pope and Patriarch?

The Reformation: Further Divisions

How did Christianity get to Britain? And what kind of Christianity was it – Church of England, Roman Catholic, or what?

The fact is, no one is exactly sure just how Christianity came to Britain. There are accounts of a Christian Roman officer called **Alban** being martyred in England in AD304, and it is thought possible that perhaps the Roman soldiers who were

The design on this fourth-century mosaic in a Roman villa at Hinton St Mary in Dorset shows that Christianity reached Britain very early in the Christian era.

posted to Britain even earlier – at the end of the first century – brought Christianity with them from Rome. If this was so, it was wiped out for a time.

However, by AD450, a British missionary called **Patrick** had crossed over to Ireland to spread the gospel there. Some time after AD500 a Welsh missionary called **David** was preaching throughout Wales. The Picts in the north (modern Scotland) were evangelized by **Columba**, an Irish Christian

Iona

Columba preaches to Picts AD 563

Synod of Whitby AD 664

Patrick to Ireland AD 450

David brings Gospel to Wales AD 500

Alban martyred AD 304

Augustine comes from Rome AD 597

who settled on the island of Iona in AD563 (following the earlier work of Ninian in 397).

Then, in 597, the Bishop of Rome sent Britain a bishop of its own – a Roman Christian called **Augustine**.

So there were two independent strands of Christianity in Britain – Celtic and Roman. They came together at the Synod of Whitby in AD664 and decisions taken then gave the Roman church the lead.

The worldwide church was governed and influenced by the two great cities of the Roman Empire – Rome in the west and Constantinople in the east. Their use of different languages (Latin in the west and Greek in the east), and their development of different ideas about beliefs and worship meant that 'Christendom' (the Christian world) developed along two separate lines (see Unit 28).

Over the centuries, the position of the Bishop of Rome (Pope) gained more and more political strength in the west, because of the church's teaching that all human creatures including kings and emperors had to be subject to the Pope in order to obtain salvation from God.

Protest

With the growth of this political power came increasing levels of corruption in the church's teaching and practice, leading to many protests from within its ranks.

● **John Wyclif** in England (1329–84) protested strongly that Jesus Christ, not the Pope, was the only 'Head of the Church', and that many church practices were not supported by the teaching of the Bible.
● **Martin Luther** in Germany (1483–1546) protested strongly that a person's salvation was not dependent upon the Pope, but was the gift of God to all who put their faith in Jesus Christ as Saviour, according to the teaching of the Bible.

Christians like these, who protested that the church was in need of reform, became known as 'protestants' or 'reformers'.

The movement is usually reckoned to have started in 1517 when Martin Luther set out his objections in ninety-five 'theses' which he nailed to the door of the church at Wittenberg.

England splits from Rome

It was against this background of protest and reformation that King Henry VIII of England severed all ties with the Roman Church and all allegiance to the Pope and declared himself the new head of the church in England in 1532.

Henry's reasons were not very religious

Tensions between church and state

Henry VIII's quarrel with the Pope which led to the formation of a separate church in England is the best-known historical example of the problem of tensions between church and state, and the one with the most far-reaching effects.

It is, though, only one example of the power struggle between church and state which began after Constantine's recognition of the church in the fourth century. Once the church had the emperor's favour, its leaders found themselves in positions of power, which often led to conflict with the state authorities.

There were times when quarrels led to the death of Christians whose beliefs were out of tune with those of their monarch or the prevailing law:

● **Thomas Becket** became Archbishop of Canterbury in 1162 under Henry II. At a time when church and monarchy were strong allies, protecting each other's wealth and power, Becket made it clear that he would always put God before king. Disputes between the two men led to Henry's outburst in 1170: 'Will no one rid me of this turbulent priest?' Four knights took him at his word and murdered Thomas Becket in Canterbury Cathedral.

● **Sir Thomas More** (1478–1535) was Lord Chancellor and **John Fisher** (1459–1535) was Bishop of Rochester when Henry VIII claimed to be head of the church in England in 1532. Neither could in good conscience support the king and both were imprisoned in the Tower of London in 1534, where they were beheaded the following year.

John Wyclif gave Britain the first Bible in English.

Sir Thomas More refused to put the king above conscience, and died for his beliefs.

The divorce of King Henry VIII led to England's separation from the Roman Catholic Church.

John Knox championed the cause of reform in Scotland.

– the Pope would not allow his marriage to be set aside so that he could take another wife. It suited the king to make use of the ferment in the church and break away from Rome.

Despite the questionable motives, the king's action was welcomed by English protestants who had wanted an opportunity for some kind of 'Reformation'. Now the Bible in English could be officially used in churches and an English Prayer Book could be compiled for church services.

The Reformation in England continued under Henry's son, Edward VI. There was a short return to Roman church rule under the next sovereign, Mary, but in 1559 under Elizabeth I the existence of a separate Church of England with the sovereign as its head was made legal by Act of Parliament. Since then, Britain has been regarded as 'protestant' rather than 'catholic'.

English Bibles and Prayer Books

English Bibles became official in English churches only after Henry VIII split from Rome. However, translations had been made before this time. In 1378, **John Wyclif** began translating the old Latin Bible into English. He escaped being condemned as a heretic because he had influential friends.

English translations were banned in 1480 because of the fear that they would be used by European reformers to stir people against the church authorities.

● **William Tyndale** (about 1492–1536) began translating the Bible into English after he realized the extent of ignorance among English people, not least the priests of the church. Faced with

opposition, Tyndale fled to Europe, where he continued his work, though always in constant danger. His task was still not finally completed when he was arrested near Brussels in 1535 and burnt at the stake the following year.

● **Thomas Cranmer** (1489–1556) was favoured by Henry VIII because of his advice and support at the time the king was seeking to divorce his first wife. Henry made Cranmer Archbishop of Canterbury in 1533, and as such it was Cranmer – not the Pope – who pronounced the king's first marriage invalid.

He continued to help the king and his successor Edward VI to shake off the supremacy of the Pope by engaging in his own

reforming projects. A new Prayer Book in English (The Book of Common Prayer still used in the Church of England) was largely his work. He made the use of the English Bible official and played a leading role in defining the beliefs of the Church of England (The Thirty-Nine Articles).

Edward was succeeded by a Roman Catholic, Mary, who found Cranmer's reforms totally unacceptable. Under threat of death he at first disavowed his reforms and declared his support for the Pope and the Mass. But he later withdrew his statement and was burned at the stake in Oxford in 1556, as were the scholar Nicholas Ridley and the preacher Hugh Latimer.

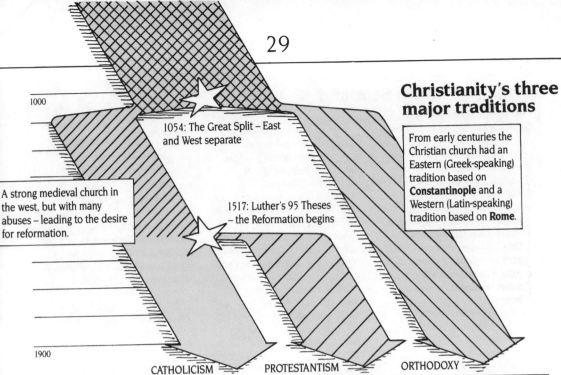

Christianity's three major traditions

1000

1054: The Great Split – East and West separate

From early centuries the Christian church had an Eastern (Greek-speaking) tradition based on **Constantinople** and a Western (Latin-speaking) tradition based on **Rome**.

A strong medieval church in the west, but with many abuses – leading to the desire for reformation.

1517: Luther's 95 Theses – the Reformation begins

1900

CATHOLICISM   PROTESTANTISM   ORTHODOXY

A 'counter-reformation' in the Roman Catholic Church in the 16th and 17th centuries emphasized the church's authority and the mystery of the Mass, often expressed in dramatic and ornate architecture. A fresh approach has emerged since the 2nd Vatican Council, 1962–1965.

Lutherans, Reformed groups, Anabaptists and Anglicans emerged from the Reformation, with others emerging later – such as Methodists and Pentecostals.

A threat from Islam in the East, but the Eastern Orthodox Church remains strong in Greece, Russia, Romania and other places.

Puritans, Presbyterians and Separatists

The Church of England was reinstated when Elizabeth I became Queen.

However, the discontent and the desire for more major reform continued both in Britain and in Western Europe.

Some thought the reforms of the Church of England did not go far enough in purifying English Christianity. These 'Puritans' wanted to get rid of every vestige of the Roman Church, including special clothes for priests and people kneeling to receive Holy Communion.

The Puritans not only believed that the Pope's authority was not an idea found in the Bible, they also claimed that the church's concept of *bishops* was not biblical either. They wanted a church governed by local elders or 'presbyters' (from the Greek word for elder).

At first, rather than splitting off from the Church of England, the Puritan-

Presbyterians tried to bring in their changes through Parliament. But neither Elizabeth nor James, her successor, was sympathetic to their cause and many Puritan-Presbyterians left the Church of England as 'Separatists'.

Non-conformists and Roman Catholics

The various church groups whose beliefs did not 'conform' to the teaching of the Church of England after the Reformation were generally known as 'dissenters'. Today, they are known as 'non-conformist' denominations.

In 1689, a 'Toleration Act' was passed, making it legal for non-conformists to meet for public worship. This ended a time of suffering and prison sentences for many, and non-conformist chapels began to be built. But Roman Catholics had to wait until 1829 for the same freedom (see Unit 30).

Presbyterians in Scotland and England

Geneva in Switzerland was a centre of Reformation thinking, particularly under the influence of the French theologian **John Calvin** (1509–64). He taught that salvation was through personal repentance and faith in Jesus, and also that God had predetermined which people would find faith in him through Jesus. Calvin's followers observed a strict moral lifestyle which did not include popular entertainment and which to outsiders seemed to be rather joyless.

John Knox was a Scottish reformer who travelled to Europe when Scotland became Catholic under Mary Queen of Scots in 1553. He spent some years in Geneva where he was influenced by Calvin, and returned to Scotland during civil war in 1559. Mary returned from France in 1561, but by that time the Roman Catholic doctrine had been replaced in Scotland by a Calvinistic Confession of Faith established by the Scottish Parliament in 1560.

John Knox and the queen represented two sides of an argument. This was not a simple matter of Protestant against Catholic. Calvinism was 'presbyterian' – congregations elected their own elders (the Greek word for elder is *presbuteros*). The Queen stood for the establishment system of bishops appointed by the monarch. The argument was about democracy as much as theology.

Despite much opposition and many difficulties, Knox's Presbyterianism survived in Scotland. Today, the largest Christian group there is the Church of Scotland, the Presbyterian church dating from John Knox's time.

In England, civil war broke out in a power struggle between king and Parliament during the reign of Charles I. Christians found themselves on both sides. Cromwell's forces won a victory for Parliament. And with the subsequent setting up of the 'Commonwealth', the Church of England (Anglican) lost out to the Presbyterianism of Cromwell's followers.

The Thirty-Nine Articles of Religion of the Church of England were replaced by the Westminster Confession of Faith (based on Knox's earlier Confession). And a Presbyterian Directory of Public Worship replaced the Book of Common Prayer.

But this strict new 'official' church was not popular with the people generally. For one thing it abolished festivals, including Christmas. So after the the king (Charles II) was brought back in 1660, the Church of England was once again legally established as the 'official' church in 1662. Many Presbyterian clergymen resigned their jobs rather than go back to what they saw as the compromises of the Church of England.

◢FOLLOW◥UP◢

1. This unit is really an overview of a long period of history. You may want to do some further research about some of the people who have been mentioned briefly.

To help you keep everything in historical perspective here is a simple chart which you can fill in to help your research:

DATE (AD)	PERSON	PLACE	DETAILS
304	Alban	England	Martyr
450	Patrick	Ireland	Missionary

2. Write a sentence which explains each of the following terms:
– PROTESTANT
– PURITAN
– PRESBYTERIAN
– SEPARATIST.

Many Branches

Here is a sketch-map of Millerbridge, an English market town of 30,000 people. Near the marketplace is the parish church, St Mary's, which is part of the Church of England (1). But that is not the only church in Millerbridge.

On the High Street, you can see another church building. The notice-board says it is High Street Methodist Church (2). Also on the High Street there is building called the Salvation Army Citadel (3). In South Street,

there's the United Reformed Church (4), and along Chapel Lane you'll find Millerbridge Baptist Church (5). St Joseph's Roman Catholic Church is in London Road (6). There's the Elim Church next to the new leisure centre (7) and something called the Friends' Meeting House near the park (8). On the corner of Victoria Road and Albert Gardens is a Gospel Hall (9).

These buildings are not very similar.

- St Mary's Church is very old, made of grey stone and partly covered with ivy. It has a tapered spire.
- The Methodist Church is nineteenth-century red-brick and has pointed windows like St Mary's, but no spire.
- The Salvation Army Citadel is red-brick too, and the front wall either side of the main door is covered with brightly-lettered posters.
- The United Reformed Church and the Baptist Church are made of stone, but the style is like the Methodist Church – they are not as old as St Mary's.
- St Joseph's is fairly new; it has a steel 'see-through' spire and modern coloured glass in the windows.
- The Elim Church is a new, low building that looks like an office complex or a health centre.
- The Gospel Hall is like a model of St Mary's – it's made of corrugated metal, painted green, and it has a small spire over the door and pointed windows.
- The Friends' Meeting House is smaller than all the others. It is an old stone building with plain rectangular windows.

All these buildings are places of worship for some of the Christians of Millerbridge. Other Christians call themselves the 'Millerbridge Fellowship' and rent a hall in the Comprehensive School for their meetings.

How did one town come to have so many different Christian groups, meeting in their different places of worship?

We'll look at each of Millerbridge's Christian groups in turn (in the order they emerged nationally) and see how they developed and how they came to be here in their different buildings.

Millerbridge Parish Church, St Mary's Church of England (Anglican)

St Mary's was built in the thirteenth century and was the only church in the town for many hundreds of years. When the Christian church in England became the 'Church of England' in the sixteenth century, the people of Millerbridge continued meeting for worship in this building, but their Bible readings and prayers for services were now in English instead of Latin (see Unit 29).

Millerbridge United Reformed Church

The 'United Reformed Church' in England was formed in 1972 when two groups joined together. They were the Congregational Church and the Presbyterian Church. Before 1972, the Millerbridge URC building was the Millerbridge Congregational Church.

The Congregational and Presbyterian churches had their origins in the general discontent among some English Christians after the formation of the Church of England at the time of the Reformation (see 'Puritans, Presbyterians and Separatists' in Unit 29).

Many Presbyterians left the Church of England as 'Separatists' in the reigns of Elizabeth and James I. Some of them later became the Presbyterian Church.

From about 1580, 'Separatist' congregations started meeting for worship. All members had equal status and each church was independent, not subject to a bishop. This movement marks the beginning of a branch of English Christianity which eventually became the Congregational Church.

Life was not easy for the Separatists. They were harrassed by English bishops and government and many fled to Holland. Others, known as the Pilgrim Fathers, sailed to America to start a new life in New England.

Millerbridge did not have a

'The Mayflower' sets out from Plymouth in 1620. On board were the persecuted 'pilgrims', seeking Christian freedom in the New World.

Presbyterian Church at the time of the union with the Congregational Church in 1972. This building was Millerbridge's Congregational Church. It was built in 1863 to replace an earlier, smaller building.

Millerbridge Baptist Church

One of the issues debated throughout Europe during the years of Reformation was the subject of baptism. Some Christians believed that the traditional church practice of baptizing babies was wrong – that baptism should only be undertaken by those who had come to full adult faith in Christ. These particular protesters were known as 'anabaptists' (*ana* is Greek for 'again') because adults who had already been baptized as babies were being baptized again after their adult profession of faith, this time by the method of 'total immersion' (where the whole body goes under the water – a powerful picture of the death of the old life and a clean new beginning), rather than the sprinkling of water on the forehead as happens in infant baptism.

Gradually, the anabaptists became known just as Baptists and they established a following in

The Baptist Church gets its name from the practice of baptizing adults by 'total immersion'.

England from 1611. Because the Church of England still practised the old Roman Catholic form of infant baptism, the Baptists separated themselves from the new English Church as well as from the old Roman Church, and they too became a separate branch of Christianity in England. Each congregation was self-governing, like the Congregational Church.

This building was built in 1878 alongside the smaller 'schoolroom' which still adjoins the church.

Friends' Meeting House

There were some Christians in the seventeenth century who rebelled against all church systems, whether Catholic or Protestant. One such group was the Society of Friends under their leader George Fox (1621–91). They renounced all formal church practices and met in 'meeting houses' to worship God informally, including using periods of silence.

To emphasize their difference, the Friends adopted a particular form of dress. The men wore broad-brimmed hats which they refused to doff to anyone, believing all to be equal. They also called each other 'thee' and 'thou' (the form of address used only among family or friends in older English, instead of 'you').

The name 'Quaker' was a nickname given to Fox himself by Justice Bennet in 1650, after Fox had exhorted the judge to 'tremble before the word of the Lord'.

The Quakers were persecuted by Anglicans and dissenters alike; Fox spent a total of eight years in prison and 15,000 Quakers are said to have died for their faith between 1650 and 1698.

Members of the Society of Friends give great importance to the 'inner light' discovered in silent prayer, believing there is 'something of God' (according to Fox) in every person. They do not observe Holy Communion or Baptism, and their marriage ceremony is a simple agreement between two people before the assembled meeting but without the presence of a minister. Friends have always had a great concern for social justice and they refuse to be part of any fighting force.

The Millerbridge meeting house was built in 1712.

High Street Methodist Church

By the mid 1700s, the Church of England had itself become corrupt

It was through the preaching of John Wesley that the Methodist Church came into being.

and ineffectual. But, once again, there were those within the Church's ranks who were anxious for improvement.

Two brothers studying at Oxford – John and Charles Wesley – began a club for any students who wanted to be more serious and methodical about their religion. Their fellow-students called them 'methodists'. Some time later, after he had served as a priest in the Church of England and as a missionary in America, John Wesley had a new experience of God which fired him up – like St Paul's conversion on the Damascus Road. (See Unit 19). He became a travelling preacher, riding from place to place throughout the country and drawing crowds to hear him. He emphasized the need for personal conversion and methodical learning and lifestyle.

His superiors in the Church of England opposed John Wesley's enthusiasm. At last circumstances forced him to take on the unofficial role of a bishop in order to ordain his own ministers to help him. From that point on Wesley's movement was no longer seen as part of the Church of England. It had become a separate branch or 'denomination'. However, John Wesley always claimed he lived and died a member of the Church of England.

In 1969, there was an attempt to unite the Methodist Church with the Church of England, but the clergy of the Church of England voted against it.

Millerbridge Methodist Church was built as a Wesleyan Methodist Chapel in 1879. It has this date and the earlier name carved on a stone lintel over the main door.

St Joseph's Catholic Church

Roman Catholics who stayed outside the Church of England after the Reformation had to wait until 1829 for the freedom to meet for worship and build churches. After this the Roman Catholic Church experienced a time of great

expansion in England – largely due to the vast numbers of Roman Catholic labourers coming to England from Ireland, where the church been untouched by the Reformation.

Roman Catholic missionaries from Italy took advantage of the new freedom and toured England, promoting Roman Catholicism. And, as all the ancient church buildings had become the property of the Church of England in 1662, the Roman Catholics also embarked on a church building programme.

However, there were very few Roman Catholics in Millerbridge until recent years. As people have become more mobile generally, changing jobs and homes in a way that was not known in previous

The Salvation Army was founded by General Booth in 1865. Its badge shows a cross and a sword, with the motto 'Blood and Fire'.

generations, the number of Catholics living in Millerbridge has increased. St Joseph's was built in 1962, for a growing congregation which had been meeting for Mass in the Corn Exchange in the town centre.

The Salvation Army Citadel

In 1861, a Methodist minister called William Booth was refused permission from the Methodist authorities to become a travelling evangelist. So Booth left the Methodists, and in 1865 established a new evangelistic movement called

'The Salvation Army', organized on military lines.

The Salvationists worked among the poorest people in England's cities and, seeing the damage caused by alcohol (at a time when people could be 'drunk for a penny, dead drunk for tuppence'), made a total ban on strong drink part of their teaching. They also taught that the inner attitudes behind Baptism and Holy Communion were more important than the practices themselves, and so abandoned the use of any sacraments at all.

The Millerbridge Citadel was built in 1922.

The Gospel Hall

Another nineteenth-century movement, the 'Plymouth Brethren', grew out of Christians breaking free of denominational barriers to meet in New Testament simplicity. More recently they have become known as the 'Brethren Assemblies'. The focus of worship is the 'Breaking of bread' (Communion Service) in which all may take part. They have no ordained ministers and are active in Bible teaching and preaching the gospel.

The Millerbridge Brethren bought this building from the Church of England in 1966. The Anglicans had built it in 1892 as a 'mission' church for the people on the far side of town from St Mary's Church.

The Elim Church

Despite the prominence given to the use of spiritual gifts in the New Testament accounts of early Christian activities, these fell out of general use as the church grew, spread and divided over the centuries.

However, in the twentieth century there has been a revival of interest in the 'gifts of the Spirit', especially the gift of 'speaking in tongues' in the way that the early Christians did.

The twentieth-century 'Pentecostal movement' is reckoned to have begun in in 1906, in a small Methodist mission hall in Azusa Street, Los Angeles, where Christians who had experienced the 'baptism of the Holy Spirit' held prayer meetings with speaking in tongues, singing 'in the Spirit' and prophecy.

The movement quickly spread to Europe, and was promoted in England from 1907 by the Rev. A.A. Boddy, Anglican vicar of All Saints' Church in Sunderland. Although the British Pentecostal movement began in the Church of England and its proponents encouraged 'pentecostal' Christians to remain as members of their traditional churches, the need for a strong organization to back up the movement's teaching led eventually to the formation of two Pentecostal Churches – the Assemblies of God, formed in 1924 with a congregational form of self-government, and the Elim Church, formed in 1926 with a centralized form of church government.

The Millerbridge Pentecostals set up their first Elim Church in a former Primitive Methodist chapel (after the Primitive Methodists united with the Wesleyan Methodists in 1932). They sold that building to developers who built a supermarket in its place. The new building was opened in 1984.

▲FOLLOW 👆UP▲

You are the chief reporter on *The Millerbridge Mercury*. Your editor wants an article (there isn't any news this week . . .) about the different churches in the town.

Plan a double-page spread to include:
● a brief description of each denomination
● space for a picture of each building
● a quote from each minister about the most important feature (spiritual or physical) of their church.
● a chart with each church in chronological order, according to when the denomination was founded – not when the Millerbridge buildings were erected!

Buildings for Worship

Some fifth formers studying Christianity conducted a survey at their school. One of the questions they asked was:

> *What is a Christian?*

There were three answers to choose from:

A Christian is someone who
☐ follows Jesus Christ
☐ does good
☐ goes to church on a Sunday

500 pupils completed the questionnaire. 35% of them thought that a Christian is a follower of Jesus Christ; 10% that a Christian is someone who does good. But all the rest – 55% – thought that a Christian is someone who goes to church on Sunday.

That wasn't really surprising because in Britain nearly every village, however small, has a church.

Strixton is a tiny village in Northamptonshire with only four farmhouses and six cottages, but it has a church.

St Romwald's Church, Strixton.

The next village to Strixton is Wollaston. Here there are four churches for a population of just under 3,000.

Wellingborough, the nearest town to Wollaston, has a population of 41,000, and all these churches:
– 7 Anglican
– 2 Roman Catholic
– 2 Baptist
– 2 United Reformed
– 5 Methodist and Wesleyan
– 1 Pentecostal
– 1 Salvation Army citadel
– 1 Society of Friends Meeting House
– 1 Church of Christ
– 2 Independent housechurches.
A total of 24 churches!

St Romwald's Church in Strixton is an Anglican church – it belongs to the Church of England. But in Wollaston there is an Anglican church, a Methodist chapel, a Baptist chapel and a Salvation Army citadel. (The Roman Catholics who live in the village use the Anglican building once a week for their Parish Mass.)

Each of these church buildings is different. It reflects the time when it was built and the beliefs of the different denominations. However, there are some features which are common to all churches, and some features which are common to most churches in a particular denomination.

The Salvation Army Citadel, Wollaston.

The Methodist Chapel, Wollaston.

The Baptist Chapel, Wollaston.

The best way to learn about church buildings is by going to look at some of them! But before you go you need to have some idea about what to look for and what the various features mean.

St Mary's Church, Wollaston

Although there are Anglican churches being built today, most Anglican churches are quite old. In fact, some of them are so old that they were Roman Catholic churches before the Reformation and then became Anglican churches. (See Unit 29).

So the main church in a village is usually an Anglican church. Here is the inside of St Mary's Church, Wollaston.

Some of the features you would expect to find in an Anglican church and which you can see in the picture are:

Altar

An altar is a table used to make an offering to a god. In Anglican and Roman Catholic churches the altar is the focus of the Eucharist or Mass based on the sacrifice of Jesus as the Lamb of God for the sins of the world. The word 'altar' emphasizes the offering of a sacrifice. Some Anglican churches would prefer to use the term 'Communion Table', which focuses on the shared meal and the fellowship. (See also Aspley Christian Centre below.)

St Mary's has two altars – a high altar at the east end of the church and a nave altar much nearer to the congregation. Most of the services take place around this altar, so that the congregation has a much greater sense of joining in with the service.

Pulpit

The sermon is preached from the pulpit. In old churches the pulpit is usually raised up – that was so that the preacher could be heard clearly. But today it does not matter so much, since many churches are equipped with microphones and loudspeakers.

Font

The font is a container for the water used to baptize babies. It is usually placed near the door, to remind people that baptism is the way to come into the church – as a member. Some fonts have covers on them to prevent people from stealing what was traditionally considered to be holy water. Orthodox churches have a much larger font as they immerse the baby – without clothes – three times in the font.

Pews

These are the seats for the congregation. They face towards the altar. Pews weren't introduced until the nineteenth century. In earlier days people stood in the open space. Pews cannot easily be moved around, so some churches have replaced their pews with chairs which can be rearranged or stacked out of the way when necessary.

Lectern

The lectern is the reading-desk from which the Bible is read aloud (an important part of all services). In St Mary's Church it is a very simple wooden one but in many Anglican churches it is made of brass in the shape of an eagle. An eagle is the symbol of St John, who wrote about the Word of God, so it is appropriate that his symbol should be used as a desk for the large church Bible.

▶▶

North and south transepts

Like many Anglican churches, St Mary's Church is built in the shape of a cross. The transepts are the 'arm' parts of the building. Here they have been filled in – with the organ on the south side and a vestry on the north side. If you looked at the church from the air you would see very clearly that it is cross-shaped – 'cruciform'.

Aspley Christian Centre, Nottingham

Aspley Christian Centre is a Pentecostal church belonging to the Assemblies of God denomination. As you can see it is very different from St Mary's Church, Wollaston. It is a much newer building – it was built in 1975. The picture shows members of the congregation actually building the church themselves.

If you look at the plan of the building you will see that it is a different shape from St Mary's – it is rectangular instead of cruciform. Many non-conformist churches are built in this shape, like a room, because they are primarily meeting-places.

Aspley Christian Centre has a **pulpit**. This is the focal point of the church, rather than being set to one side. The non-conformist churches usually emphasize the importance of preaching from the Bible and so they give the pulpit the focal point in their buildings.

There is a simple **Communion Table**. Pentecostal Christians often call their Communion Service the Lord's Supper, as a reminder of the Last Supper which Jesus ate with his disciples. This Communion Table has the words which Jesus spoke to his disciples carved on the front: *This do in remembrance of me.*

What you can't see from the main picture of the inside is the **baptistry**, where adults are

baptized by total immersion. This is at the back of the church on the right hand side. There is no particular reason for it being there – many baptistries are at the front. This one is usually covered over with carpet and chairs, but when there is a baptismal service it is uncovered and filled with water, which is then heated!

In this church there are **chairs** instead of pews. These chairs can be moved around and placed in different formations or moved out of the way if a large space is required. When church members have a meal together, or a party, they move the chairs back and put long tables down the middle of the church.

This makes the church building much more flexible than a cruciform building with pews. When a new church is built today, one of the main concerns is to make a place which can adapt to all the different needs of the congregation. Also, it is now thought to be important that everyone can see everything that happens. Look at the picture of a modern church on a housing estate. What differences can you see here, compared with the two church buildings we have looked at?

In some places churches of different denominations have joined together to worship in one building. This might be for financial reasons or because the people in those two or three churches want to break down the barriers which are caused by their denominational differences. (See Unit 30.) Obviously, there are problems to be overcome. If Baptists or Pentecostals join together with Anglicans they may need both a font *and* a baptistry.

Cathedrals

A cathedral is actually only a church where the bishop has his chair, or *cathedra*. Originally a cathedral was a place for the bishop to celebrate Mass with his household of priests.

Gradually, however, cathedrals grew bigger until the bishop's church with his *cathedra* was only a small part of a much larger and grander building. Some cathedrals were originally the church of a monastery which was extended and developed.

Traditionally a cathedral was cruciform in shape, as you can see from the plan of St Paul's cathedral in London.

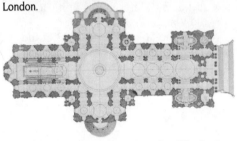

Cathedrals often became a focus for all kinds of activities (the nave was often used by traders) and it became necessary to screen off the altar area so that there would be somewhere separate where the Mass could be celebrated. Elaborate screens were built to separate the chancel from the nave. These were called *rood screens* because they often had a cross or 'rood' on top of the screen.

However, today people often want to be nearer to the altar, to feel part of the service taking place. When the Roman Catholic church wanted to build a cathedral in Liverpool the archbishop asked architects to submit a plan for a building which could seat between two and three thousand people, all of whom should be able to see the altar with no one sitting more than twenty-three metres away.

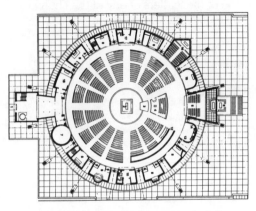

The Church of England and the Roman Catholic church are divided into *dioceses* to make administration as simple as possible. In each diocese there is a cathedral presided over by a *diocesan bishop*. Sometimes the bishop has assistant bishops to help him. These are called *suffragan bishops*.

Cathedrals today are used on a variety of occasions as well as the regular services. People from all over the diocese go to the Cathedral for special services and occasions. After the Hillsborough football disaster in 1989 there was a special Requiem Mass held at the Roman Catholic Cathedral in Liverpool and a memorial service at the Anglican Cathedral.

▲FOLLOW UP▲

Look back at Unit 29. Choose two denominations and design a joint place of worship for them, to be built in a new shopping precinct. In your design you need to consider the following points:

● Would these two denominations actually be likely to join together? (If not, choose two that would!)
● What is the main belief of each denomination?
● How is this expressed in their own buildings?
● How can you express these beliefs in a shared building?
● What is going to be the shared focal point of this church?

● Can everyone see this focal point easily?
● What Christian symbols do you want to include in your building?
● What advantages does your design have over the two separate buildings these congregations have been worshipping in previously?
● What will attract shoppers from the precinct to come into your building?
● What accommodation is there in your plan for activities other than the Sunday services?

Leaders of the Church

If you were asked to think of a name for some of the leaders of any of the churches, what would you come up with?

– bishop?
– priest?
– vicar?
– captain?
– elder?
– moderator?
– Pope?
– deacon?
– archbishop?
– minister?

Could you group the names under the churches to which they belong?

– Church of England
– Roman Catholic Church
– Non-conformist or Free churches

Look at the chart later in this unit. How many did you get right?

Now for the $64,000 question! Could you say which of those titles are used in the New Testament for the leaders of the early church?

The early church

There are in fact four titles generally used for leaders in the New Testament:
– apostle
– elder or bishop
– deacon

● **Apostle.** The word apostle literally means someone who is sent out, a messenger, especially someone who has been authorized to act in a particular way by the one who sent him. After a night of prayer, Jesus chose twelve of his disciples to be apostles:

'When day came, he called his disciples to him and chose twelve of them, whom he named apostles.'
Luke 6:13

Later on in the New Testament other names are added to the list of apostles; Matthias takes the place of Judas Iscariot and Paul calls himself an apostle.

The job of an apostle is very straightforward – it is to preach the

Good News of Jesus Christ, especially to those who have not yet heard the message. Paul starts his letter to the church at Rome with these words:

'From Paul, a servant of Christ Jesus and an apostle chosen and called by God to preach his Good News . . . God gave me the privilege of being an apostle for the sake of Christ, in order to lead people of all nations to believe and obey.'
Romans 1:1,5

In Paul's letters and the account of the early church in the book of Acts it is clear that the apostles had overall authority in the church. Any major problems, such as whether Gentiles should be included in the church, were discussed and decided upon by the apostles.

● **Elder or bishop.** The New Testament does not provide us with a neat list of definitions of ministers! We have to try to work out a pattern

from a variety of references. The apostles had to circulate and move about because they were the original witnesses who had known and been taught by Jesus. But there were also people appointed as overseers of each individual church or as overseer of a group of churches. These ministers were responsible for looking after the group, sorting out problems and helping their churches to grow. One of the words which is used of these bishops or elders is the same word which is used of a shepherd looking after his flock of sheep.

When Paul is saying goodbye to the elders of the church at Ephesus he says:

'Keep watch over yourselves and over all the flock which the Holy Spirit has placed in your care. Be shepherds of the church of God, which he made his own through the death of his Son.'
Acts 20: 28

One of the duties of a bishop today is to confirm new members of the church.

How a bishop is chosen in the Roman Catholic Church

When a bishop retires or dies, the Pope appoints a new bishop. However, as the Pope cannot know all the possible candidates personally, he takes advice from other people.

His representative, or Pro-Nuncio, has the job of finding priests who might be good bishops and he asks for other people's opinions. This is all done confidentially but anyone is free to send a nomination or suggestion about the kind of person they would like as a bishop to the Pro-Nuncio.

Eventually the Pro-Nuncio sends three names to the Congregation for Bishops in Rome. They discuss the nominations and maybe add other names before passing the list to the Pope, for him to make the final decision.

● **Deacon.** As the early church in Jerusalem grew the apostles found that they did not have time to look after all the problems that were arising because they were so busy preaching the word of God. Refer back to Unit 20 and read Acts 6:1–6 to see how the first seven deacons were chosen, to take care of practical matters. (This special responsibility did not prevent them from preaching too.)

The deacons, or church helpers, here and in other parts of the New Testament did not have the same authority as the apostles, bishops and elders, but they did have an important practical role in the church. Paul gives very clear instructions to his younger helper Timothy about the kind of person who might be entrusted with this responsible job.

'Church helpers must also have a good character and be sincere; they must not drink too much wine or be greedy for money; they should hold to the revealed truth of the faith with a clear conscience.'
1 Timothy 3:8–9

Stephen, who died for his faith, was one of the first seven deacons. Phoebe, who served the church at Cenchreae, is singled out for praise by Paul in his Letter to the Romans (16:1).

Gradually these ministries changed until by the end of the second century AD the pattern of bishops, priests and deacons had been accepted. It is still in use in the Roman Catholic, Anglican and Orthodox churches. But the roles are now clearly distinguished.

The church today

● **Bishops.** The bishops soon became the main leaders of the church. They were seen as part of the chain of leadership which stretched back to the apostles. Today they have the authority to:
● ordain priests
● administer Communion
● pronounce forgiveness of people's sin, on Christ's behalf
● baptize and confirm new members of the church
● control the finance of the church
● settle matters of dispute.

At the ordination of a bishop to the Anglican Church, the archbishop sets out the following description:

A bishop is called to lead in serving and caring for the people of God and to work with them in the oversight of the Church. As a chief pastor he shares with his fellow bishops a special responsibility to maintain and further the unity of the Church, to uphold its discipline, and to guard its faith . . . He is to ordain and to send new ministers, guiding those who serve with him and enabling them to fulfil their ministry.
  He is to baptize and confirm, to preside at Holy Communion, and to lead the offering of prayer and praise. He is to be merciful, but with firmness, and to minister discipline, but with mercy. He is to have special care for the outcast and needy; and to those who turn to God he is to declare the forgiveness of sins.

From *The Alternative Service Book*

In both the Roman Catholic and the Anglican churches the bishops are seen as part of the **apostolic succession** which stretches back to the first apostles. The Archbishop of Canterbury claims to trace his succession back to the archbishops before him and through them to Augustine and to Gregory who sent Augustine to England and from Gregory back to Peter and Paul. Similarly the Pope claims to be able to trace his succession back in a direct line to the apostle Peter. For many Christians the authority this gives is vitally important. For others it matters much less.
  Each bishop is in charge of a **diocese** – an area based around a cathedral (where the bishop has his chair or *cathedra*). Dioceses are organized into a province which is under the jurisdiction of an archbishop.

● **Priests.** When you looked at the list of functions of a bishop you may have thought that your local

A priest's duty is to 'proclaim the Word of the Lord'. This is done, not just in church from the pulpit (as here) but in all his or her work amongst people.

vicar, rector or priest does a lot of those jobs. He administers Communion, pronounces the forgiveness of sins and tries to sort out the problems of the church!

In fact the bishop entrusts those roles to the priest (vicar or rector) at his ordination. But they are roles which can only be taken by someone who has been ordained by a bishop – no one else can 'preside', or be in charge, at a Communion Service for example.

A priest is called by God to work with the bishop and with his fellow-priests, as servant and shepherd among the people to whom he is sent. He is to proclaim the word of the Lord, to call his hearers to repentance, and in Christ's name to absolve, and declare the forgiveness of sins. He is to baptize, and to prepare the baptized for Confirmation. He is to preside at the celebration of the Holy Communion . . .

The Alternative Service Book

Each diocese is divided into parishes and a priest is the representative of the bishop in a parish. His role is to be a shepherd or pastor of that parish, helping his people to grow in their Christian lives.

● **Deacons.** Traditionally, being a deacon has been thought of as the first step towards becoming a priest. But it is a ministry in its own right and some deacons never go on to become priests. In the Roman Catholic Church, where priests have to be celibate (see Unit 51), it is possible for a deacon to be a married man. And in the Anglican Church where, at the moment, only men may become priests, a growing number of women have become deacons.

The role of a deacon is to provide support for a priest. A deacon is:

called to serve the Church of God, and to work with its members in caring for the poor, the needy, the sick, and all who are in trouble . . . A deacon assists the priest under whom he serves, in leading the worship of the people especially in the administration of the Holy Communion. He may baptize when required to do so. It is his general duty to do such pastoral work as is entrusted to him.

The Alternative Service Book

Obviously the 'he's in this quotation also now apply to 'she's! The Church of England is developing a new Prayer Book which will have all-inclusive language. They hope to publish this new book of services in AD2000.

Leadership in the Free churches

There is a very different structure of leadership in the Free churches. Although each denomination has its own particular pattern, they are all based on the same two principles:

● All Christians are of equal status. There is no apostolic succession which marks anyone out as having a special ministry.

● The Communion Service is a meal of remembrance, not a re-enactment of a sacrifice, and so does not need a priest to preside over it. In theory anyone could administer Communion – although usually only those who are recognized as ministers of a particular denomination actually do so. See picture on page 146.

What those two principles mean in practice is that the Free churches:

● have no bishops. They have Moderators, Superintendents and Presidents (who often have the same pastoral role as bishops but whose control depends on the system of church government).

These officials have no sacramental ministry – anyone can give Communion, baptize and pronounce God's forgiveness for sins.

● recognize that anyone, male or female, single or married, can be called by God to become a minister.

● involve church members much more in the life of the church. The Methodist church, for example, often has a minister who looks after four, five or even more churches within his/her 'circuit', and then a system of trained church members who visit the different churches to take the services and preach.

However, although in theory anyone can minister in the Free churches, each denomination has its own pattern of training which is just as thorough as the training which priests undergo. For example, a minister in an Assemblies of God church may go to Bible College for three years and then have a further two years' probation in a church before he is a fully accredited minister.

Lay ministry in the church

'Lay' means those who are not trained/ordained ministers. In all the churches there are many working people who have a special role or special responsibility in the work of their church. In Roman Catholic churches it is now possible to train and be licensed to be a 'Eucharistic minister' – to help the priest with the Communion at a Parish Mass.

In the Church of England a person may become a Reader – someone who is specially licensed by the bishop to take services, preach and visit the sick. Brian Coupland is a Company Director who is a Reader in the Diocese of Peterborough. His licence says:

As you can see, Brian is given authority to assist in most of the duties of the priest. He can only assist though – he can't preside at a Communion Service.

One of the main duties of a Reader is to take services at churches which do not have vicars – either because they are waiting for a new one or because they share a vicar with three or four other parishes.

Of course it is not only specially trained people like Brian who are involved in the ministry of the church. Many churches (like the Brethren and the newer, fast-growing Community churches) have no minister, and members share all the responsibilities, under the leadership of Elders. More and more lay people today want to play

an active part in the church – they are not content to simply be pew warmers. They also realize that it is impossible for a minister or vicar to be a successful:

- priest
- pastor
- counsellor
- man who services the church boiler
- sick visitor
- worship leader
- preacher
- Bible study leader . . . etc., etc.!

The jobs are shared around among as many people as want to be involved and who have talents in a particular area. For example, a school teacher may prove to be very good at leading Bible study groups.

DIOCESE OF PETERBOROUGH

READER'S LICENCE

Issued to :

JOHN BRIAN COUPLAND

on

7th. MAY 1989

WE authorise you to carry out the following duties at the invitation of the incumbent or those authorised to invite you :

read, conduct or participate in such services as may be approved by us and are authorised or allowed by the Canons of the Church of England ;

publish Banns of Marriage (on occasions when a layman is legally allowed to do so);

read and expound the Scriptures;

preach at Services, including Holy Communion;

teach the people according to the doctrines of the Church of England;

assist in the administration of the sacrament of Holy Communion in Church;

conduct funerals with the goodwill of the family of the deceased.

FOLLOW UP

Complete the chart below for as many denominations as possible. (You might also want to look back at the section on denominations on Unit 30.)

For each denomination complete the sections for as many leaders as possible. For example, under the Church of England section you will need to include the following:
- archbishop
- bishop
- priest
- deacon
- reader.

The section entitled 'exclusive functions' means: what jobs is that leader allowed to do, which other leaders in that denomination are not allowed to do?

DENOMINATION	TITLE OF LEADER	SEX	EXCLUSIVE FUNCTION

Creeds and Councils

Right from their very beginnings, Christians were people who believed certain things about God.

We know what these beliefs were from two things –
- what Christians said about God when they preached to non-Christians
- what Christians said about God to other Christians.

The beliefs contained in the preaching or proclamation (Greek *kerygma*: see Unit 15) of the Gospel can be summarized like this:

> - The man Jesus was God's chosen one, Messiah/Christ – Son of God *and* fully human.
> - Through Jesus, God made himself known.
> - Jesus was crucified, but God raised him from the dead.
> - God appointed Jesus to be judge of all people.
> - Through Jesus, God offers people forgiveness of sin, the gift of the Holy Spirit and new (eternal) life.

There are many 'statements of belief' woven into the New Testament apart from these *kerygma* sections. Some are thought to be fragments of the 'confession of faith' a new convert would have to make at his/her baptism. Other bits seem to come from formalized summaries of Christian beliefs that were taught to new Christians. And there are compact statements of belief tucked into what Christian writers said to their readers:

6 There is for us only one God, the Father, who is the Creator of all things and for whom we live; and there is only one Lord, Jesus Christ, through whom all things were created and through whom we live. 9
I Corinthians 8:6

6 There is one God, and there is one who brings God and mankind together, the man Christ Jesus, who gave himself to redeem all mankind. 9
1 Timothy 2:5–6

6 Jesus is Lord. 9
I Corinthians 12:3

6 He appeared in human form,
was shown to be right by the Spirit,
and was seen by angels.
He was preached among the nations,
was believed in throughout the world,
and was taken up to heaven. 9
1 Timothy 3:16

6 When the kindness and love of God our Saviour was revealed, he saved us. It was not because of any good deeds that we ourselves had done, but because of his own mercy that he saved us, through the Holy Spirit, who gives us new birth and new life by washing us. God poured out the Holy Spirit abundantly on us through Jesus Christ our Saviour, so that by his grace we might be put right with God and come into possession of the eternal life we hope for. 9
Titus 3:4–7

By the end of the second century AD, a summary of basic Christian belief known as the 'Rule of Faith' was in circulation, in various versions. This 'Rule' had two main purposes:

- **it preserved true teaching** (doctrine)
- **it refuted false teaching** (heresy).

It became the practice for new converts to declare their belief in God – Father, Son and Holy Spirit – before being baptized. In third-century Rome, new Christians had to answer 'I believe' to questions based on the 'Rule of Faith'.

Later, this question-and-answer form was replaced by a straight statement of belief by the baptism candidate, beginning 'I believe . . .' (*Credo* in Latin). This gave the name 'Creed' to any statement of belief.

Not all 'creeds' are religious: here are some that are popular today:

The Apostles' Creed – so-called because it preserves the teaching of the first apostles – is thought to be based on the third-century question-and-answer baptism creed, but the earliest text in this straight statement form dates from about AD400.

You might find that not all your friends agree about today's popular 'creeds'. Well, there wasn't always universal agreement about Christian beliefs in the early days, either.

When the Emperor Constantine became

The Apostles' Creed

I believe in God, the Father almighty, creator of heaven and earth.

I believe in Jesus Christ, his only Son, our Lord.
He was conceived by the power of the Holy Spirit
and born of the Virgin Mary.
He suffered under Pontius Pilate,
was crucified, died, and was buried.
He descended to the dead.
On the third day he rose again.
He ascended into heaven,
and is seated at the right hand of the Father.
He will come again to judge the living and the dead.

I believe in the Holy Spirit,
the holy catholic Church,
the communion of saints,
the forgiveness of sins,
the resurrection of the body,
and the life everlasting. Amen.

The Alternative Service Book

a Christian the church expanded throughout the Roman Empire. It was governed, like the Empire itself, from two centres – Rome in the west (which was Latin-speaking) and Constantinople in the east (which was Greek-speaking). With Christians from so many different races, cultures and backgrounds it was almost inevitable that there would be disagreement about some points of belief.

Questions arose about the person of Jesus Christ:

How could Jesus Christ be both Son of God, and fully God?

How could Jesus Christ be fully God and fully human?

Two crucial doctrines (teachings) were fashioned from the discussions that followed:

● *the doctrine of the Trinity*: belief in the three persons of the one 'Godhead' – God the Father, God the Son, God the Holy Spirit.
● *the doctrine of the Person of Christ*: (sometimes called 'Christology').

Arius

In about AD318, a priest called Arius, whose parish was in Alexandria in Egypt, claimed that only the Father was God. Jesus was a lesser being because (Arius reckoned) he had been created by God – even though it was before everything else was created. Was this right? Or was it heresy?

A decision had to be made for the whole church.

This wasn't the first time the church had had to take action in order to come to some agreement and standardization of accepted teaching. In the very early days, when Peter and Paul were preaching in different places, they each had to 'report back' to the church leaders in Jerusalem to explain just what they were preaching and why.

● Read Acts 11:1–18 for Peter's explanation of why he had been preaching to Gentiles (non-Jews).
● Read Acts 15:1–21 for Paul's explanation of why he was not insisting that Gentiles should become Jews (by circumcision) in order to be saved by Jesus.

As the first-century Christians had done, so, when they were confronted by the 'Arian heresy', the church leaders in the fourth century also called a meeting, a council of bishops, to discuss the problem.

It was held in Nicea in 325, and the result was a new credal statement. Father and Son were said to be 'consubstantial' – that is, both of the one substance.

The new statement was fairly complex, and it also dealt with other aspects of belief, so the decisions made at Nicea were reconsidered later and were not made official until the Council of Constantinople, AD381. Today, there is no trace of any statement put out after this second council, but a statement put out after a much later council, held at Chalcedon in AD451, summarized the original Nicea beliefs and

this has become known as the Nicene Creed.

The Nicene Creed

We believe in one God,
the Father, the almighty,
maker of heaven and earth,
of all that is,
seen and unseen.
We believe in one Lord, Jesus Christ,
the only Son of God,
eternally begotten of the Father,
God from God, Light from Light,
true God from true God,
begotten, not made,
of one Being with the Father.
Through him all things were made.
For us men and for our salvation
he came down from heaven;
by the power of the Holy Spirit
he became incarnate of the Virgin Mary,
  and was made man.
For our sake he was crucified under
  Pontius Pilate;
he suffered death and was buried.
On the third day he rose again
in accordance with the Scriptures;
he ascended into heaven
and is seated at the right hand of the Father.
He will come again in glory
to judge the living and the dead,
and his kingdom will have no end.

We believe in the Holy Spirit,
the Lord, the giver of life,
who proceeds from the Father and the
  Son.
With the Father and the Son he is worshipped
  and glorified.
He has spoken through the Prophets.

We believe in one holy catholic
  and apostolic Church.
We acknowledge one baptism for the
  forgiveness of sins.
We look for the resurrection of the dead,
and the life of the world to come. Amen.

The Alternative Service Book

The Nicene Creed established the teaching that Jesus was fully God, just as the Father was fully God.

The first great Church Council at Nicea (325) is pictured by a sixteenth-century artist.

Athanasius

There were frequent troubles in the time between the Councils of Nicea and Constantinople, especially in the east, where Arius had many loyal followers. The Arians might have brought about an 'east-west' split had it not been for the lone voice of Athanasius, Bishop of Alexandria, who consistently defended the Council of Nicea and attacked the growth of Arianism.

Five times Athanasius was banished by leaders who were Arian sympathizers, but he was convinced that if Christ were less than God he could not be the Saviour of . mankind.

It was largely due to the persistence of Athanasius that the original agreement of Nicea was confirmed at Constantinople and the Nicene Creed became – after Chalcedon – the universal statement of belief for the whole Church, east and west.

But there was still that other problem of belief to be cleared up. If Jesus was fully God, how could he also be fully human?

Around AD350, Apollinarius – Bishop of Laodicea in Syria – taught that Jesus Christ could not have possessed a human soul because the human soul is basically corrupt. Christ (said Apollinarius) had only one nature – his divine nature 'enfleshed' in a human body. Again, decisions had to be made about this.

Nestorius

Apollinarius' teaching was most strongly opposed by the church leaders in and around Antioch in the years between the Council of Constantinople (381) and the Council of Ephesus (431).

One of the theologians involved was Nestorius, a deacon of Antioch who became Bishop of Constantinople in AD428.

Although Nestorius believed that Christ was both God and man, he went so far as to claim that these two natures were quite separate, almost as if Jesus Christ were two beings – Son of God and Son of Mary.

Nestorius insisted that God could never be a baby a few days old, so the two natures must have remained separate when God became human in Jesus.

He also claimed that Mary was the mother of the *human* Jesus, but not the 'bearer of *God*'.

This division between the human and divine nature of Jesus was out of step with the picture in the Gospels. But political rivalry between the leaders in Antioch and Alexandria was what really led to Nestorius being condemned as a heretic by the Council of Ephesus in AD431.

Like Arius before him, Nestorius had a loyal following who continued to promote

Some early false beliefs

Some people believed that acceptance by God depended on gaining special knowledge. This belief is called 'gnosticism', from the Greek *gnosis* which means 'knowledge'. Gnostics saw access to God as a kind of spiritual ladder of secret knowledge shared with the angels. The human body, they said, was a hindrance to spiritual progress, and therefore God would never have become human. Paul warns against this false teaching in his letter to the Colossians (see Colossians 2:8–9).

Some people believed that Jesus was not in fact fully human, that he only appeared to be human but did not truly share humanity's natural frailty. This belief is called 'docetism', from the Greek *dokein* which means 'to appear'. John warns against this false belief in his first letter (see 1 John 4:1–2).

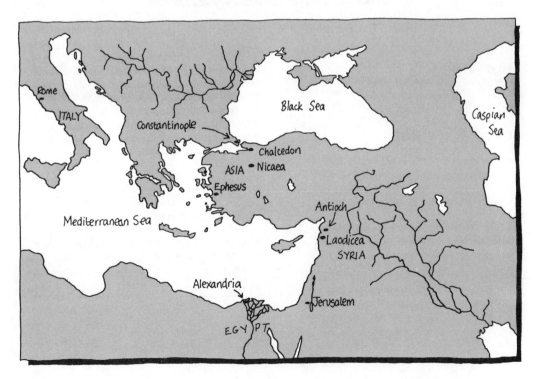

his teaching, and the debate about the human and divine natures of Christ erupted again when these Nestorian sympathizers were challenged by an elderly Constantinople monk called Eutyches.

Again, a council was called! At the great Council of Chalcedon in AD451, more than 400 bishops worked out the agreed wording for the earlier creeds of 325 and 381 (the Nicene Creed), and a new 'confession' which stressed the union of Christ's two natures in one person.

Other Councils met as years went on, as they still do from time to time today. But it was these first four 'worldwide' or 'universal' councils that determined the 'worldwide' or 'universal' beliefs taught and accepted by the whole of the Christian church.

● **Council of Nicea** AD325
dealt with the teaching of Arius (who claimed that only the Father was really God)
● **Council of Constantinople** AD381
reaffirmed conclusions of Nicea (that Jesus was both God and human) and dealt with further errors
● **Council of Ephesus** AD431
dealt with the teaching of Nestorius (that Jesus was both God and man, but with two separate natures) and reaffirmed credal statements
● **Council of Chalcedon** AD451
finalized the wording of earlier creeds, and issued a 'confession' concerning the nature of Christ as God and man (two natures which exist without separation)

The Apostles' Creed and the Nicene Creed are still accepted by Christians throughout the world as summaries of basic Christian beliefs. And they serve the same two purposes as the original credal statements of the first Christians:

● The Christian Creeds preserve the true doctrines of the Church.
● The Christian Creeds protect the Church from the invasion of heresy.

▲FOLLOW☞UP▲

1. Write a one-sentence definition for each of the following:
● doctrine
● heresy
● creed
● christology.

2. Explain the main beliefs of:
● Arius
● Athanasius
● Nestorius.

3. Copy out one of the creeds from this section.

4. Now work through this unit and find references from the Bible which support each credal statement.

5. Today the creeds are used as an affirmation of faith by Christians around the world. However there are some credal statements which could potentially divide rather than unite some Christians:
● God as the Creator of heaven and earth
● the virgin birth of Jesus
● the physical resurrection of Jesus
● the resurrection of the body.
(Check that you understand what the Creeds mean by these terms!)

Conduct a poll among your friends – make sure you include some Christians – to see what they believe about these credal statements.

6. To what extent is knowing, and regularly reciting, a creed helpful to a believer? Give reasons for your answer.

The Trinity:
The Three-in-One God

It is no wonder that there were centuries of discussions, debates, arguments and Councils about the doctrine of the Trinity – about how God is one, yet three-in-one: Father, Son and Holy Spirit. It is obviously not an easy concept to grasp, or to teach to new believers.

The thing to note is that the church leaders who formulated the creeds were trying to preserve what was *true*, not what was merely *understandable*! The idea of the Trinity (like the idea of God becoming human in Jesus) is a *mystery* which words can never fully describe.

And the truth as they saw it was that the Creator of the world was God the Father, Jesus Christ was God revealed to mankind, and the Holy Spirit was God in action within and among his people.

Where did the church leaders first discover this difficult 'truth' about God? They found it in the Bible.

The doctrine of the Trinity is not actually spelt out in the Bible. But it is easy to see what the Bible writers believed about God. For one thing, they stuck firmly to the belief that God is *one*. It was this view of God which separated the ancient Jews from the other nations.

> 'Israel, remember this! The Lord – and the Lord alone – is our God!'
> Deuteronomy 6:4

This is the most famous Jewish statement of belief, the 'Shema' (the word with which the verse begins in Hebrew).

The Shema

The Shema, Deuteronomy 6:4–9, is the most important prayer in the Jewish religion. It contains the belief that God is one and emphasizes
● the importance of whole-hearted devotion to God
● the importance of knowing, obeying and teaching God's commandments.

The Shema contains practical instructions about where the words of God's commandments are to be placed:
● in little boxes (phylacteries or *tefillin*) on the forehead near the mind and on the left upper arm near the heart
● in a tiny scroll-case (*mezuzah*) fixed to the doorpost at the entrance to the home.

The Shema is the first thing spoken to a new-born Jewish child and the first prayer the child learns to say. Jews say the Shema before going to bed, and they hope it will be the last thing they say before they die.

But it is also obvious that when the Bible writers talked of Jesus as the 'Son of God', they were attributing to him all the same characteristics as God:

READ MATTHEW 16:15–16; JOHN 20:24–29

where Peter and Thomas identify Jesus as God

READ JOHN 1:1–14; PHILIPPIANS 2:5–11

where John and Paul portray Jesus as God in human form

Similarly, the Bible writers' experience of the Holy Spirit was reckoned by them to be an experience of God himself:

 READ EZEKIEL 36:27; JOEL 2:28–29

for ancient prophecies about people receiving God's Spirit

READ ACTS 2:14–38

for Peter's claim that God's Spirit has been 'poured out' on his people

 READ ACTS 5:1–4

for Peter's claim that to deceive the Holy Spirit is to deceive God himself.

There are also places in the Bible where all three Persons of the Trinity are described or referred to:

 READ GENESIS 1:1–5

for Creator, Word and Spirit at work in Creation ('power of God' = 'Spirit of God')

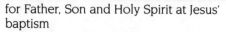 **READ MATTHEW 3:16–17**

for Father, Son and Holy Spirit at Jesus' baptism

READ 2 CORINTHIANS 13:13

for Paul's prayer for the blessing of Jesus, the love of God and the fellowship of the Holy Spirit on his readers.

It was against this biblical background that the Nicene Creed came into being, to promote and preserve the truth that

● the Creator Father is God
● the Son Jesus is God from God
● the Holy Spirit is God (Lord, giving life, to be worshipped).

Christians believe that each of the three Persons of the Trinity is fully God, not one-third of God. But each Person of the Trinity shows God relating to the world in a different way:

● creating and sustaining the world (Father)
● revealing himself to the world (Son)
● achieving his purposes in the world (Spirit)

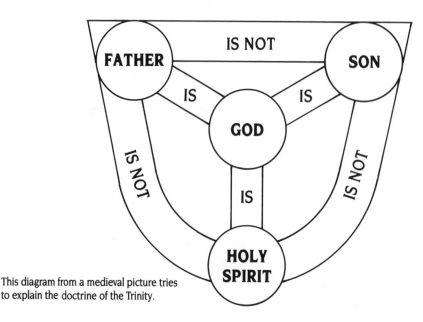

This diagram from a medieval picture tries to explain the doctrine of the Trinity.

The Athanasian Creed

An unknown theologian living in southern Gaul at the end of the fourth century produced a statement of belief which began, 'Whoever will be saved . . .', and went on to say what such a person must believe. The writer was apparently influenced by the teaching of Augustine of Hippo in his document called *De Trinitate*. He emphasizes the unity and equality of the three Persons of the Trinity and also the unity and equality of the two natures of Jesus Christ, human and divine. This creed was wrongly associated with Athanasius, hence the name. Because it was not the product of a worldwide Council it never attained the authority of the other two creeds.

FOLLOW UP

1. What does the word 'Trinity' mean?

2. Draw a picture or diagram which would help someone to understand the Christian doctrine of the Trinity.

3. What are the individual roles of each of the Persons of the Trinity?

4. Look at the story of the baptism of Jesus in Matthew 3:16, 17. What does this occasion tell us about the different roles of the Trinity?

5. How helpful do you find the idea of God in three Persons? What are the strengths of this idea? Are there any weaknesses?

Issues of Belief: Creation and Evil

Creation: how things began

'I believe in God, the Father . . .' So begins the Apostles' Creed. The Christian concept of God as 'Father' has two strands in it, one reflecting the teaching of the Old Testament, and the other reflecting the teaching of the New Testament.

According to the Old Testament, God is Father of all humanity because he made humankind in his likeness (Genesis 1:26) and gave life to them (Genesis 2:7) – just as human parents give their *likeness* and *life* to their baby. This is what is meant by the phrases 'family of man' and 'brotherhood of man'. All human beings – men and women – are bound together, belonging to the one family, originating from the same source.

This shared brother/sister relationship of all humanity under God as Father has

Christians believe that all human beings are bound together in one family.

implications recognized by both Christians and non-Christians. It means that no person can claim to be better than another person on grounds of race, colour, religion, education or status. Belief in God as Father of the whole human race requires that all people should respect others and care for them as 'family'.

For Christians, there is also the additional New Testament meaning behind the idea of God as Father.

According to the New Testament, those people who accept Jesus as Lord and Saviour (i.e. all Christians) are 'adopted' into God's close family (Galatians 4:4–7). They are accepted by him and become 'children of God' for ever (John 1:12–13; Romans 8:12–17; 1 John 5:1, 11–12).

' . . . God, the Father almighty, creator of heaven and earth'. According to their creeds, Christians believe that our world

was created by God. The creation account in the Bible pictures God's acts of creation taking place in a sequence of six days. Some Christians understand this literally as twenty-four hour days. But there are other interpretations. All Christians agree that whatever the process and timing, God created our universe – and all that he made was good.

Scientists, both Christian and non-Christian, put forward various theories about how it all began.

A 'Big Bang'?

Most scientists say that there was a massive explosion, a 'Big Bang'. From this point in time and space the universe has expanded ever outwards. It is still expanding today, like a balloon being blown up.

A moment of initial creation helps some to believe in a Creator. But it does not *prove* the existence of God. We cannot go back beyond the Big Bang or test whether it was caused by God. Perhaps it 'just happened'.

The Big Bang theory says that the stars and planets (including planet Earth) formed very slowly. It took billions of years for matter to join together to make the Earth, and billions of years for life to form. The theory of evolution says that all life on Earth today has come from a very long series of modifications and improvements to the original life-making chemicals.

Evolution does not rule out God. Traditionally, Christians working in science have understood their work as discovering how God himself is working in the world. What we call scientific laws (for example, the laws of gravity) are summaries of what we observe happening. Apples always fall to the ground. But what is gravity? A Christian can say that God is the ultimate cause of events – he makes gravity 'work'. In science we are recording how God runs the world.

Different views

Christians hold different views on this point. But they are clear that science cannot prove or disprove God. And many work within science in order to be able to say, 'So *that's* how God does it!'

Some see evolution as a major difficulty for believers in God. In the last century, Charles Darwin suggested that all animal and plant life had gradually evolved from simpler forms. His theory is widely accepted today, and scientists try to discover how simple chemicals over many thousands of years have developed into mankind. But the latest scientific discoveries do not make Christian belief more difficult. Evolution may in the end turn out to be God's method, or mechanism, of creation.

Some Christians cannot accept this. They believe the first two chapters of Genesis say that God created distinct 'kinds' which cannot change into other completely different forms. They also see the six days of creation as six periods of twenty-four hours, or six periods of time. They believe the Earth was created thousands, not millions, of years ago. Creation was by a series of special miracles, which go beyond the laws of science as we see today.

No Christian doubts God created the world. The arguments between the 'creationists' and those who believe God created by evolution is an argument over science and the interpretation of Genesis. They do not argue over whether or not God is the Creator. On that they are agreed, but they cannot agree over how and when he did it.

What Genesis says

The creationists believe the first chapters of Genesis give the historical sequence of creation. Everything happened just as Genesis says. Others say that Genesis is a poetic account which tries to highlight the meaning of creation, not its science. Not to read Genesis in this way is, they say, to miss the point. And they emphasize how the first three days of creation beautifully echo the last three. God first creates realms of creation (light, sky/water, earth) and then the occupants for these realms (stars, birds/fishes, people).

Mount St Helens Volcano, Washington, USA, erupts. The human suffering which results from natural phenomena raises an age-old problem for those who believe in a good God.

The Bible story of creation stresses:

God created the universe from nothing.

God's world is good, and is complete. God needed no outside help.

God created humankind, giving them a special place in creation.

People are responsible to God and must care for the rest of nature.

This is what Christians affirm when they begin to say their creed.

The problem of evil

If God, who is good, made and sustains this world, why does it contain so much suffering?

The Bible's answer, in Genesis chapter three, is that after God had made the world – and everything he made was good – people rebelled against God and that perfect creation was spoiled.

All religions (and all people) have to account for evil in the world. The Christian doctrine claims to account more satisfactorily than others for both the glory and evil in the world.

The most obvious question is: how do we account for 'natural disasters'?

● **God created the world and sustains it in a life-supporting state.** The Bible claims that God made the world; the scientists from their observations suggest how it was done.

In order for the various life-forms to appear and exist (whether suddenly or gradually), the planet Earth had to be at just the right point between molten hot and cooled solid. The crust has cooled to the point where it can and does continue to support life. But it is only a crust, a cooled outer layer, and as such it moves, cracks and buckles from time to time, causing earthquakes – and volcanic eruptions when the molten inner core sometimes breaks through the surface.

Although earthquakes and volcanic eruptions are called 'natural *disasters*' because of the harm they can do to people, they are in fact 'natural *phenomena*', indicators which show that the earth is in a life-supporting state.

But evil affects people in other ways, apart from natural disasters.

● **People make wrong choices which bring their own evil consequences.** Some of the suffering in the world is cause by human negligence, weakness and greed – the results of deliberate choices people have made.

For example, millions starve because wrong choices dictate political and economic structures, so that while there *is* enough food for everyone on the planet, the *rich* nations don't like to risk a fall in world prices by releasing their 'surplus mountains'. In the meantime, people starve in some badly-governed *poor* countries where war, exploitation of natural resources or exploitation of cheap labour take priority over planning for self-sufficiency. Human selfishness and greed are to blame – not God.

Thousands die in 'natural disasters' because re-locating them away from known earthquake lines, volcanoes and flood zones – or housing them adequately to ensure survival – takes money and political will.

● **God is not indifferent to suffering.** Both Old and New Testaments are clear that God is not indifferent to suffering. He *cares* what happens to the poor and needy. He hates injustice and the self-interest that inflicts suffering on others.

Christians believe that the suffering and death of Jesus show that God knows what it is to suffer. He identifies with and sympathizes with people in their suffering. Christians point to the resurrection of Jesus as proof that God's purpose of love and life

---

Christians believe that the essential truths about creation and evil are contained within the accounts of Genesis 1–3.
● God made our world and it was good.
● People rebelled against God and that perfect creation was spoiled.

The picture language allows for a variety of interpretations of these truths, but they are not diminished by being compared with an honest observation of the world and its people. Genesis 1–2 can be seen as a poetic description of the way life emerged, and Genesis 3 can be seen as a poetic description of what happens when people make wrong choices.

---

for mankind can never finally be overcome by evil. Through the suffering and death of Jesus, those who believe in him are saved from the power of death. In the life beyond death there will be no more pain or tears. God's new world will be wholly good, as he intended our world to be (Revelation 21:3–4).

This belief helps Christians to look for good coming out of evil, to accept that suffering can produce hope, faith and love – both in those who suffer and also in those who care for them. Some Christians spend their lives helping people who suffer, in the firm belief – that God cares, and that evil will never overcome good (see Units 55 and 58). All the means we have of relieving suffering, such as medicines and hi-tech treatments, are seen as part of God's creation to be used for the benefit of all people.

Food is distributed at a refugee centre in Sudan, as people respond to disaster.

● **God has a wider purpose for humankind beyond earthly existence.**
Christians believe that the physical world that can be observed and monitored by scientists is not the *whole* of God's creation.

Although Christians take seriously the role of 'steward' given by God to mankind, and will therefore work to make the world a better place ecologically, politically, economically and medically, they also see

Why doesn't God *do* something? When confronted with suffering – disasters, injustice, illness, wars – people often wonder why God does not intervene to stop the suffering or even prevent it happening in the first place. Christians believe that this too is answered in the Genesis creation accounts.

When God made human beings, he gave them a nature which allowed them to think and act independently, making their own choices, rather than creating them like pre-programmed robots or puppets that could only ever do what God made them do.

Christians call this freedom to make choices 'free will' and they see it as an indication of God's love for people, that he allows them this freedom and maturity so that they can order their own lives. The risk is that people will exercise free will in ways that can hurt other people, the environment and God.

Sometimes God *does* intervene in a direct way; miracles happen and people are healed. These occasions are exceptional. They help to build up people's faith by giving glimpses of the power of God which is not limited by the laws of nature. But they have to remain the exception rather than the rule if God is not to become a puppet-master.

the death and resurrection of Jesus as an assurance of a life with God that begins now and continues beyond death for all who believe in Jesus as the way to God.

FOLLOW UP

CREATION
1. Watch someone using a computer game, preferably of the action type rather than an adventure game. Write down some of the rules: how do you move the character? What happens when a character meets an alien?

Now list some rules or scientific laws of the real world, just as a scientist would do.

Split into groups and discuss who wrote the rules of the computer game. What does this tell us about scientific laws in our world?

2. Divide into two groups.
Group A: Make a list of the order in which the school was built. What work did the builders do first, what last?
Group B: List the school buildings as though trying to impress anxious parents about to send their child for the first time. What would they be looking for?

Come together and discuss your lists. Which list is 'correct'?

Taking your two lists as examples, what do you think the first chapter of Genesis is trying to teach us?

EVIL
1. 'If there was a God my daughter wouldn't have died.' You are a vicar. What would you say to this mother whose 2-year-old daughter has just died of cancer?

2. There are other issues you may want to discuss. Here are some words which may act as a trigger to your discussion:
AIDS
DOWNS SYNDROME
HIROSHIMA
ETHIOPIAN FAMINE
HOLOCAUST

Issues of Belief:
Incarnation and Salvation

Incarnation

'We believe in one Lord, Jesus Christ,
the only Son of God,
eternally begotten of the Father,
God from God, Light from Light,
true God from true God,
begotten, not made,
of one Being with the Father.
Through him all things were made.
For us men and our salvation
he came down from heaven;
by the power of the Holy Spirit
he became incarnate of the Virgin Mary,
      and was made man.
For our sake he was crucified under
      Pontius Pilate;
he suffered death and was buried.
On the third day he rose again
in accordance with the Scriptures;
he ascended into heaven
and is seated at the right hand of the
      Father.
He will come again in glory
to judge the living and the dead,
and his kingdom will have no end.'
Part of the Nicene Creed

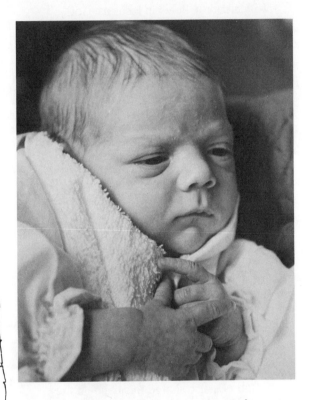

Christians believe that God took on human nature in the birth of Jesus. They call this 'incarnation'.

Christians believe that Jesus of Nazareth was not merely God's special 'anointed one' (Messiah/Christ). They claim him to be 'Son of God'. And they base that claim on what the first disciples observed and recorded about Jesus' *own* understanding of his relationship to God.

According to the Gospels, at Jesus' baptism and his transfiguration, a voice from heaven declared 'You are (this is) my beloved Son.' And Jesus constantly referred to God as 'my Father' (Matthew 7:21;10:32,33; 11:27), emphasizing that,

because of his special Father–Son relationship with God, he was now the supreme channel of communication between God and mankind. More than this, in Jewish thinking the father is seen in the son – so the idea of Jesus as Son of God means that in Jesus we see what God is like.

The early disciples realized that a belief in Jesus as Son of God has implications. The most obvious thing is that such a unique relationship could not be limited by human time or a human life-span. Which is why Jesus' first followers came to see him as someone whose life with them was the earthly 'embodiment' of a heavenly existence going back to before the creation of the world.

Another word for 'embodiment' is 'incarnation', which means 'becoming flesh'. The Christian belief in Jesus as the Son of God is known as the doctrine of the incarnation. Belief in Jesus as 'God incarnate' (God become flesh/human) is central to the teaching of the New Testament.

It is seen most clearly in John's Gospel, especially the Prologue – 'the Word – that is, God – became flesh' (John 1:1–14). (See Unit 17.)

Paul, in his letters to new Christians, portrays Jesus as God's Son, sent by God into the world, giving up the riches of heaven to become human, but still expressing every aspect of the nature of God (Philippians 2:6–7; Colossians 1:19). (See Unit 18.)

> 'He always had the nature of God, but he did not think that by force he should try to become equal with God. Instead of this, of his own free will he gave up all he had, and took the nature of a servant.'
> Philippians 2:6–7

The unknown writer of the letter to the Hebrews also shared this belief in the incarnation, showing Jesus as the exact likeness of God himself (Hebrews 1:1–4).

> 'He reflects the brightness of God's glory and is the exact likeness of God's own being, sustaining the universe with his powerful word.'
> Hebrews 1:3

Although these New Testament writers express this teaching or 'doctrine' of the incarnation very clearly, some Christians in recent times have not shared the same belief. They think that the New Testament writers had a primitive way of describing

? ? ?

In an Easter TV programme in 1989 the Anglican Bishop of Durham, Dr David Jenkins, claimed that Christian faith does not require a belief in the physical resurrection of Jesus. He said: 'I don't think it means a physical resurrection', and went on to talk about the need for something more than 'the revival of a corpse'.

The broadcast provoked an immediate response, and not just from church people. One Member of Parliament, Neil Hamilton, summed up what many people felt – that bishops ought to strengthen people's faith, not shake it. 'His religion is full of doubts' said Mr Hamilton.

truths, and that this is no longer appropriate to Christian belief.

Some modern theologians dispute the idea of Jesus being God in human form. They reckon that the New Testament claims are merely a poetic way of presenting what they would prefer to call 'the human face of God'.

These are some of the ways in which Christian groups see Jesus as alive today:

● **Jesus is alive today in his church which is 'the body of Christ'** (an idea that comes from 1 Corinthians 12:12–27 and other New Testament passages)

The sixteenth-century nun, St Teresa, expressed it like this:

Christ has no body now on earth but yours
No hands but yours,
No feet but yours.
Yours are the eyes through which is to look
out Christ's compassion on the world.
Yours are the feet with which he is to go
about doing good.
Yours are the hands with which he is to bless
men now.

● **Jesus is alive today as he is met personally, by each individual believer who accepts him as 'Lord'.**

● **Jesus is alive today through the power of his Holy Spirit at work in believers.**

● **Jesus is alive today in the sacrament of Holy Communion.**

Similarly, some modern theologians see the New Testament resurrection accounts as a poetic way of presenting the disciples' continuing experience of the presence of God after Jesus had died.

It is, however, always important to listen to those who knew Jesus on earth. They are in a better position than later Christians to know what happened – especially since they were prepared to stake their lives on it.

There will always be controversy and debate. The ideas of incarnation and resurrection are great mysteries which no one can fully understand. Nonetheless, all the main Christian churches today still accept and teach the doctrines of the Creeds. They also try to express the present-day significance of Jesus, his incarnation and resurrection.

Salvation

The 'significance of Jesus for today' teaching is also expressed in the various churches' ideas about how Jesus saves and redeems his people.

The New Testament writers saw Jesus as the one who came to 'save' people who were doomed because they had been cut off from a holy God by their sins. In taking the punishment for people's sins by dying on the cross, Jesus was 'saving' them from being cut off from God for ever.

There are various New Testament 'pictures' which give some ideas about how salvation works. Jesus' death is described as a **victory** over evil (see Colossians 2:15) which sets people free from slavery to the devil and his ways.

Jesus' death is described as a **penalty**, a sentence in law, which God has passed on guilty humanity, but which Jesus has paid on our behalf (see Romans 5:8–9).

(It is part of God's perfection and holiness that he is both totally loving *and* absolutely just. Any human judge who fails to sentence for a serious offence is labelled unfair and unreliable in his decisions. It is because God is perfectly fair that he passes sentence on guilty humanity. But it is because he perfectly loving that he pays

the penalty himself, in the person of his Son Jesus.)

Jesus' death is described as a **sacrifice**, a perfect offering made to God on behalf

In his work of salvation God bridges the gap between himself and humankind.

of humanity to make up for all wrongdoing (see Hebrews 10:10–12). This picture is a reflection of the Old Testament sacrifices which 'atoned' for the sins of the Jews. Jesus' sacrifice was the 'atonement' people needed to make them 'at one' with God (see Unit 12).

There is another New Testament picture of salvation which reflects God's dealings with his people in the Old Testament. It is the picture of Jesus' death being a way of **rescue** for mankind, like the Exodus, God's rescue of the Jews from slavery in Egypt.

(See Matthew 1:21; John 3:17; Acts 2:47; Romans 5:9–10; Romans 10:9; 2 Peter 1:11; 1 John 4:14.)

The New Testament writers also use a whole range of word-pictures to express what Jesus has done to rescue mankind. One word is **redeem**. (See Mark 10:45; 1 Peter 1:18.) To 'redeem' something which belongs to you, you have to buy it back. A

These are some of the ways Christian groups teach about Jesus 'saving' and 'redeeming' today's world:

● **Jesus saves and redeems today's world as believers who follow his teaching and example make the world a better place to live in.**

● **Jesus saves and redeems today's world as believers bring care and comfort to the suffering, inspired by his example.**

● **Jesus saves and redeems today's world as individuals come to him for cleansing, forgiveness and assurance of eternal life.**

● **Jesus saves and redeems today's world as the sacrifice of the body and blood of Jesus is offered for the sins of the world in the bread and wine of the Holy Communion.**

piece of jewellery, left with a pawnbroker in exchange for some cash, is 'redeemed' later when the cash is paid back. In dying on the cross, Jesus was paying the price to 'buy people back' for God.

Sometimes the word **ransomed** is used – like a kidnap victim being bought back for cash.

FOLLOW UP

1. One of the titles given to Jesus in the Bible is 'Emmanuel', which means 'God with us'. What do Christians today mean when they use that title?

2. In what sense do Christians believe that God is with them today? (Look back at Unit 22.)

3. Draw a circle and divide it into four sections. In each section draw a picture which illustrates one way in which Christians believe that Jesus is alive today. Draw another circle in the centre of the first one and write the words 'Jesus is alive today'.

4. Write four captions which start with the words 'Jesus saves'. Each must express a different way in which Christians believe Jesus saves and redeems. (Try to make your caption as witty and catchy as an advertising slogan – 'Zippo fills you with zest!')

Holy Communion:
The Last Supper and Modern Communion Services

The Last Supper

The day before his death, Jesus had a meal with his disciples. This was a special meal, not just because Jesus knew he was going to die, but because it was the Jews' most important festival meal, celebrated every year.

This Passover meal was a reminder of the Exodus, when God had brought their ancestors out of Egypt and taken them to a land he had promised to them – the land where Jesus and his disciples were now living.

At the annual Passover meal, the Jews remembered two particular things from the original Passover:

> Each household had to kill a lamb. They put its blood on the doorposts and above the doors of their home, to protect them from the Angel of Death who would see the blood and 'pass over'. That night they roasted and ate the meat.

> The meal was eaten with bread made without yeast. They were to eat quickly: there was no time to make bread that needed to rise.

Like generations of Jews before them, Jesus and his disciples had celebrated the Passover since they were young children. But this year Jesus made it into a different occasion.

Read Mark's account of this meal, which Christians now call the 'Last Supper' because it was just before the death of Jesus. You will find it in Mark 14:12–26.

Can you see what Jesus did? When his disciples were expecting him to talk about the sacrificed Passover lamb, he talked

about his own death. And when he broke the bread for them to eat, he talked about his body being broken – instead of reminding them of their ancestors' dramatic journey of escape from Egypt.

Look again at what Jesus said:

> '. . . this is my body . . . this is my blood which seals God's covenant . . .'

'Covenant' is a technical word which means an agreement or contract. Another word for it is 'testament'.

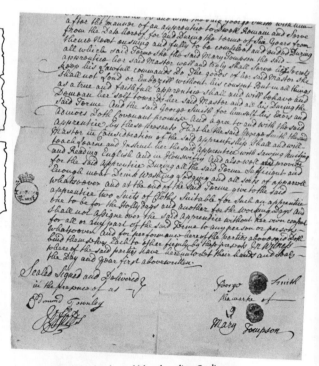

Jesus spoke of his body and blood sealing God's new covenant-agreement with humankind, like the formal seals on this contract.

After the exodus from Egypt, the Bible records the agreement between God and his people at Mt Sinai – *if the Jews obeyed him they would be his special people.* They looked back to the lambs that were sacrificed at the first Passover as a symbol of this agreement or covenant.

The problem with this covenant was that the Jews found it very difficult to obey God's commandments. They had to keep on sacrificing animals, to show God that they were sorry for their sins and to ask for his forgiveness. (See Unit 12.)

Now, at the Last Supper, Jesus talks about a *new* covenant.

Christians believe that Jesus' death was a sacrifice or offering for the sins of the whole world. That is what makes it a *new* agreement between God and his people, a *new covenant.* Instead of people having to sacrifice an animal every time they have sinned, they can now ask God to forgive them because of the death of Jesus. The new covenant replaces the old, ineffective covenant as the way of salvation – putting people right with God.

When Christians hold a Communion Service, they use bread and wine in the same way as Jesus did at the Last Supper – as symbols of his body and blood, his life given for them.

But the bread and the wine are *also* reminders of the Passover meal Jesus was celebrating the night before he died. At that meal, they would eat lamb as a reminder of the lambs that were sacrificed to save the people. The bread was a reminder of the food they ate on their journey to the Promised Land.

At a Communion Service in a Christian church the 'meal' of bread and wine reminds Christians of the death of Jesus, sacrificed to save his people, *and* helps them on the journey they are making, as Christians, to their 'promised land' – life with God for ever.

Different Communion services

Different branches of the Christian church have different Communion services. Some have one every day or every week, some once a month or even less often. And some have no Communion Service at all.

A Free Church Communion Service.

Baptist Minister,
Graham Sansom.

We are going to look at two Communion services at either end of the spectrum – one a fairly typical Baptist Communion Service and the other a Roman Catholic Communion Service (usually known as 'Mass').

We interviewed two ministers, and discovered the following differences between their Communion services:

GRAHAM SANSOM

Baptist Minister-in-Training, and Pastor of Wollaston Baptist Church

What do you call the service?
'Communion' mostly; sometimes 'The Lord's Supper'.
How often is it held?
Twice-monthly, as part of the Sunday worship, once in the Morning Service, once in the Evening Service.
Who can receive Holy Communion?
It varies from one Baptist Church to another, but it's usually an open invitation to those who know and love the Lord as their own personal

Roman Catholic priest,
Father Keith Sawyer.

Saviour and are in a right relationship with their fellow-Christians.
Where do you stand for Communion?
Behind the Communion table at the front of the church.
Where do the people stand to receive Communion?
They remain seated and are served by the deacons. Or (more recently) the bread and wine are passed from one person to another along the pews.
What do you use for bread and wine?
We're moving away from diced sliced bread! We have a home-made

A Roman Catholic priest conducts Holy Communion at Parish Mass.

▶▶ loaf which is broken, then the two halves are put on two plates and passed round. And we now use a non-fermented wine, rather than Ribena.

How do you serve the wine?
In small individual communion glasses – a twentieth-century hygiene-conscious tradition. But at my college and some Baptist churches, the single chalice of earlier centuries is back in use, symbolizing the 'one body', 'one cup' and 'one sacrifice'.

Is this your most important service?
I think it ought to be more of a focal point than it tends to be. We don't have any 'more' or 'less' important services. Communion is part of our regular service which includes preaching and teaching.

Can 'lay' people help with the service?
Certainly. Our deacons are lay people; they not only serve the bread and wine, but a deacon may also preside in the absence of a minister.

Note Although many Baptist churches belong to a Union, they do have a great deal of freedom in structuring their services, so Mr Sansom's answers would not necessarily apply 100 per cent to other Baptist churches.

FATHER KEITH SAWYER
Roman Catholic Priest at Our Lady's and St Edmund Campion, Wellingborough

What do you call the Service?
'Mass' or (more recently) 'Eucharist'.
How often is it held?
Sundays, plus Holy Days of Obligation. And priests are encouraged to celebrate Communion daily, if possible.
Who can receive Holy Communion?
Any Catholic who has reached the age of understanding – usually about eight years.

Where do you stand for Communion?
Behind the altar, facing the people.
Where do the people stand to receive Communion?
They come up in a queue to the priest, who moves in front of the altar to serve them.
What do you use for bread and wine?
Unleavened bread, in the form of wafers, and alcoholic wine.
How do you serve the wine?
From a chalice which is handed to the people in turn by the priest – or a deacon or a commissioned lay person.
Is this your most important service?
Yes – there is an obligation for Catholics to attend.
Can 'lay' people help with the service?
Yes – altar servers assist throughout the service, and 'special ministers of the Eucharist' can administer the chalice if there isn't a second priest, or a bishop or deacon, present.

We then asked them some further questions:

1. Can you explain the importance of the 'Breaking of Bread' or the 'Eucharist' for your congregation?
2. What do the bread and wine symbolize in your church?
3. What is the most important part of your Communion Service?
4. What happens to any bread or wine which is left over?

Here are the answers we were given:

Graham Sansom:
1. It's an act of remembrance (in obedience to Jesus' words, 'Do this in remembrance of me'), a recognition of the cost of our salvation, and a meeting with the risen Jesus in a very special way. For some, there's a sense of anticipation of the heavenly banquet which Jesus looked forward to sharing with his followers.
2. They are symbols of the broken body of Christ and his shed blood. But there's an increasing awareness (possibly more so at college) of these symbols speaking of Christ's continuing presence with his people.
3. We tend not to emphasize any one part more than another, though we do all wait for everyone to be served the wine in the small glasses and then we drink together – that can be a very powerful moment for some people, a reminder that we're at one with Christ.
4. It's discreetly disposed of after the service.

Father Keith Sawyer:
1. Well, at one level they come because the church says they should – there's an obligation. But they see it as an occasion for receiving a sacrament of grace. In Communion, they are caught up with Christ in dying and rising – dying to selfishness and rising to live his life in the world. And they'd also see it as an act of union with the worldwide Catholic Church.
2. They are reminders of what Jesus used at the Last Supper. But they're not just a 'photographic' symbol. Because of Jesus' words ('this is my body' – 'this is my blood') the Communion bread and wine make present what they symbolize – that is, the whole Christ, both in the form of bread and in the form of wine. Which explains why the traditional Catholic Communion, where the people only received the bread, would still be fully valid.
3. The Narrative of the Institution – the repeating of the words Jesus used at the Last Supper.
4. Any unused wafers (bread) are reserved in a 'Tabernacle' for later use in private Communions – for the sick and housebound, for example. If there isn't a Tabernacle, the priest eats the unused bread. And the priest drinks the unused wine.

Bread and wine represent the broken body, the shed blood, of Jesus on the cross.

We chose these two ministers to interview because their answers show up the one main difference in the kind of Communion Service you would find in the different denominations . . .

Some churches focus their Communion Service on the idea of the *sacrifice* of Jesus and so they use an *altar*. Other churches have what they would call a *memorial meal* which remembers the Last Supper and so they use a *table*.

You can see which church follows which tradition from the chart at the end of this Unit. The chart lists many features and shows what different denominations usually do, but beware – there are always exceptions. When you are writing about the differences make sure you don't write sentences which start, 'All Baptist churches . . .'

Look at the answers given by Graham Sansom and Keith Sawyer. You can see that they are quite close in their beliefs about the Communion Service. Now look at the chart. There are a lot of differences between the official doctrines of the Roman Catholic Church and the Baptist Church, but within each church there is a wide range of views held by individuals.

▲ FOLLOW UP ▲

Use the following questions to help you make a set of notes on the important features of this Unit:

● What was the name of the Jewish festival which Jesus was celebrating with his disciples?
● What event in Jewish history did this remember?
● What does *covenant* mean?
● Where was the Promised Land for the Jews?
● What did Jesus mean when he said: 'This is my body'. 'This is my blood of the new covenant'?
● In what ways was this a remembrance of the events of the Passover?
● In the Anglican Communion Service there is a prayer which says:

'Lamb of God, you take away the sins of the world: have mercy on us.'

What do you think that means?

Modern Communion services.
● Why do some churches use an altar?
● What does the phrase 'memorial meal' mean?
● What is the most important service for Baptists?
● List five similarities between the Baptist and Anglican services.
● An Anglican minister is also called a priest. Can you explain why, from the information you have here?
● Look at the chart in this Unit. Make two lists; one of denominations where the Communion Service is a reminder of the sacrifice of Jesus and one where they are having a memorial meal.
● Imagine you have just joined an Anglican church. Write a letter to a friend explaining why the Communion Service is important. Make sure you give examples from the service which show this.
● Design a leaflet to be given to visitors at a Baptist church explaining their church policy on the Lord's Supper. Remember, you want the visitors to feel welcome even if they can't join in the Lord's Supper!

	BAPTIST	CHURCH OF ENGLAND	HOUSE CHURCH	METHODIST	PENTECOSTAL	ROMAN CATHOLIC
Name(s) of Service?	Breaking of Bread Lord's Supper	Eucharist Holy Communion	Communion	Holy Communion Lord's Supper	Lord's Table Communion	Mass
Frequency of service?	Monthly	Twice weekly or weekly and special days	Monthly	Monthly	Weekly	Daily
Qualification necessary to receive?	Church Membership	Confirmation	Personal conversion	Confirmation Full membership	Personal conversion	Baptism
Altar used?		•				•
Table used?	•	•		•	•	
Set form (liturgy) used?		•				•
Main Service?		•			•	•
Ordained Minister necessary?		•		•		•
Lay Assistants permitted?	•	•	•	•	•	•
Bread used?	•	•	•	•	•	
Wafers used?		•				•
Fermented wine used?		•	•			•
Unfermented wine, fruit juice used?	•			•	•	
Shared chalice?		•	•			•
Individual glasses?	•			•	•	
People go to Altar/Table to receive?		•		•	•	•
Stay in seats to receive?	•		•			
All drink at same time?	•					•
Bread & wine/juice left over eaten by minister(s)?		•	•			
Bread left over given away?	•		•	•	•	
Wine/juice left over returned to bottle?	•			•	•	
Bread & wine kept as 'reserved sacrament' for infirm in parish?		•				•

NB: Salvation Army and Society of Friends (Quakers) don't have Communion

• = Yes

Rites of Passage

Have you read the book *The Pilgrim's Progress* by John Bunyan? It is the story of one man's journey from earth to heaven as a Christian and it describes various things which happen to him on the way. The man, who is actually called 'Christian', sets off from his home to find eternal life. After many adventures he finally arrives at heaven and is welcomed in.

Christians today often think of their lives as a journey. They see the events of their Christian life as being part of their journey home, to be with God. On this journey there are important 'staging-posts' to remind them of the purpose of their journey, and that they are not travelling on their own but are part of a large community of Christians making the same journey. The main staging-posts for Christians are:

- birth or joining the faith
- making an adult commitment to the faith
- marriage
- death.

Did you expect those to be the staging-posts? After all, most people get married and certainly everyone is born and later dies! There is nothing especially Christian about those events. The only special religious event on that list seems to be joining the faith or making an adult commitment to Christianity.

But look at these extracts from some of the special services for those staging-posts:

Evangelist points out the way to Christian, in *The Pilgrim's Progress*.

'We welcome you into the Lord's family . . .'

'Almighty Father, we thank you for our fellowship in the household of faith with all those who have been baptized in your name . . .'

'In marriage husband and wife belong to one another, and they begin a new life together in the community.'

> 'May God in his infinite love and mercy bring the whole Church, living and departed in the Lord Jesus, to a joyful resurrection . . . .'

All these extracts come from *The Alternative Service Book* of the Church of England, used by many Anglican churches. Can you see that in each case there is an emphasis on the Christian being a part of a group of people who together make up the whole Christian community? That is very important to remember when you are studying these events. Because you need to be able to make a distinction, between – for example – committed Christians who have a wedding ceremony in church, and other people who want to be married in church because they want a traditional ceremony and pretty surroundings.

Rites of passage

We call these staging-posts 'rites of passage'. A rite is something required in a solemn or religious event – an order of service for each of these Christian staging-posts. The 'passage' is a reference to the idea of a journey – that life is a passage from birth to death . . . and beyond.

All religions have these events and many cultures also have special rites – particularly to mark the change from childhood to adulthood. They are particularly important in a society or a tribe which expects its adult members to take an active part in the life of the community – by hunting or fishing for example.

But for most people today who don't have any religious commitment there probably won't be any ceremony to mark their becoming an adult until their eighteenth birthday party. And they will probably think of themselves as adults long before that time!

Symbols

In the church, each of these rites of passage has its own symbols – actions or words which show what is happening in the Christian's life at this particular point. A symbol is something which stands for something else. Symbols can be names, pictures, logos (the car manufacturer's badge, for example), words, actions . . .

Symbols are used a great deal in religion, because they provide a simple way of expressing difficult ideas. A symbol is often a 'shorthand' form of expression.

Here is a Christian symbol:

It is a very simple one, which represents the light of Jesus in the world. In a service of infant baptism the priest often hands a candle to a parent or godparent with these words:

> 'Receive this light.
> This is to show that you have passed from darkness to light.
> Shine as a light in the world . . .'

MILESTONES

Passing your test...

Leaving school...

Voting for the first time...

STAMP! STAMP!

BALLOT BOX

Most of the Protestant churches believe that there are only two sacraments which were ordained by Jesus and are therefore necessary for Christians: baptism and Communion. The Roman Catholic and the Orthodox Churches observe seven sacraments:

- baptism
- Holy Communion
- confirmation
- marriage
- ordination (to the priesthood)
- penance
- extreme unction.

Sacraments

A sacrament is a dramatization of something which is happening spiritually within a person. St Augustine called it 'an outward sign of inward grace'.

That might sound very difficult, but it isn't really. One sacrament observed by nearly all Christians is Communion. In a Communion Service, Christians remember the meaning of the death of Jesus (and what difference that death has made in their lives) through the symbols of bread and wine. Here is part of the Anglican Communion Service:

'In the same way, after supper he (Jesus) took the cup and gave thanks; he gave it to them, saying, Drink this all of you; this is my blood of the new covenant, which is shed for you and for many for the forgiveness of sins.'

From *The Alternative Service Book*

Christians don't believe that, as they drink the wine or grape juice at Communion, the liquid actually washes their sins away inside their body. What they are acknowledging is that Christ is present with them and in them through that action, and that the death of Jesus means that their sins can be forgiven.

Summary

Rite of passage = a ceremony which marks a stopping or changing-point on a spiritual journey.

Christian rites of passage are held at:
- birth or joining the faith.
- an adult commitment to the faith.
- marriage
- death.

Symbol = something which stands for something else.

Sacrament = a dramatization of a spiritual happening.

⬆FOLLOW UP⬆

1. This unit mentioned light as a Christian symbol. Here are some other symbols connected with Christian rites of passage. Work through this unit and try to find out what each one means – or symbolizes.
- water
- ring
- cross
- earth
- bread
- wine

2. Draw a picture for each of these symbols which either
- illustrates its meaning

or
- shows its use as a symbol for Christians today.

Infant Baptism and Dedication

The first rite of passage which many Christians go through is one which they don't (usually) remember at all! This is the naming ceremony which follows their birth. For some Christians the ceremony is called **baptism**. For others it is called **dedication**.

Baptism

In an infant baptism ceremony the priest will pour water from the font onto the baby's head and say 'I baptize you in the name of the Father and of the Son and of the Holy Spirit.'

The ceremony means that the baby is now thought of as belonging to the Christian church, the family of Christ. Obviously, because the baby isn't able to understand what is happening, other people have to take responsibility for the child at this stage. Usually a baby will have three godparents to stand as sponsors and to make the baptismal vows on the child's behalf.

Before the baptism takes place the priest will ask the parents and godparents if they understand what they are doing:

> You have asked to have your child baptized. In doing so you are accepting the responsibility of training him(her) in the practice of the faith. It will be your duty to bring him(her) up to keep God's commandments as Christ taught us, by loving God and our neighbour. Do you clearly understand what you are undertaking?
>
> *Parents:* We do.
> *Priest (to godparents):* Are you ready to help the parents of this child in their duty as Christian parents?
> *Godparents:* We are.

From an Order of Service for a Roman Catholic baptism.

The parents and godparents then have to make three vows. Later, when the baby has grown up s/he will have to *confirm* these same vows for her/himself (see Unit 40).

For some Christians the first 'rite of passage' is infant baptism (pictured here). Others hold a service of dedication.

In the Church of England, the three vows are made like this:

> Priest (*to parents and godparents*): . . . I ask these questions which you must answer for yourselves and for this child.
>
> Priest: Do you turn to Christ?
> Answer: I turn to Christ.
>
> Priest: Do you repent of your sins?
> Answer: I repent of my sins.
>
> Priest: Do you renounce evil?
> Answer: I renounce evil.

Then the actual baptism of the child takes place. Because Jesus was baptized in water, water has become a symbol of the start of a new life in Christ. A candle may also be given to the parents or godparents as a symbol that the baby has now passed from darkness into light.

You may be thinking that we have missed out the most important part of the ceremony. If you've ever been invited to a baptism service you perhaps didn't call it a baptism but a 'christening'. This is a very old English word which means 'making a person a Christian'. Before the days of government registrars it was at this service that the baby was given its 'Christian' name. And 'to christen' came to mean 'to name', in a general way, not 'to make Christian'.

Finally all the congregation say to the newly baptized baby:

> All: We welcome you into the Lord's family.
> We are members together of the body of Christ;
> we are children together of the same heavenly Father;
> we are inheritors together of the kingdom of God.
> We welcome you.

Usually after the ceremony there is a family party with a special Christening Cake. Sometimes this will be the top layer of the parents' wedding cake, saved specially!

Dedication

In some churches parents believe that they should allow a child to make its own decision about whether or not to become a Christian. So after the baby's birth they hold a 'dedication' service – not a baptism. (In some churches, this is called a 'Service of Thanksgiving'.) At this service the parents thank God for the birth of their child. They dedicate the child to God and dedicate themselves to bring her/him up in a Christian home. In these churches the service will usually include some form of words like this:

> Minister (*to congregation*): Christian parents desire to acknowledge God in all their ways and to give thanks to Him in His House for the joy of parenthood. In the presence of fellow believers they seek His grace, guidance and wisdom to train their children in the ways of the Lord. We therefore welcome in Christ's name our friends who have brought their child to be dedicated to the Lord.
>
> Minister (*to parents*): In presenting your child to the Lord do you promise by prayer, precept and example to instruct him(her) and bring him(her) up in the ways of the Lord?
> Parents: We do.
>
> (*After appropriate comments the minister should take the child in his arms and, pronouncing the child's name aloud, offer prayer, dedicating the child to God and to His service in the Name of the Father and of the Son and of the Holy Spirit.*)

From A *Manual for Ministers*, Assemblies of God

▲FOLLOW UP▲

Design a baptism certificate for a baby which includes the following:

- name of church
- date
- name of child
- name of parents
- names of godparents
- a paragraph which explains the meaning of baptism
- decoration using symbols which have meaning for a baptism (for example, a candle)

If you think your certificate is good, perhaps you might like to show it to your local vicar. Maybe the church will adopt your certificate!

UNIT 40

Believer's Baptism and Confirmation

Anne and Sarah are two fourth-years studying Christianity in a group that consists of Christians and non-Christians, so there's often a lot of lively discussion about whether or not it is stupid to be a Christian. Here is the group in one of the moments when they're not arguing!

Sarah became a full member of her church when she was confirmed by the bishop.

Although Anne and Sarah are Christians they go to different churches. Sarah attends the Anglican church in her village and Anne goes to a Baptist chapel near the farm where she lives. When they were both thirteen years old they each went through a ceremony of initiation – Sarah was confirmed and Anne was baptized. Here are their answers to some questions about their experiences:

When were you baptized or confirmed?

Anne: Two years ago.
Sarah: Two years ago.

How old were you then?

Anne: I was thirteen years old.
Sarah: So was I.

Why did you decide to be baptized or confirmed?

Anne: I had just become a Christian and wanted to show my faith through this act of obedience to the command of Jesus.
Sarah: I wanted to understand more about God and be closer to him.

> What preparation did your minister give you before the ceremony?

Anne: There were two of us who wanted to be baptized and he gave us books to read and then we had some special classes.

Sarah: There were four people in our Confirmation Class. We had some sheets to work through about the Creed, the meaning of confirmation and generally about church life.

> Did you do anything yourself to prepare for the ceremony?

Anne: I prayed a lot about the step I was taking and I read my Bible.

Sarah: I read my little red Bible and attended church regularly.

> What did you wear for the ceremony?

Anne: A long white gown!

Sarah: I wore a black skirt and a white blouse. The older women who were confirmed also wore a white veil.

> How many other people were baptized or confirmed with you?

Anne: Just one other; a boy a year older than me.

Sarah: There were 67 candidates for Confirmation. Some of them were children but many of them were adults.

> Can you say (briefly!) what happened at the ceremony?

Anne: I went down into the baptistry and the minister asked me quietly (because I was nervous!) some questions about being a Christian. He then said that on the declaration of my faith he baptized me in the name of the Father and of the Son and of the Holy Spirit. At that point he tipped me backwards and I went right under the water before he lifted me back up.

Sarah: We went up in turn and knelt in front of the bishop. He put his

Anne made a public declaration of her faith in baptism by immersion.

hands on our heads and he said, 'Confirm, O Lord, your servant Sarah with your Holy Spirit.'

> How did you feel after the ceremony?

Anne: Happy and excited.

Sarah: I felt very happy and different – I think that was the Holy Spirit in me.

> What difference has it made in your life?

Anne: The ceremony hasn't changed my life – God had already done that, which was why I got baptized. It was a big step to take as I was made a church member at the same time. I already took Communion before my baptism.

Sarah: It has made me think more about my life and more about Christ and I now take Communion.

> Would you recommend baptism or confirmation for anyone else?

Anne: It needs to be their own personal decision but I would certainly pray for them.

Sarah: Yes, if they want to be nearer to God.

> When do you think that someone is ready for baptism or confirmation?

Anne: When they are certain about their faith.

Sarah: When they have found Christ and are certain about their faith.

> What is your best memory of that day?

Anne: Saying my vows and actually going under the water.

Sarah: When I went up to the bishop and was confirmed.

Although baptism and confirmation seem to be very different ceremonies there are a lot of similarities. During her confirmation Sarah had to repeat the vows that were made for her when she was a baby:

> Do you turn to Christ?
> I turn to Christ.
>
> Do you repent of your sins?
> I repent of my sins.
>
> Do you renounce evil?
> I renounce evil.

When the minister asked Anne about being a Christian before he baptized her, he was really asking her the same sort of questions that Sarah had to answer.

The meaning of adult baptism is broadly the same as the meaning of infant-baptism-plus-confirmation. Confirmation is the adult's acceptance of what was done on her/his behalf at baptism. And whichever practice is followed, churches which observe the sacrament of baptism would say that it involves four things:
● washing away sin
● dying to the old way of life
● starting a new life in Christ
● receiving the Holy Spirit.

Some people believe that all these things happen at the moment of adult baptism. Some believe that they happen either for the first time or in a new way at the moment of confirmation. But others believe the ceremony of adult baptism or confirmation is only a symbol of what should have taken place in the candidate's life before the event.

Adults are not usually allowed to have 'believer's baptism' (which is what adult baptism by total immersion is often called) until all of the above things have taken place. Similarly with confirmation – a person is believed to have received the Holy Spirit at baptism and is now being given power for work in the church.

Once a person has been confirmed or baptized s/he is regarded as a full member of their church. Sarah, for example, can now take Communion and Anne is a church member and can vote at church meetings when they make decisions about church life and practice.

Because confirmation in the Church of England marks the point where a person makes his/her own adult commitment to keep the vows made on their behalf in infancy, this has seemed an appropriate point at which they are also reckoned to be able to understand and receive Holy Communion.

So, traditionally, people who have not been confirmed have not taken Communion. This has sometimes led to the belief that once you've gained your right to take Communion – by getting confirmed at thirteen or fourteen – you can then stop going to church!

To counter this tendency in his Diocese (where Sarah was confirmed), the Bishop of Peterborough is trying an experiment.

He is giving permission for some children to take Communion much earlier – from seven onwards – provided that their vicar believes them to be Christians. Then the bishop will confirm them at a later age, about eighteen, when they are ready to make an adult commitment to the church and have got over any period of being fed-up with church-going!

▲FOLLOW↓UP▲

For this work you will need to interview ten different people who have either been baptized or confirmed.

1. Ask them the same questions that Anne and Sarah answered.

2. Now try to collate the information you have received under the following headings (you may like to show your findings in the form of pie charts):

● number confirmed
● number baptized by total immersion
● number who still attend church regularly
● How many had preparation classes beforehand?
● Write a list of what they thought to be the main meaning of baptism or confirmation.
● Summarize your results and write a conclusion
● Thank the people who helped you and show them your conclusions.

Marriage

If you were asked to describe a Christian wedding ceremony what would you include in your description?

- a long white dress for the bride?
- bridesmaids?
- a best man?
- confetti?
- the bride's father to give her away?
- the 'Bridal March' being played on the organ . . .?

Christian marriage involves vows made before God and all the wedding guests. It is a commitment to lifelong faithfulness.

And what about the actual words of the ceremony? Do you know what has to be said and what can be left out? You may know that a wedding ceremony usually starts with words something like these:

> 'Dearly beloved brethren we are gathered together in the sight of God and in the face of this congregation to join together this man and this woman in holy matrimony . . .'

The Book of Common Prayer

In fact neither these words nor any of the 'traditional' things listed above are necessary for a wedding in a church – or a wedding anywhere else. The only *necessary* things are:

● a bride and a bridegroom who make certain legal statements
● witnesses
● someone who is authorized to conduct the wedding.

This is usually the minister or priest but if he/she has not been authorized, then a registrar will attend the wedding to sign all the legal documents. As well as signing the documents, the minister or registrar has to check that there is no good reason why the couple cannot be married – maybe one of them is already married?

The only words which have to be used are those which form the vows between the bride and the bridegroom and a response by the minister. The vows usually go something like this:

> 'I, Peter, take you, Jane
> (I, Jane take you, Peter)
> to be my wife (husband),
> to have and to hold
> from this day forward;
> for better, for worse,
> for richer, for poorer,
> in sickness and in health,
> to love and to cherish,
> till death us do part,
> according to God's holy law;
> and this is my solemn vow.'

The Alternative Service Book

Then the minister declares that Peter and Jane are now man and wife and adds the statement:

> 'That which God has joined together, let not man divide.'

The Alternative Service Book

The minister also reminds the congregation of what has taken place:

> 'In the presence of God, and before this congregation, Peter and Jane have given their consent and made their marriage vows to each other. They have declared their marriage by the joining of hands and by the giving and receiving of a ring and I therefore proclaim that they are husband and wife.'

The Alternative Service Book

The first part of that statement is very important. Peter and Jane have not just made vows to each other which they hope to be able to keep; they have made vows in the presence of God and the congregation. Before their wedding day they will have had some preparation classes, so that they know what a Christian marriage should be like.

Are the words 'marriage' and 'wedding' interchangeable?

Not really.

A *wedding* is the marriage ceremony which takes place on a particular day. A *marriage* is the relationship which starts for those two people on that day and hopefully lasts for the rest of their lives.

The fact that the relationship has been started in the presence of God is very important. Did you notice what the minister says after the vows have been made?

> 'That which God has joined together . . .'

It's not the couple who have joined themselves together but God who has made their union complete. That is why in the Roman Catholic church marriage is considered to be a sacrament – it is the outward sign of an inward work which has been completed by God.

Many Christian couples, especially Roman Catholics and Anglicans, will choose to have a brief Communion Service for themselves, or sometimes for the whole congregation, at the end of the formal wedding service. They feel that this emphasizes the spiritual meaning of their wedding ceremony. It is easy to lose sight of the spiritual meaning of a marriage in all

the details about who pays for what and who stands next to the bride's mother for the family photographs!

As with all the rites of passage there is usually a meal afterwards for family and friends – though the wedding reception is probably the most important and often the most expensive of all.

Christians and divorce

All Christians believe that marriage should last for a lifetime. The vows which a couple make include the phrase 'till death us do part . . .'

However there are times when a marriage totally breaks down . Many churches today are having to face the problems of broken marriages, divorce and remarriage.

Some churches refuse to perform a marriage ceremony for someone who has been divorced and others will only perform a service of blessing after a registry office wedding.

In the Church of England the decision about whether someone should be remarried in church is made by the vicar of the parish where the couple want to be married. He has to decide if the reasons for the breakdown of the marriage are valid and whether the divorced person intends these new vows to be permanent.

Divorce and remarriage are two serious problems for the church at present. Each of the denominations is working on statements of what is believed to be the best pattern for dealing with this situation.

▲ FOLLOW UP ▲

1. Explain what you understand by the following sentence:

'Marriage is a sacrament; an outward sign of an inward work which has been completed by God.'

2. Discuss whether or not you agree with the following statement:

'It doesn't matter how bad their marriage is; Christians should never get divorced.'

3. Read the newspaper account of the wedding of Kenneth Branagh and Emma Thompson.
● Do you think it is a good idea to separate the religious and the legal parts of a wedding ceremony as they have done?
● Which part do you think should come first?

OUR PHONEY WEDDING, BY EMMA

by EMMA LEE-POTTER

SHOWBIZ stars Kenneth Branagh and Emma Thompson are not legally married at all yet, it was revealed last night.

The theatrical couple had claimed their £30,000 star-studded ceremony at Cliveden House on Sunday was 'the real McCoy.'

But as they prepared to go on stage in London's West End last night, they admitted the legal knot had yet to be tied.

'As far as we are concerned, Sunday was our marriage – we were married in the sight of God and the presence of our families and friends,'

they said. 'But the legal ceremony will take place privately abroad next month.'

More than 100 friends and relations attended Sunday's service at Cliveden, scene of the 60s Profumo scandal.

Many were convinced they were seeing the real thing as Emma, 30, and Kenneth, 28, exchanged rings before joining a spectacular reception at the £370-a-night hotel.

'It was a full wedding ceremony,' insisted best man Brian Blessed

yesterday. 'All I know is that I was the best man.'

But East London vicar Rev Malcolm Johnson, who conducted the service, confirmed it had only been a blessing.

'They were married ecclesiastically,' he said. 'You can only be married in a church or a register office. You couldn't be married legally at Cliveden.' The couple left the hotel yesterday afternoon for London's Lyric Theatre, where they are starring in Look Back In Anger.

Today, Tuesday 22 August 1989

Death

When a Christian dies a funeral service is held a few days later, either in church or at the chapel of a crematorium. The funeral service is usually quite short, with some readings and prayers, and possibly a talk by the minister about the person who has died. Then the coffin which contains the body is either taken outside and buried in the ground or cremated (burned in a purpose-built incinerator).

When the coffin is placed in a hole in the ground one of the relatives of the dead person may be asked to throw a handful of soil on top of the coffin while the minister recites:

> 'We have entrusted (Michael, Jane) to God's merciful keeping, and we now commit his/her body to the ground: earth to earth, ashes to ashes, dust to dust in sure and certain hope of the resurrection to eternal life through our Lord Jesus Christ . . .'
>
> From *The Alternative Service Book*

For a Christian, death is not the end of the journey. Because they believe that Jesus rose again from the dead, Christians believe that they will rise again, too, to live with him for ever.

As the coffin is brought into church the minister makes this tremendous statement:

> Jesus said, I am the resurrection, and the life; he who believes in me, though he die, yet shall he live, and whoever lives and believes in me shall never die.

Strange words for a funeral service, when someone has died. But the

Christians may choose to be buried (as here) or cremated. Their belief is that death is not the end.

resurrection of the dead is the most important belief when a Christian dies.

The minister may say:

> We believe that Jesus died and rose again, and so it will be for those who died as Christians. God will bring them to life with Jesus. Thus we shall always be with the Lord. Comfort one another with these words.

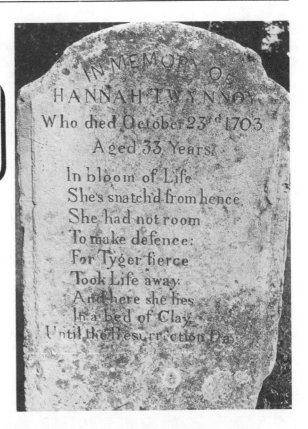

If you walk around a churchyard you will see this belief expressed on many of the tombstones.

Of course, Christians still grieve the death of those they love. But their firm belief that this is not the end, that their loved ones now enjoy life with Christ and free of pain, and that they will one day meet again, is a source of deep comfort and even joy.

The funeral service is a way of saying goodbye to the person who has gone ahead on his or her 'pilgrim's progress' to God. The early Christians used to say 'goodnight' instead of 'goodbye' because they were so sure of seeing their friends again after the 'sleep' of death.

Here is a verse from an old hymn which is sometimes used at funeral services:

> Only 'goodnight' beloved – not 'farewell'!
> A little while, and all God's saints shall dwell
> In holy union, indivisible –
> Goodnight, Goodnight, Goodnight!

In the Salvation Army, where members are given titles such as Captain or Lieutenant, when someone dies they are 'promoted to glory' and relatives and friends try to be more happy about that promotion than about expressing their own sorrow at their loss.

FOLLOW UP

1. Visit your local churchyard or cemetery.

Copy down anything engraved on the tombstones which you think expresses Christian beliefs about:
● death
● life after death.
   Explain what these beliefs mean.

2. Now try to write a hymn which could be sung at a Christian funeral service. You should try to include the following key ideas:
● thanksgiving for the life of the person who has died
● belief in the resurrection of Jesus
● belief in the resurrection of all Christians
● something to help the mourners cope with their grief.

This is a very hard assignment — check back in this unit to make sure that you understand what Christians believe about death and an afterlife. You might like also to read again Units 14 and 26.

Christian Festivals: The Church's Year

Is there a calendar on the wall of your classroom? Is there one at home? Most homes have one pinned up somewhere, and very often it has enough space on it to write in important events that have to be remembered – like family birthdays or dental appointments.

Some calendars have special information already printed on them. Gardening calendars will tell you what to plant when, and what jobs you should do in your garden each month. A 'pop fan's' calendar will incude birthdays of well-known singers and musicians, with details about them and their chart successes.

An 'anniversary' calendar is packed with information about important people and events from the past, printed day-by-day on the date of their annual 'anniversary'. Broadcasters and journalists make very good use of 'anniversary' calendars, informing their audiences of significant or humorous occasions in years gone by . . .

Christianity has a kind of 'anniversary' calendar: throughout the year there are special days or even longer periods when Christians remember important people and events. It's known as 'The Christian Calendar' or 'The Church's Year'.

Christians began ear-marking some days as 'special' very early in their history. They had inherited the seven-day week from Judaism, but whereas the Jews kept the seventh day (Saturday) as their holy day or 'Sabbath', the Christians designated the first day of the week (Sunday) as the regular day to meet for worship. This was because

● Jesus rose on the first day of the week
● the first day symbolizes the new beginning, or new life, offered to people who believe in Jesus.

All Christians recognize the concept of Sunday as a day of rest and re-creation, but different branches of the Christian church observe Sunday in different ways. For example, in many countries which are predominantly Roman Catholic, religious services are confined to Saturday night and Sunday morning and the rest of the day is given over to leisure and sports. On the other hand, very strict Protestant or Reformed denominations keep Sunday in a similar way to the Jewish Sabbath – all work is forbidden. And other denominations simply set aside Sunday as a day for attending church, perhaps especially for the Holy Communion service.

Apart from Sundays, the most important Christian special days – festivals – are connected with either the *birth* or the *death* of Jesus Christ. There are also special days which celebrate the life and example of

The Church's Year

Name of Season	Date	Special Day(s)	Original Event	Bible Passage	Church's Teaching	Traditional Customs
ADVENT	Starts Sunday nearest 30 November	Advent Sunday	Prophecies about the coming king	Isaiah 52:7–10	Christians prepare for the anniversary of Jesus' coming as a baby, and think about his coming again as King	Advent wreath; Advent calendar
CHRISTMAS	25 December (Western Church only)	Christmas Day	Jesus is born	Luke 2:1–15	God sends his Son into the world to save people from their sins	Crib; gifts; special food
EPIPHANY	6 January		Visit of the Wise Men	Matthew 2:1–12	People of all nations can see God's glory in his Son Jesus	
	Day before Ash Wednesday	Shrove Tuesday				Pancakes before the fasting of Lent
LENT	Starts Ash Wednesday, 6½ weeks before Easter	Ash Wednesday	Jesus' time in the desert	Matthew 4:1–11	Christians remember Jesus' fast with penitence (saying sorry to God) and self-denial	Ash on forehead, a sign of penitence
	Sunday, one week before Easter	Palm Sunday	Jesus rides into Jerusalem on a donkey	Matthew 21:1–11	Christians follow Jesus' example of humility	Distribution of miniature crosses of palm
	Thursday before Easter	Maundy Thursday	The Last Supper; Jesus washes the disciples' feet	John 13:1–15, 34–35	Christians remember the origins of Holy Communion and also Jesus' teaching about loving and serving each other	The monarch distributes 'Maundy Money'
	Friday before Easter	Good Friday	Jesus' crucifixion	Matthew 28:1–10	Christians remember Jesus' sacrifice, the price paid for their reconciliation with God	Procession to local 'Calvary'; hot-cross-buns
EASTER	Starts Sunday after the calendar full moon falling on or after 21 March (Western Church only)	Easter Day (always a Sunday)	Jesus' resurrection	John 18–19:37	There is new (eternal) life for all who come to God through Jesus	Easter eggs to end the fasting of Lent
	5½ weeks after Easter	Ascension Day	Jesus returns to his Father in heaven	Acts 1:1–11	God places Jesus higher than all creation because of what he has done	
PENTECOST	Sunday ten days after Ascension Day	Pentecost Sunday (old Whitsunday)	The disciples are filled with the power of the Holy Spirit	Acts 2:1–21	God gives his power to people so that they can be witnesses for Jesus	Whit walks of witness
TRINITY	Sunday, one week after Pentecost	Trinity Sunday		Matthew 28:19	Christians believe in the three-in-one God: Father, Son and Holy Spirit	
	1 November	All Saints' Day		Hebrews 12:1–2, 18–24	All Christians, past and present, are in unity. Christians follow the example of the saints	Churches decorated with white lilies to represent Christians who have died

Sunday

The word 'Sunday' is older than Christianity. It was the name given in Greek and Latin to the ancient weekly festival of the sun-god, celebrated on the first day of the week.

In New Testament times it became the appropriate day for Christians to meet together, as it marked the day of Christ's resurrection (Mark 16:9; 1 Corinthians 16:2). It was called 'the Lord's day' (Revelation 1:10).

The Christian interpretation of the Old Testament book of Malachi 4:2 – 'my saving power will rise on you like the sun and bring healing like the sun's rays' – was that this was a prophecy about Jesus. There were many reasons why Christians found it easy to take over the name 'Sunday' for their festival. A second-century Christian writer called Justin refers to the day by its ancient name:

'And on the day which is called the day of the sun there is an assembly . . .' (*Apology* 1.67).

some of Jesus' followers (saints). So the Christian calendar is largely made up of three 'blocks' or 'cycles' (because they come round each year) –

● The Christmas cycle (centred on Christ's birth)

● The Easter cycle (centred on Christ's death and resurrection)

● The saints' days cycle (remembering significant followers of Jesus)

In addition to the days in these three cycles, Christians also celebrate other special days, such as Pentecost or Whitsunday and Corpus Christi, which you will find in Unit 45 at the end of the Easter cycle.

Harvest Festival

One of the most ancient festivals which has been celebrated all over the world for thousands of years is the thanksgiving for the year's harvest. But the Christian 'Harvest Festival' is quite a recent 'hi-jack' of a pagan festival. It was first celebrated in 1862 as a Christian version of the traditional 'Harvest Home' celebrations with their feasting and merrymaking. Each church chooses its own day for a Harvest Thanksgiving service, usually in September or October.

The Church's Year

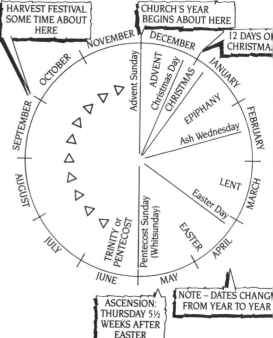

HARVEST FESTIVAL SOME TIME ABOUT HERE

CHURCH'S YEAR BEGINS ABOUT HERE

12 DAYS OF CHRISTMAS

ASCENSION: THURSDAY 5½ WEEKS AFTER EASTER

NOTE – DATES CHANGE FROM YEAR TO YEAR

1. A key word associated with most festivals is **celebration**.

Conduct a brainstorming exercise in your group.
● Write the word CELEBRATION in the middle of a large piece of paper.
● Appoint one person to be scribe and write down what *everyone* says.
● Allow everyone to contribute words or ideas which they associate with celebration. For example: parties, fun . . .
● Don't discuss any of the words until you have run out of ideas.
● Now try to link up words that go together – let your scribe join them up.

2. Can you write a definition of celebration from the ideas you have collected?

Write your group definition down so that you can refer to it as you work through the next three Units.

3. Now turn your large piece of paper over and try to make a group picture which will immediately suggest the word CELEBRATION to anyone who looks at it.

Have fun!

The Christmas Cycle

No one knows exactly when Jesus was born. The ancient Romans used to celebrate the winter solstice (shortest day) on 17 December and the festival of the god Mithras on 25 December. Mithras was also known as *Sol Invicta*, meaning 'unconquerable sun'. This name, and the gradual increase in daylight after the winter solstice, led to Roman Christians celebrating the birth of Jesus, 'the light of the world', at this time.

The Eastern Church, however, originally chose 7 January to celebrate both the birth and baptism of Jesus, and this tradition is still maintained in the Orthodox churches.

But the Church's Year doesn't begin on either 25 December or 7 January (or even on 1 January, like the calendar on your wall).

The Church's Year begins by *looking forward* to the *coming* of Jesus. The first day of the year is therefore Advent Sunday ('Advent' means 'the coming').

Advent

Advent Sunday is always the Sunday nearest to 30 November. The season of Advent includes four Sundays and lasts until Christmas Eve, 24 December.

During this time, Christians remember how the Old Testament prophets foretold the coming of a King, and also how the New Testament writers foretold the *second* coming of Jesus as King and Judge at the end of time. So Advent is a time of preparation:

making ready to celebrate the coming of the baby Jesus – practical preparations for Christmas such as food, presents, etc.

The Advent 'crown' has four candles, to be lit on the four Sundays leading up to Christmas.

making ready to receive Christ once again at Christmas, in renewed personal commitment to serve and live for him

making ready for the Second Coming of Christ, when he will come as King and Judge, and will gather up his true followers to be with him for ever. (See Unit 27.)

You will see that the main teaching of Advent is serious, suggesting the need for self-examination and penitence (saying sorry to God). Some Christians make Advent a special time of prayer and fasting; church altars may be covered in cloths of purple or violet (the traditional colour of penitence). In some churches flowers are not used for decorating the church building during Advent.

Children gather round a group of figures representing the events at the birth of Jesus. The candles symbolize the belief that Jesus is 'the light of the world'.

But there is another side to Advent, the exciting sense of looking forward to something. This is encouraged by the use of an Advent wreath containing four candles which are lit in turn on each of the four Sundays in Advent. And, of course, children love the excitement of an Advent calendar, opening a little picture-window each day until on Christmas Eve they uncover a picture of the baby Jesus.

Christmas

What most people call Christmas (Christ's 'Mass' or 'Festival'), actually has two other important names.

● First, there is the more technical title, the 'incarnation' (which means 'becoming flesh') and refers to the Christian belief that God himself became a human being in the person of Jesus (John 1: 14). (See Unit 17.)
● Then there is the more descriptive title, the 'nativity' – which just means 'the birth'.

Most of the available details about the actual birth of Jesus are in Luke's Gospel. Some scholars think that Luke – who was a doctor – knew Jesus' mother Mary well, and that she told him many things about her son's birth and early days.

These are the 'facts' from Luke:

● The Angel Gabriel told Mary she would give birth to God's Son.

● Mary went with her husband Joseph from their home in Nazareth to the town of Bethlehem, as required for a Roman census.

● Mary's baby was born at Bethlehem, where a 'manger' for animal food served as a cot. There was no room in the inn, so it is assumed that the birth took place in an animal shed or cave – or maybe the family part of a peasant house, shared with the animals.

● On the night of Jesus' birth, an angel told some local

shepherds that the long-awaited Messiah had been born in 'David's town' (Bethlehem).

● The shepherds went to visit Jesus.

● Jesus was circumcised at eight days old, according to Jewish practice.

● Jesus was taken to be presented at the Temple in Jerusalem, in accordance with Jewish practice for a male first-born: he was recognized as Messiah by Simeon and Anna.

Luke was a Gentile who wrote a Gospel for Gentiles (see Unit 16). His information about the birth of Jesus (in an animal-shelter, visited by humble shepherds) emphasizes the fact that this is a significant event for ordinary people, not just for Jews or important people.

The only other further information we have about the birth of Jesus comes from Matthew's Gospel:

● Jesus' family-tree is traced from Abraham through King David to Mary's husband Joseph.

● An angel told Joseph that Mary's baby – seemingly illegitimate – was the child of the Holy Spirit, and this baby would save his people from their sins.

Matthew was a Jew who wrote a Gospel for Jews (see Unit 16). His information about the birth of Jesus (descended from King David, come to save people from their sins) emphasizes the fact that this is a significant event for Jews awaiting their kingly Messiah.

For Christians, Christmas is more than a celebration of the birth of the founder of their religion. Christians believe that the baby Jesus was unique in having both human and divine origins. He was the expected Messiah, the Saviour from sin, God present with his people ('Emmanuel'), God in human form – come to make peace between the Creator and his creation.

The 'gift' of peace with God through

Jesus, has made Christmas a time of goodwill between people. The giving of Christmas presents (once part of the Roman festival of Saturnalia) has become a Christian expression of joy and love.

In the northern hemisphere, churches are decorated with greenery and Christmas lights – often with a crib as the focal point. Christmas carols are sung at church services and family gatherings, and many churches hold midnight Communion services. Christmas is a time of great joy, and also a time of caring and sharing.

Epiphany

If you have seen the traditional 'nativity play' (or taken part in one), you will now be wondering what's happened to three of the main characters.

According to Matthew's Gospel, around the time of Jesus' birth, wise men from the East came looking for a new King whose arrival they had deduced from observing the stars. Matthew does not say how many wise men there were, just that they brought three gifts for this new King.

But two small details in the Gospel account have led the church to make this incident a separate event from the nativity:

This is the way the Christmas cards represent the visit of the three wise men.

● The wise men found Jesus and his family in a 'house', not an animal shelter.

● The local ruler, Herod – whose help they had sought – was so enraged at the idea of being ousted by a new king that he ordered the death of all Jewish boys in and around Bethlehem under the age of two years (not just new-born babies).

So it's quite possible that the wise men visited Jesus a long time (anything up to two years) after the shepherds.

But there is an even more important distinction between the two groups of visitors. The shepherds were Jews, visiting their Messiah. But the wise men were non-Jews, Gentiles, worshipping the new King of the Jews. Christians see this as an indication that right from his birth, Jesus was recognized as Saviour and Light of the whole world. So they call their celebration of this visit, and the season which follows, 'Epiphany' which means 'becoming apparent/seen/clear/obvious'. In the Western Church, Epiphany is celebrated on 6 January and marks the end of the Christmas season (the twelve days of Christmas). The season of Epiphany continues until the start of the Easter cycle.

➤FOLLOW UP➤

1. Work through this unit on Advent, Christmas and Epiphany and make a list of all the ways in which Christmas is celebrated which are based on the biblical accounts of the birth of Jesus. (Check your references with the chart in Unit 43.)

Now make a list of all the other ways in which Christmas is celebrated which have no religious significance.

Can you draw any conclusions by looking at your two lists? What are they?

2. Do you think that people who are not Christians should celebrate Christmas? Why? Give reasons for your answer.

The Easter Cycle

The second main feature of the Christian Calendar is the death and resurrection of Jesus Christ. This event is easier to pinpoint than the birth of Jesus. The Gospels record that Jesus was executed during the Jewish festival of Passover, on the day before the Jewish Sabbath.

So the first followers of Jesus, who were Jews, simply added their new festival to the old one, which always took place at the first full moon of the first month of Spring. This is why the Christian celebration of the death and resurrection of Jesus – Easter – doesn't have a fixed date each year. But the crucifixion is remembered on a Friday and the resurrection on a Sunday – the actual days of the week on which the original events took place.

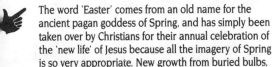

The word 'Easter' comes from an old name for the ancient pagan goddess of Spring, and has simply been taken over by Christians for their annual celebration of the 'new life' of Jesus because all the imagery of Spring is so very appropriate. New growth from buried bulbs, new creatures from hatched eggs, and so on.

The chick emerging from the egg is a popular Easter symbol of new life.

Like Christmas, Easter begins with a period of preparation before the main festival.

Lent

Lent is an old English word for the season of Spring, but on the Christian Calendar it refers to the forty days which lead up to Easter Day (not counting the Sundays). This is the time when Christians remember the forty days at the beginning of Jesus' ministry when he was tempted by the devil, after his baptism.

Many Christians commemorate Jesus' fast by undertaking some kind of fasting themselves – traditionally this meant giving

Fasting

Jesus went without food during his forty days and nights in the desert (see Luke 4:1–2). The word for deliberately giving up eating is 'fasting'. Here are some reasons for fasting.

● Going without food makes the mind and spirit more alert.

● Going without food shows a willingness to follow a disciplined lifestyle.

● Going without food is a sign that spiritual things take priority over material things.

● Going without food, occasionally, is good for the body's digestive system.

up meat and all rich foods. The fasting is accompanied by self-examination and penitence (saying sorry to God). Today many people give up other things than food (it may be a bad habit!), and some 'give up' in order to 'give to' those in need.

Shrove Tuesday

The day before Lent starts is called Shrove Tuesday. Perhaps you know it as Pancake Day. It doesn't mark any particular event associated with the death of Jesus, but it became special because of the day's two traditional preparations for the start of Lent:

● People had to use up all their rich foodstuffs before the fast (hence the pancakes).
● People confessed their sins to a priest. They obtained God's forgiveness and were given a spiritual task ('penance'). This was called 'being shriven', hence 'Shrove Tuesday'.

Ash Wednesday

The day on which Lent starts gets its name from an old custom, when part of a sinner's

A 'Pancake Day' race.

'penance' might be to appear in public wearing sackcloth and ashes. Today, Christians in some churches have their foreheads marked with ash at a special church service on Ash Wednesday, as a sign of their penitence. The ash is sometimes made from burning the previous year's palm crosses (see Palm Sunday).

Mothering Sunday

The fourth Sunday of Lent was once called 'Refreshment Sunday', and the tradition was for Christians to gain spiritual refreshment by visiting the 'mother' church

In the nineteenth century it became the custom for young girls who worked away from home to take a simnel cake to their mothers on a special visit home on 'Mothering Sunday'.

on this day – that would be a large area church or a cathedral. It was a day for physical refreshment, too, when the Lent fast was suspended and special simnel cakes were eaten.

These days, Mothering Sunday is an

occasion when Christians give thanks for mothers and families.

Palm Sunday

The week running up to Easter Day is known as Holy Week and it begins on Palm Sunday. Christians remember Jesus arriving in Jerusalem riding on a donkey, and the people greeting him as a king by waving palm branches and crying 'Hosanna!' Some churches have a procession to act out the event. Many churches give out little crosses made of folded palm-leaf strips.

Maundy Thursday

Although it is not entirely clear from the Gospels exactly which night of the week it was that Jesus ate his Last Supper with his disciples (see Unit 21), the Christian Calendar remembers the event on Maundy Thursday, the day before the crucifixion anniversary, Good Friday.

At this Last Supper, Jesus changed the words of the traditional Passover meal and instructed his followers to break and eat bread and to drink wine in memory of him in future. This is the origin of the Holy Communion service (see Unit 37).

On the same occasion, Jesus also gave his disciples a new commandment, to love each other as he had loved them. As an example of humble service he washed their feet.

The word 'Maundy' comes from the Latin word for 'commandment'. It used to be the tradition that priests washed their parishioners' feet on this day, and sometimes the Pope will still do this. An English tradition is for the reigning monarch to give special coins – 'Maundy Money' – to elderly people at a special service, the number of coins matching the monarch's age.

Because Jesus and his disciples went from the Last Supper to the Garden of Gethsemane, where he was arrested, some churches switch out the lights during the final hymn of their special evening service, and the worshippers make their way out of the building in darkness.

Palm Sunday marks the beginning of the week leading up to the death and resurrection of Jesus (the Easter events). Churches often give out palm-leaf crosses to the congregation.

Good Friday

Despite its name, this day marks the anniversary of the death of Jesus by Roman crucifixion. It is called 'Good' (or 'God's') because Christians believe that out of that awful execution came the conquest of sin

Hot cross buns, spiced buns marked with a cross, were the traditional way to break the Lent fast and are still popular.

and the chance for all people to be reconciled with God.

At special services, Christians remember all the stages leading up to Jesus' crucifixion, and in some places there is a procession to recall these 'stations of the cross'.

Easter Eve

On the Saturday between Good Friday and Easter Day, Orthodox, Roman Catholic and (some) Anglican churches keep an Easter Vigil, where Christians remember the time Jesus' body lay in the tomb. Orthodox churches have a coffin decorated with flowers as a reminder of Jesus' dead body before the resurrection. Late in the evening, the people leave the church and all the lights are put out.

Then at midnight, outside the building, a large Paschal candle is lit, sometimes from a special bonfire. ('Paschal' is a corruption of *Pesach*, the Hebrew word for Passover.) The priest shouts: 'Christ is risen!' and the people reply: 'He is risen indeed!'

The Paschal candle is carried into the dark building, with the people following. The opening of the church doors symbolizes the stone rolling away from Jesus' tomb, and the candle coming into church symbolizes the light of Jesus' resurrection overcoming the darkness of the tomb.

Starting from the Paschal candle, worshippers with small candles pass the light from person to person. This is to symbolize the spreading of the good news that Jesus, Light of the world, has risen from the dead.

Candles blaze at an Easter service, marking the triumph of light over darkness in the resurrection of Jesus.

Some churches have a dawn service at sunrise on Easter Day, to celebrate Jesus' rising from death as the sun rises over the horizon.

Easter Day

The commercial emphasis on Christmas tends to obscure the fact that *Easter* is the most important festival on the Christian Calendar! On Easter Day, Christians celebrate the resurrection of Jesus from the dead, the assurance of 'new life' and access to God.

Of all the 'new life' symbols, the egg is the most popular. People give each other gifts of chocolate eggs or decorated eggs; in some places hard-boiled eggs are used in knock-out competitions like conkers, or they are rolled down hills with a prize for the first to the bottom.

Churches are decorated with flowers for the celebration services, and there may also be a little model garden showing the three crosses (Jesus was executed with two robbers) and the empty tomb.

Ascension

Forty days after the Sunday of Easter Day comes Ascension Day, always on a Thursday. This is when Christians remember Jesus' return to be with his Father in heaven, after spending the forty days following his resurrection appearing to many of his followers and teaching them. Before he 'ascended' into the clouds, he told them to wait in Jerusalem for the coming Holy Spirit who would empower them to spread the news about Jesus.

Pentecost

'Pentecost' means 'fifty days' and it is the name of the Jewish festival which comes fifty days after Passover. It was during the time of this festival in Jerusalem that the first followers of Jesus, who were Jews, received the power of the Holy Spirit.

The Christian festival commemorating this event became a popular time for baptizing new members, and because of the white baptism robes which symbolized

One custom associated with the festival is Whit Walks – processions by church members through their village or parish. Local to Derbyshire is the practice of well-dressing, when springs are marked with canopies covered with pictures of Bible scenes made entirely of small flowers. In church services, teaching focusses on God the Holy Spirit and his work in and through believers.

new life, the day became known as White Sunday or Whitsunday.

Trinity Sunday

The Sunday after Pentecost has become the special day for remembering the Christian belief in God as Father, Son and Holy Spirit.

Corpus Christi

The Thursday after Trinity Sunday is kept in Roman Catholic churches as a special day of thanksgiving for the sacrament of Holy Communion, where the bread and wine become for believers the body and blood of Christ. *Corpus Christi* is Latin for 'body of Christ'. Some churches have processions, when the consecrated bread is carried reverently through the streets.

Corpus Christi is also celebrated by some Anglican churches.

FOLLOW UP

Copy out this chart and complete it, using the information in this section.

THE EASTER CYCLE	
OCCASION	HOW IT IS REMEMBERED
Lent	Fasting Self-examination Penitence
Shrove Tuesday	
Ash Wednesday	
Mothering Sunday	
Palm Sunday	
Maundy Thursday	
Good Friday	
Easter Eve	
Easter Day	
Ascension	
Pentecost	
Trinity Sunday	
Corpus Christi	

The Saints' Days Cycle

The word 'saint' is related to the word 'sanctify', which means 'to set aside for special use'. In one sense, all Christians have been set aside for the special purpose of being faithful followers of Jesus; that is why St Paul addressed many of his letters to 'the saints at such-a-town'. He meant *all* the Christians there.

But from earliest times, Christians have remembered the life and example of particular followers of Jesus, who were special and have consequently become known as 'the saints'. Christians today are inspired by the example set by these special Christians of the past.

The first saints to be remembered were Christians who had died for their beliefs – martyrs. There is a tradition, for example, that the apostles Peter and Paul were executed at Rome on the 29 June in AD67. So that date is kept as the 'Feast of St Peter and St Paul' on the Christian Calendar.

Other New Testament Christians are remembered as saints, not just those thought to have been martyred. However, as time passed, local congregations started honouring the memory of so many different Christians who had lived their lives close to God and set an example to others, that an official list was drawn up (called a 'canon') of those Christians worthy of the title 'saint'.

The canon was made before the Reformation and since that time the Church of England has not added to it.

The Roman Catholic Church, however, has continued to add names to the list, but only after the most stringent examination of the claims made for a person's 'canonization'. Christians can be considered only after their death, when the whole of their life can be judged as an example. The case for their canonization is heard by a

A twentieth-century saint

The Roman Catholic Church recently canonized a Polish Catholic priest called Maximilian Kolbe. In 1941 he persuaded guards at Auschwitz concentration camp to let him stand in for a married man with a family, when ten prisoners were selected to be starved to death as a punishment for another prisoner escaping. Kolbe comforted the other nine as they died one by one until only he was left. Eventually, the guards were so disturbed by his serenity and faith that they injected him with poison.

special council in Rome. Proof of saintliness is required, usually including well-attested miracles associated with the Christian being considered. The discussions may take several years while the evidence is examined, and in the end it is the Pope who finally decides whether or not a Christian can be honoured and listed as a saint.

The countries of the British Isles each celebrate a historic 'patron' saint:

1 March   St David (Wales)
17 March   St Patrick (Ireland)
23 April   St George (England)
30 November   St Andrew (Scotland)

The Christian Calendar celebrates All Saints' Day on 1 November, remembering all Christian saints, known and unknown.

Because the word 'saint' in the Bible applies to *all* believers, many of the non-conformist denominations do not celebrate any special saints' days.

In 1969, St George was one of several saints removed from the official canon because there was no reliable evidence for who they were or whether they actually existed. Their names had been included centuries ago, on the flimsy basis of popular legends.

Each saint appearing on the present-day canon (in both the Anglican Church and the Roman Catholic Church) is remembered on his or her special day each year.

Many churches are dedicated to a particular saint, and their congregations will hold a special 'patronal festival' on their patron saint's day.

In the New Testament, the word 'saints' refers to all Christians. In the Apostles' Creed (see Unit 33), the 'communion of saints' means the family unity shared by all Christians, living and dead. There is a bond between all true believers, of all races and all generations. (See Colossians 1:12; Hebrews 11:39–12:1).

FOLLOW UP

1. Choose one of the saints and find out as much as possible about them.

2. Now design a festival service for a church which is dedicated to that saint. For example St Mary's church in Millerbridge (Unit 30) is dedicated to Mary, the mother of Jesus.

Try to include ideas of celebration from your work in Unit 43 as well as more traditional ideas for a church service.

Your final service draft should include:
● celebration
● thanksgiving for the life and work of the saint
● prayers
● hymns – perhaps you could write a special one? Here is a hymn dedicated to Saint Stephen (whose special day is 26 December) to give you an idea!

Yesterday with exultation
Joined the world in celebration
   Of her promised Saviour's birth;
Yesterday the angel-nation
Poured the strains of jubilation
   O'er the Monarch born on earth:

But to-day, O deacon glorious,
By thy faith and deeds victorious,
   Stephen, champion renowned,
Thee we hail who, triumph gaining,
Mid the faithless faith sustaining,
   First of martyr saints wast found.

For the crown that fadeth never
Bear thy murderers' brief endeavour;
   Victory waits to end the strife:
Death shall be thy life's beginning,
And life's losing be the winning
   Of the true and better life.

Interpreting the Bible

All Christians agree that the Bible is the word of God. But the sixty-six books of the Bible were written by a large number of different writers, spread over many centuries. So the Bible has both a God dimension and a human dimension.

When we look at the **human dimension** of the Bible we have to take into account a number of factors, such as:
- the personality of the writers
- the cultural and historical setting and the world-view of the particular book
- the kind of writing (history, poetry, wisdom, letter . . .)
- apparent contradictions
- translation.

We can never understand the Bible properly without taking this vital human factor into account. The Bible writers were not *less* human because they were inspired by God, but *more* human . . .

When we look at the **God dimension**, some of the factors we need to take account of are:
- the inspiration of the Bible
- the unity of the Bible
- the power of the Bible to move people and to speak to every age-group and every generation and culture.

We can never understand the Bible properly if we leave out this God dimension. The Bible is *not* like any other book.

Let us look at some of these factors more closely.

The human dimension
- **The personality of the writers.** If you look back at Unit 15 you will see that the Gospels of Matthew, Mark and Luke are called the synoptic Gospels because they have a similar viewpoint of the life and ministry of Jesus. At the same time, however, each writer has a particular viewpoint and style which makes his Gospel different from that of the other two writers. Even where they are writing about common subject matter the personality of each writer shows through.

Similarly, because the writers of the Bible had a different perspective from that of other contemporary writers, it is possible to compare some parts of the Bible with other historical documents written at the same time. Sometimes these documents confirm what is written in the Bible and sometimes they give us a very different view.

For example, in 1 Kings chapter 16 we read a short account about King Omri who reigned for twelve years. According to historical documents, Omri was a very successful king who brought a lot of strength and prosperity to Israel. But to the writers of Kings he was a bad king because he 'sinned against the Lord more than any of his predecessors' (1 Kings 16:25). So to the writers his achievements were unimportant in comparison with the fact that he did not follow God.

- **The cultural and historical setting and the world-view of the particular book.** The Bible was written in different cultures from our own. If you are ever the honoured guest of one of the Arab sultans you may be offered (as Queen Elizabeth II was) the wonderful delicacy of a sheep's eye. If someone in England offered you a sheep's eye for dinner you would probably think it was an insult.

Waiter! There's a contact lens in my soup!

Different cultures have different customs. For example, when Paul wrote to the Corinthian church he told them that women should have their heads covered. In the culture of first-century Corinth, women who went about with their heads uncovered were women of fairly dubious character to say the least! But today that doesn't apply in Western society. You would feel very strange putting on a veil to go to the paper shop.

If we are to regard the Bible as being relevant for today's world we have to look for the principle behind Paul's words. The truth of the Bible is unchanged by its cultural setting – we have to bring that truth into our own culture and experience.

Many people are prepared to disregard the Bible because of the accounts of the creation of the world which they read in Genesis. They believe that science has proved the Bible to be wrong and that because there might be evidence of life on earth stretching back for hundreds of thousands of years the Bible must be a collection of fairy tales.

But Christians believe the truth of the the Bible. Although the cultural setting is different – most if not all of the writers of the Bible would have believed that the earth was flat – the truth that God is the Creator of the world remains.

● **Type of literature.** When we read the Bible we have to take into account the different types of literature which have been included. If you look back to Unit 1 you will see the variety of literature in the Bible – poetry, history, wisdom, letters, for example. If we are to discover the meaning of the Bible for today's world we have to make an attempt to understand these different styles of writing. The Bible is like a library of books on one particular topic – like the Library of Natural History – where all the books have a different and unique approach to the same theme.

● **Apparent contradictions.** People who are not Christians often point out that there seem to be contradictions in the Bible. For example, the Gospel accounts of the resurrection of Jesus all contain different, and in some cases contradictory, information.

> 'After Jesus rose from death early on Sunday he appeared first to Mary Magdalene . . .'
> Mark 16:9

> 'The women hurried away from the tomb . . .suddenly Jesus met them.'
> Matthew 28:8–9

> 'The Lord is risen indeed. He has appeared to Simon!'
> Luke 24:34

In John's account Jesus also appears first to Mary Magdalene. What are Christians to make of these differences? Is there any way that all of them can be true? Clearly all the accounts agree that Jesus rose again from the dead and was seen by several people on that first Easter morning. The seeming differences do not contradict the meaning of the Bible – the truth of the Bible remains unchanged.

Also there are bound to be differences which creep in during the copying and transcribing processes. Look back at Unit 2 to see the stages that the Bible has gone through from when it was first written until today. Remarkably, none of these small errors affects any important Christian teaching.

● **Translation.** The Bible was originally written in Hebrew, Greek and Aramaic. Fine – no problem. All we have to do is is to translate the words into English, French, Swahili and so on. Except that it isn't quite that easy . . .

For example, you perhaps know that *dans* in French means *in*, and *le vent* means 'the wind'? But put them together, and you get a phrase, *dans le vent*, which actually means 'trendy'!

There are similar difficulties in translating the Bible. You can't convey the meaning if you translate it word by word. Obviously the work of a translator is more complex than that and involves understanding the complete meaning of a passage or book.

The translation of the Bible is also made difficult by the fact that the latest book to be written was completed approximately 1900 years ago. If you have ever read any of Shakespeare's plays you will know how many strange words there are and how some words have changed their meanings. And that's with something written in English less than 400 years ago!

Also – we don't have the originals of any of the books of the Bible. Look back at Units 2–4 to see some of the problems we have when it comes to translating copies of copies of copies. When Christians say that

Around the world the work of translating the Bible continues, so that the Good News can be available to everyone in their own language.

the Bible is the word of God do they mean the Bible which we have copies of? (And which translation of those?) Or do they mean the Bible in its original form – which no longer exists?

Another problem with translation is that the translators are human beings not computers. So when they have a choice of words to use for a translation they have to choose which one to use. Usually, a particular translation of the Bible isn't the work of one person, but a group of translators who are as committed to the preservation of the complete word of God as they are to producing the best translation possible.

The God dimension

When we look at the 'God dimension' of the Bible we discover that some of these problems are turned upside down!

● **The inspiration of the Bible.** The personality of each writer of the Bible comes through their writings. But so does the inspiration of God to those writers. The presence of God is felt very clearly through the pages of both the Old and the New Testaments. Some Christians believe that each word of the Bible is inspired by God while others believe that the message of the Bible is divinely inspired and that the individual writers expressed that message in their own particular way. Paul, writing to Timothy expresses the Christian belief about the inspiration of the Bible:

'All Scripture is inspired by God and is useful for teaching the truth, rebuking error, correcting faults, and giving instruction for right living.'
2 Timothy 3:16

● **The unity of the Bible.** The Bible has a central theme and overall message which is continued by each writer in turn. The basic story of the Bible is how the love of God for humankind sent Jesus into the world. John's Gospel describes this very succinctly:

> 'For God loved the world so much that he gave his only Son, so that everyone who believes in him may not die but have eternal life. For God did not send his Son into the world to be its judge but to be its saviour.'
>
> John 3:16,17

This theme of salvation can be traced right through the Bible from Genesis to Revelation. Look at Isaiah chapter 53. Christians believe that this is a passage describing the suffering and death of Jesus. Compare it with the last few chapters of one of the Gospels and see if you can see the common threads?

If you look at a Bible *concordance* you can trace some of the key themes of the Bible

for yourself. Look up the following words in the concordance and read through the list of references:

- salvation
- sin
- redemption
- forgiveness.
- love

● **The power of the Bible to move people and to speak to every age-group and every generation and culture.** Here are two examples of people who found the Bible relevant to their lives. Bilquis Sheikh met God through reading the Bible and Corrie ten Boom and her sister were able to introduce other people to the love of God expressed in the Bible. They are included here to give you some idea of how the Bible – despite the various difficulties we have mentioned – affects people's lives.

Bilquis Sheikh is a Pakistani woman who was brought up as a Muslim. After she was left by her husband she retreated to her family estate to find peace. But the real peace which she wanted seemed to escape her. Searching through the Muslim holy book, the Qur'an, she found many references to Jesus. Out of curiosity she obtained a Bible.

That Bible was to transform her life as she learned to call God her Father and came into a living relationship with Jesus Christ.

The next day just before a visit from Tooni, a little Bible mysteriously appeared on my downstairs drawing room table. I picked it up, and examined it closely. Cheaply bound in a gray cloth cover, it was printed in Urdu, a local Indian dialect. It had been translated by an Englishman 180 years before and I found the old-fashioned phraseology difficult to follow. Manzur had evidently got it from a friend; it was almost new. I leafed through its thin pages, set it down and forgot about it.

A few minutes later Tooni arrived. Mahmud ran in just behind her, squealing, because he knew his mother would have brought him a toy. In a minute Mahmud raced through the French doors to the terrace with his new airplane, and Tooni and I settled down to our tea.

It was then that Tooni noticed the Bible resting on the table near me. 'Oh, a Bible!' she said. 'Do open it and see what it has to say.' Our family views any religious book as significant. It was a common pastime to allow a holy book to fall open, point blindly at a passage to see what it said, almost like having it give a prophecy.

Lightheartedly, I opened the little Bible and looked down at the pages.

Then, a mysterious thing happened. It was as if my attention were being drawn to a verse on the lower right hand corner of the right page. I bent close to read it:

I will call that my people, which was not my people; and her beloved, which was not beloved. And it shall be, that in the place where it was said unto them, Ye are not my people, there shall they be called sons of the living God.
Romans 9:25–26

I caught my breath and a tremor passed through me. Why was this verse affecting me so! I will call that my people, which was not my people . . . In the place where it was said unto them, Ye are not my people, there shall they be called sons of the living God.

A silence hung over the room. I looked up to see Tooni poised expectantly, ready to hear what I had found. But I could not read the words out loud. Something in them was too profound for me to read as amusement.

'Well, what was it Mother?' asked Tooni, her alive eyes questioning me.

I closed the book, murmured something about this not being a game anymore, and turned the conversation to another subject.

But the words burned in my heart like glowing embers. And they turned out to be preparation for the most unusual dreams I have ever had.

Corrie ten Boom is known to many people because of a book and film about her experiences in a German concentration camp. Corrie and some of her family were imprisoned because they hid Jews from the Nazis during the Second World War. In this extract from her book, *In My Father's House* Corrie explains how a simple childhood game enabled her sister to share the love of God with other prisoners and guards in the concentration camp.

With the dishes cleared off and the kitchen duties accomplished, the oval table could be turned into a place for games. We didn't play cards (for that was considered a form of gambling), but we had a lasting enjoyment in the type of games which taught us something.

Different languages were introduced as a game, not as a forced study. When I was in the fourth grade, we began to learn French. As I remember, I loved the melodious sounds of this beautiful language, but it was and remained a difficult language for me. The next year I started English, which was easier, but I wondered as I struggled with all the different English meanings for words if I would ever go to England or America and have an opportunity to use the language.

Father wanted me to learn English well, and he gave me a little Sunday-school booklet in English which was called 'There's No Place Like Home.' I read it over and over again.

The greatest fun in language-learning came during our Bible study. The entire family would take part, each one of us having a Bible in a different language. Willem usually had the original in Hebrew and Greek; I would have the English; Mother the Dutch; Nollie the French; and Betsie or Father, German. It was a special and joyous time for us.

Father would begin by asking what John 3:16 was in English. I would answer from my English Bible, Mother from her Dutch Bible, and Betsie would reply in German.

When I was so young, it didn't seem possible that Betsie would ever have a chance to use a Bible verse in German. We didn't know any Germans then! However, God uses such seemingly insignificant ways to prepare us for the plan He has for our lives. Over forty years later, in a concentration camp in Germany, Betsie was able to use that verse – and many more – to speak to the prisoners and the guards about God's love.

▲ FOLLOW ☞UP ▲

A world without tears

Just think of a world without tears
Where a man can live for a million years (John 17:3)
With never a grief, an ache or a pain (Isaiah 33:24)
And never a thought of dying again. (Revelation 21:34)

Think of a world without bloodshed and strife
Where no man dare take another man's life (Micah 4:3)
Where man unto man will unite in peace (Isaiah 9:7)
And malice and hatred for evermore cease. (Susanna 2:14)

Now a world without tears is not just a dream.
As many persons might make it seem (Revelation 21:5, 6)
For just as sure as the Bible is true (Hebrews 6:18)
A world without tears now lies before you. (Luke 21:28)

And since such a world before you now lies (Luke 31:31)
Wouldn't you like to live in this Paradise? (Isaiah 66:17)
And share all the blessings that God has in store (Psalm 72:7, 8)
For all who do His will evermore. (Matthew 6:10)

Here is a passage which could be read in a church service. At the end of each line there is a Bible reference (Susanna is in the Deuterocanonical books, which may not be included in your Bible). The writer wanted to show that the Bible could address the problems of today's world as clearly as it did when it was written – and still provide answers!

In pairs:

● look through the references and jot down what each reference says.
    For example: 'where a man can live for a million years? (John 17:3)'
    If someone knows God through Jesus Christ they will live for ever (have eternal life).

● Do you think that the world which this passage describes is possible?

● What would have to happen for a world like this to become a reality?

Using the Bible in Christian Life and Worship

The Bible in public worship

If you visit a church on a Sunday you will see or hear the Bible being used in a number of different ways.

Let's imagine that you have been given an assignment to visit your local Baptist church and see what you can discover about how they use the Bible in public worship.

When you go through the front door someone shakes you by the hand and gives you a hymn book. As you flick it open you see a hymn you know:

> The Lord's my Shepherd, I'll not want
> He makes me down to lie
> In pastures green; He leadeth me
> The quiet waters by.

You know that this hymn is based on Psalm 23 in the Bible. Maybe there are other hymns which are also based on verses from the Bible?

By now you are sitting down in a pew and you can have a look around. On the front wall above the pulpit are two beautiful banners:

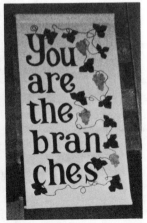

'I am the vine', 'You are the branches' are words of Jesus – from the Bible.

At this point someone comes to the front of the church and turns on an overhead projector. These words appear on the projector screen:

> Seek ye first the Kingdom of God
> And his righteousness,
> And all these things shall be added unto you,
> Hallelu, hallelujah!

A young man comes to the front with a guitar. He introduces the song by explaining that these are words of Jesus from the Sermon on the Mount. More from the Bible!

After the congregation has sung several more songs, the minister (a woman) comes and stands by the side of the Communion Table at the front. She welcomes everyone to the service and announces the first hymn.

When this hymn is over, she leads the congregation in prayer, finishing with the Lord's Prayer – the prayer which Jesus taught his disciples.

> Our Father, who art in heaven,
> Hallowed be thy name.
> Thy kingdom come, thy will be done
> On earth as it is in heaven.
> Give us this day our daily bread,
> And forgive us our trespasses
> As we forgive them that trespass against us.
> And lead us not into temptation, but
> deliver us from evil.
> For thine is the kingdom and the power
> and the glory,
> for ever and ever,
> Amen.

48

The Bible is of central importance to Christians, as the pictures in this unit show.

It is read aloud in church services.

Individuals study it on their own.

Groups of Christians get together to share its teaching.

Key verses may be highlighted for special treatment.

This too, of course, comes from the Bible.

After this the man sitting at the end of your row gets up and goes to the reading-desk. He reads a passage from the Bible, from Isaiah chapter 43, and everyone listens. (You finally manage to find Isaiah in the Bible in front of you on your pew, just as he is finishing the reading!)

Then the minister tells a story to the children about a tax collector called Zacchaeus who was so small that he had to climb up into a tree to see Jesus. The children act out the story while she tells it. At the end of the story they sing a song about Zacchaeus:

Now Zacchaeus was a very little man,
And a very little man was he;
He climbed right into a sycamore tree
For the Saviour he wanted to see.

Then the notices about the week's activities are read out. As far as you can see, this is the first item which hasn't included anything from the Bible! During the next hymn the collection is taken – is this practice also in the Bible?

Now the minister preaches the sermon. Most of the people around you follow in their own Bibles while she explains the reading from Isaiah 43. She talks about when it was written, and what it would have meant to the people for whom it was written. Then she goes on to talk about what it means for the congregation today. In particular she concentrates on verse 2:

'When you pass through deep waters, I will be with you; Your troubles will not overwhelm you.'
Isaiah 43:2

She talks about God being with Christians in whatever situation they have to face. Not that God makes everything dead easy for Christians but, better than that – he never leaves them on their own. It's rather like the Liverpool football fans' anthem: 'You'll never walk alone.'

. At the end of the sermon three scouts come out to the front and pray some prayers which they have written down. Then it's the final hymn and the 'benediction' – yet again from the Bible:

The Lord bless you and watch over you,
The Lord make his face shine upon you
and be gracious to you,
The Lord look kindly on you
and give you peace;
and the blessing of God almighty
the Father, the Son, and the Holy Spirit,
be among you and remain with you always.

At school the next day you compare notes with your friend who visited the local Roman Catholic church. They had three readings from the Bible and when they had the reading from the Gospel there was a procession of people to the front of the church.

A young boy carried a crucifix, two more carried lit candles; and someone waved incense in front of the person carrying the Bible. Everyone in the congregation stood up at this point and the priest kissed the Bible before reading the Gospel passage. At the end of the reading there was the same procession to take the Bible away again.

Your friend was very impressed by this. It made the Bible seem extremely important and very holy. The service he attended was a Parish Mass and the Communion part was based around the Last Supper that Jesus had with his disciples. Some of the actual words of Jesus at that meal were included in the 'liturgy' (the set form of words which the priest used).

The Bible used by individuals

In some world religions the sacred scriptures are kept in the place of worship and very few people have their own copies at home. The most important role for the scripture is within public worship, with passages of scripture being explained by a specially trained official.

Most Christians, however, have their own copy of the Bible in the home, and many will read it regularly on their own. The Bible has been translated into nearly every language in the world, so people are able to read it in their own language without having to learn a special 'scripture language' to understand it.

Janet Tebby is 36, single, and a Christian. She teaches very young children and is also director of music at her parish church. Here Janet answers some questions about her use of the Bible at home . . .

Q: *Have you always been a Christian, Janet?*
A: No – I became a Christian when I was a student. I was twenty at the time.

Q: *Do you have a Bible of your own at home?*
A: Yes, several. I have a small leather-bound Bible which is a particular favourite – it was a twenty-first birthday present. I keep that next to my bed so that I can read it at night before I go to sleep. I also have a large 'study Bible' which has lots of helpful notes and references, and I have two or three different translations of the Bible which I also use for study.

Q: *Do you read the Bible at any other time than at night?*
A: I try to spend some time each week studying a particular book or theme from the Bible. At the moment I am looking at the idea of 'sacrifice' in the Bible.

Q: *Do you use anything else to help you understand the Bible?*
A: At night I use some Bible-reading notes called 'Guidelines' which have a reference of several verses or a chapter from the Bible and then a few paragraphs explaining what that passage means. I find these notes help to concentrate my thoughts when I'm getting sleepy! I also buy books which are commentaries on particular parts of the Bible – I've just finished working through 1 Corinthians with a commentary.

Q: *How important is the Bible to you?*
A: Very, very important. As a Christian I believe it is the word of God and therefore that God can speak to me through it. I try to base my life on the teaching of the Bible; although that isn't always easy . . .

Q: *Some people memorize large portions of their sacred scriptures. Do you know any parts of the Bible off by heart?*
A: When I was small, we learned things like the twenty-third psalm at school. And when I first became a

▶▶

Christian, I did try to learn lots of 'key' verses about the faith and living as a Christian. A lot of the songs we sing at church are taken straight from the Bible, and they stick in my mind very well. I think I've probably got a lot of bits of the Bible in my head by now, but I can't always remember the references!

Q: *Are there any other ways you use the Bible apart from just reading and studying?*
A: I belong to a study group with eight other people. We talk about passages from the Bible and our Christian lives – maybe at work or family pressures. It's very informal but it's a good way of learning to apply what the Bible says to our ordinary lives instead of it just being something which is read in church on Sunday.

Not all Christians use the Bible in the same way as Janet – some will do more serious study, others will only use it in times of particular need, or only in church services.

The Bible itself speaks of different ways in which it can be used:
- for guidance:

'Your word is a lamp to guide me and a light for my path.'
Psalm 119: 105

- guidelines for Christian living:

'All Scripture is inspired by God and is useful for teaching the truth, rebuking error, correcting faults, and giving instruction for right living.'
2 Timothy 3:16

- for teaching:

'Everything written in the Scriptures was written to teach us, in order that we might have hope through the patience and encouragement which the Scriptures give us.'
Romans 15:4

▲FOLLOW UP▲

1. Make a list of ways in which the Bible is used in church services.

2. Read Psalm 23. As a group, try to work out a sermon which a minister could preach about that psalm.

Pilgrimage

An illustration of Chaucer's pilgrims, on their way to Canterbury.

The festivals of the Church's Year are very important times of celebration. They break the pattern of the ordinary Sunday routine and help to focus the minds of many Christians on particular aspects of their faith.

Christmas and Easter, especially, remind Christians of the main roots of their faith: the birth, death and resurrection of Jesus. During the preparation periods of Advent and Lent people have a chance to look forward and to anticipate the joy of the festival celebrations.

In the same way, Christians who go on pilgrimages find that their faith is increased and strengthened by the pilgrimage. They usually come back from a visit to a special holy place spiritually refreshed and wanting to try to be more single-minded Christians.

It is not essential for a Christian to go on a pilgrimage. Many Christians would never think of making such a visit. This is unlike Islam; all Muslims have to go on a pilgrimage to Mecca, their holy city, once in their life. Only if they can find someone to go in their place may they be excused this spiritual journey.

In the Middle Ages, pilgrimages were very popular and people often made vows to go on a pilgrimage if their prayers had been answered. Also, the risks in making a long pilgrimage – for example, to Israel, the Holy Land, – were considerable. This made the successful completion of a pilgrimage more important than it is today when you can go to the local travel agent and conveniently make all the arrangements in advance.

Not all pilgrimages were long ones – there were hundreds of minor pilgrimage places which attracted pilgrims because of stories about healings or miracles which had taken place there. Some places became famous and attracted pilgrims from all over Christendom; others faded into insignificance.

Most people prefer to go as part of a guided group, so that they can gain as much benefit as possible from the journey. There is something very special about being able to have an informal Communion service together, sitting on the shores of Lake Galilee.

But how is this different from someone going on a package holiday to Israel? What exactly is a pilgrimage? Or a pilgrim? Here are two dictionary definitions:

Pilgrimage: the journey of a pilgrim.

Pilgrim: one who journeys to a sacred place as an act of religious devotion.

People have gone on pilgrimages almost since Christianity began – and continue to go today. Why is this?

Some reasons for Christian pilgrimage

People go on pilgrimage:

- to visit a holy place where God seems especially present;
- as an act of thanksgiving to God;
- for physical healing;
- for spiritual healing;
- to fulfil a vow or promise made to God or a saint;
- as an act of penance for sin;
- to visit the places connected with the life, death and resurrection of Jesus;
- to strengthen personal faith;
- to strengthen relationships within a group of people;
- to have a holiday in spiritual surroundings;
- to pray to God for help.

Some possible benefits of Christian pilgrimage

These include:

- a sense of spiritual growth;
- physical healing;
- spiritual healing;
- lovely memories!
- the repayment of a vow;
- strengthened relationships within a group;
- a sense of spiritual restoration.

As you read through the descriptions of various pilgrimage places keep looking back at these two lists. Which words or phrases might apply to which particular place? For example, someone visiting Jerusalem might feel that they are coming to a holy place where God seems to be specially present and that they will be able to visit the places Jesus visited.

Modern pilgrims gather at Walsingham in Norfolk.

FOLLOW UP

1. Look at the list of reasons for going on a Christian pilgrimage in this unit. Put them into your own order of importance.

2. Now put them into an order of importance which you think a Christian might choose.

3. Are there any differences between your two lists? Can you think why?

Christian Places of Pilgrimage

The Holy Land is probably the most frequently visited pilgrimage place in Christianity today. Many Christians experience a tremendous excitement at the thought of being able to visit places that Jesus would have visited and to trace his spiritual journey from the years in Galilee to his death and resurrection in Jerusalem.

Here is how one Christian, Stephen Orchard, felt as he arrived:

'I walked down the dark street with a travel bag in my hand. It seemed right to set off for Jerusalem on foot rather than to call a taxi. Fifteen minutes' walk to the station is not quite how the medieval pilgrims started out but I thought of them as I moved beneath the night sky. What did they carry in a travel bag to see them through the months of journeying to the Holy Land? It could not have been less than my bundle of belongings, soon to pass through El Al security at Heathrow. What did they need to hump along in the days before package tours and travellers cheques?

At the airport I met my fellow-travellers. Some were old friends, some strangers, all to be united by the distinctive badge of our travel company. It was strange to meet another old friend with a different badge and a different group also bound for Israel. Why were we all going? I told the security guard it was a study tour but he said that meant a pilgrimage. But what is a pilgrimage after all? For some a time of prayer and meditation; for some a search for the concrete evidence to support their faith; for some, and I think me, an adventure, not knowing quite what will be found.

I have not been to Israel before, though friends assume it. I have been to Madrid and it is of that I think as our bus drives away from Ben Gurion airport through the dusty suburbs of Tel Aviv. It is a dry landscape at the end of summer, dotted with small-windowed houses and scrubby trees. We recover from our night flight with a day at the Mediterranean resort of Netanya. The beach hotel and swimming pool could be on any tourist shore but a group of fishermen emptying their nets on the sand give a sudden hint of Galilee to come . . .'

Here are some of the most popular pilgrimage places.

Bethlehem

At Bethlehem is the Church of the Nativity – built on the traditional site of the birth of Jesus. Most of the Christian pilgrimage sites in the Holy Land are shared by different branches of the church and the Church of the Nativity is no exception – it has altars which are looked after by the Greek Orthodox Church, Roman Catholics, Egyptians and the Syrians.

This is how Simon Mayo describes it:

66 It really is a cave – except that the rock walls have been covered in some very dirty, gloomy old tapestries, heavy with the smell of centuries of incense. There's enough incense down there to turn you into a secondary smoker.

At the foot of the steps, there's a small area on the left called the Chapel of the Manger. Here Mary is said to have placed Jesus after he was born. And then to your right is the place of the birth, where there is a big indentation in the rock.

If it doesn't sound too irreverent, this actually looks like a very large fireplace.

You have to get down on your hands and knees to look inside.

What you see there is an old, cracked marble slab with two candles burning on it.

A whole collection of tinsely oil lamps hang over the top like a cluster of bats.

In front of the candles, set into the marble, there is a large silver star. Written around the star in Latin are the words, "Here Jesus Christ was born of the Virgin Mary".

All this isn't exactly everyone's cup of tea – and the place can be profoundly disappointing.

It is supposed to be one of the holiest pieces of ground in the world, and yet at the busiest times

▶▶ of the year you can be herded in as if you're entering Santa's Grotto. The cave itself felt as packed (and about as holy) as a tube train.

What makes it worse is that various branches of the Christian Church jealously guard their rights here. The Armenians, the Greek Orthodox and the Roman Catholics all have their own zones within the church.

They have been known to hold long and bitter disputes over who should mop step number six, who should stand where in processions, and where the no-go areas are.

On the plus side, it seems that the cave really could be where it all happened. Many Bethleham houses had caves in the time of Jesus. Houses were built on top of them, and the cave was used as a sort of downstairs, where the animals slept at night.

From the very early days of the Christian faith, this particular cave was identified as the place where Jesus took his first lungful.

If you can forget the religious squabbles and see through all the marble, incense and silver trinkets, then it's amazing to think that Jesus might have been born here. **99**

Nazareth

Nazareth is another important place for Christians to visit, because the Gospels tell us it is where Jesus grew up and where Mary, his mother, was told about the special baby she would have.

However, you have to make a choice when it comes to where the Angel Gabriel might have visited Mary! There are two churches which claim the site – the Basilica of the Annunciation and the Church of Saint Gabriel. One of the problems with all the pilgrimage sites in Israel is that nearly everything is based on tradition. There is no historical documentation outside the Bible. Different branches of the church each claim that their site is the real

one! For some this is important, but for many it is enough to be in the place where a key event happened. It is often easier to imagine the real thing away from the razzmatazz and commercialization of official sites.

Jerusalem

There are many important places to visit in Jerusalem – perhaps the most important are the site of the death of Jesus and the empty tomb where his body was laid. The Church of the Holy Sepulchre contains a tomb cut out of the rock and, to the right of the tomb area, is the traditional site of Calvary, where Jesus was crucified. This site is also covered over by a church.

Further away is another rock-cut tomb – this time in a quiet garden. The tomb was only discovered comparatively recently by an officer in the British army. Although it does not in fact date back quite as far as the first century it has become a place for prayer and devotion for many Protestants. It is easy to picture the events of the first Easter day in this peaceful place.

Many pilgrims choose to walk along the Via Dolorosa (Way of Grief), following the journey Jesus is said to have taken to his death. The Via Dolorosa is marked with the 'Stations of the Cross' – the places where, according to tradition, Jesus stopped on his journey to the cross, and places for remembering the crucifixion and the placing of the body in the tomb.

There are traditionally fourteen 'Stations of the Cross' and inside many churches, particularly Roman Catholic ones, there are pictures or statues representing the events remembered at each point. During Lent, people often walk around the church in procession, stopping at each station to pray and think about the suffering of Jesus (see Box).

Many pilgrims visit Jerusalem at Easter so that they can walk the Via Dolorosa on Good Friday and then

The Church of the Holy Sepulchre, marking the traditional site of Jesus' burial, is still a place of pilgrimage today.

celebrate the resurrection of Jesus on Easter morning – possibly by attending an Easter Eucharist in one of the churches.

One of the problems with visiting any of the holy places in Jerusalem is that, because they have so many visitors, they have also become tourist traps – guides almost fight to gain custom and there are souvenirs on sale everywhere. But this is a problem for any pilgrimage place of any religion. Christians going on a pilgrimage to Jerusalem must remind themselves that they are pilgrims and not merely tourists if they are to benefit spiritually from their journey. The crowds are also a reminder of what the city was like at festival times in Jesus' day, with trouble always ready to break out.

Lourdes

Lourdes, in France, is a very different kind of pilgrimage place from any of the places in the Holy Land. Lourdes only became a place of pilgrimage in the nineteenth century, and most of the pilgrims who go to Lourdes go for a very specific purpose – to seek healing.

On 11 February 1858 a fourteen-year-old girl was walking by a grotto

Stations of the cross

Fourteen 'stations of the cross' are represented in some churches. Each marks a stage on Jesus' last journey. As you will see from the list, and the Bible references, some of these incidents are 'apocryphal' – they represent a tradition, although there is no evidence for them in the Bible itself.

1. Jesus is condemned to death
Matthew 27:15–26; Mark 15:6–15; Luke 23:17–15

2. Jesus receives his cross
John 19:17

3. Jesus falls beneath the cross for the first time
(apocryphal)

4. Jesus meets his mother
(apocryphal – see Matthew 27:55–6; Mark 15:40; John 19:25–7)

5. Simon of Cyrene helps Jesus to carry the cross
Matthew 27:32; Mark 15:21; Luke 23:26

6. St Veronica wipes Jesus' face
(apocryphal)

A Good Friday procession in Jerusalem reaches the third 'station of the cross'.

7. Jesus falls a second time
(apocryphal)

8. Jesus comforts the women of Jerusalem
Luke 23:27–31

9. Jesus falls a third time
(apocryphal)

10. Jesus is stripped and soaked with bitter wine
Matthew 27:28–31, 33–4; Mark 15:16–20

11. Jesus is nailed to the cross
Matthew 27:33; Mark 15:24; Luke 23:33

12. Jesus dies on the cross
Matthew 27:45–56; Mark 15:33–41; Luke 23:44–9; John 19:28–30

13. Jesus is taken down from the cross and laid in his mother's arms
(apocryphal)

14. Jesus is laid in the tomb
Matthew 27:57–61; Mark 15:42–7; Luke 23:50–56; John 19:31–42

in Lourdes when she had a what she believed to be a vision of the Virgin Mary. The apparition appeared to the girl, Bernadette Soubirous, on several more occasions and eventually revealed her identity as the Virgin Mary. She also told Bernadette that people would be healed if they visited the spring of water which appeared miraculously out of the ground.

Pilgrims gather in the grotto at Lourdes. Many Christians journey to Lourdes in search of healing.

As a result of Bernadette's visions and subsequent claims of healing, Lourdes has become a major centre for people seeking to be healed. Hundreds of thousands of people go on a pilgrimage there every year. Each evening during the pilgrimage season there is a huge torch-lit procession through the town. Prayers, hymns and finally a Communion service are relayed over loudspeakers, so that everyone can join in as they march around the town. Those who can't walk are pushed through the streets in wheelchairs by volunteer helpers.

During the daytime pilgrims visit the grotto and some have a special bath in water from the spring. Anyone who believes that he or she has been healed at Lourdes has to undergo very strict examination by both the Roman Catholic medical authorities and independent medical sources.

If both these groups agree that there has been a cure then the ▶▶

▶▶ Roman Catholic church will investigate the claims and pronounce whether a healing has taken place. Only if there was no chance of the person getting well by any other means and if the cure is instant, total and permanent will it be recognized as a genuine miracle.

Canterbury

Thomas Beckett, the Archbishop of Canterbury was murdered on the steps of Canterbury Cathedral by the assumed order of King Henry II in 1170. (See Unit 29.) Only three years later he was declared to be a saint because of all the accounts of miraculous happenings connected with him: blind people recovering their sight, lame people walking and even a drowned boy coming back to life.

Canterbury became one of the most popular place of pilgrimage for the Christian church in the Middle Ages with pilgrims visiting it from all over the Christian world. Geoffrey Chaucer wrote his famous *Canterbury Tales* about an imaginary group of pilgrims travelling from London to Canterbury.

Today not many people make an individual pilgrimage to Canterbury; but is quite common for church groups to walk at least part of the way there and maybe sleep rough in church halls along the routes.

Iona

Iona is a very small island off the west coast of Scotland. In AD563 St Columba settled there with a group of monks from Ireland, with the aim of spreading the Gospel. (See Unit 28.)

Today Iona seems very far removed from the busy motorways and communication networks of Britain but in the sixth century it was on the sea route between Ireland and other parts of Christendom.

In 1938 a decision was made to restore the eleventh-century abbey and make Iona a place where lay people and ministers could mix together easily and learn to understand one another better.

Today it is a place that many Christians visit for refreshment and renewal. It is a mixture of the old and the new and provides spiritual healing for many people. Here is what one person, Fiona Williams Hulbert, felt about Iona:

'Clearly there are many ways that Iona is significant to those who come. There is the simple need to rest and enjoy the sea and seals and silly sheep. There are needs for healing, for knowing one's life to be meaningful, for thinking with others about God's mystery and strange ways of working in the world. There is a spectrum of meanings that Iona the island and Iona the community with ancient roots has for its pilgrims.'

Lindisfarne

Another ancient place which used to be a great pilgrimage centre is Lindisfarne, an island off the Northumbrian coast, sixty miles from Newcastle. In 634 a group of Irish monks led by St Aidan came from Iona to set up a community. Having established a monastery and a school they travelled around the north of England, spreading the gospel and encouraging people to become Christians.

Today hundreds of thousands of visitors come to the island – which is cut off for about five hours each day by the sea. However, at low tide you can walk across the sand to the island. Some of the visitors are tourists but many are pilgrims; they pray in the church and visit the ruins of the priory and maybe take a break in their holiday in Northumbria to spend time in quiet meditation.

Taizé

A very popular place of pilgrimage for young people today is Taizé in France. You can read more about Taizé in Unit 52.

▲FOLLOW✋UP▲

1. Using an atlas, mark all the pilgrimage places mentioned in this unit on a blank map of the world.

2. Complete the following chart:

Pilgrimage place	Country	Reason for pilgrimage	Activities
Bethlehem	Israel	Birth of Jesus	Visit Church of Nativity
Nazareth			
Jerusalem			
Lourdes			
Canterbury			
Iona			
Lindisfarne			

Monasticism

Most Christians today live ordinary lives, working, bringing up families . . . But there are some who leave home and family to join a Christian community. They leave their ordinary lives for many reasons – some feel they need to escape from the 'world' – but many join a community because they believe they have a vocation – that God has called them to enter into a special life of service for and worship of him.

They usually join together with others who have a similar vocation. Anyone who joins a religious order as a nun or a monk has to make three traditional vows – of poverty, chastity and obedience.

Poverty

This means giving up all your possessions before you enter the order. You might think that your house or your car would be the most difficult thing to part with, but most monks and nuns find that it is the small things which have sentimental value which are the hardest to give up. It is also quite difficult to give up all the clothes which express your individual personality and accept robes which make you look like everyone else!

Chastity

You might have thought that this would be the most difficult vow to keep, but in fact most monks and nuns find it the easiest. Chastity is more than not having a physical sexual relationship with someone. It is also an attitude of mind which stops the monk or nun from forming a closer relationship with any person than they have with God. Of course this should be true of all Christians!

A Benedictine monk gets to work on a diseased tree.

○ **Celibacy**

To be celibate literally means being unmarried but
○ traditionally in the Church it has become used for
   someone who has dedicated their life to God.
   Although you might think of celibacy as 'giving up
○ sex', monks and nuns who make a vow of celibacy see
   their vow in a much more positive light. What they are
   doing is committing themselves to a relationship with
○ God which will be the most important relationship in
○ their life.

Obedience

At its simplest, this means obeying the
rules of the religious community and being
obedient to God. At its hardest, it means
not making your own decisions about how
you spend your time or what work you do
within the community. A doctor who
becomes a nun in a contemplative order
may find herself digging the garden or
scrubbing the floors as an act of obedience
to God and the community.

There are communities of monks and
nuns in the Roman Catholic, the Orthodox
and the Anglican churches. They all make
the same three basic vows, although some
orders also make extra vows. The colour of
their robes may be different – for example
some Benedictine monks are called 'black
monks' because of their black robes and
the 'white sisters' are members of 'the
congregation of the daughters of the Holy
Ghost' who wear white robes.

Traditionally nuns have dressed like
the nun in the picture. Her hair is
covered with a veil as a symbol of
modesty. In the past, nuns had to
have their hair shaved off to show
that they had made a complete
break from the world, but many
orders no longer follow that rule.

Her clothes, which cover as
much of her body as possible, are a
reminder of her vow of chastity.
They are made of plain hard-
wearing material to symbolize her
poverty. The rope belt around her
waist has three knots to symbolize
the three vows of poverty, chastity
and obedience.

On her wedding finger she wears
a ring which shows she is 'married'
to God and the church. A traditional
title for a nun is a 'Bride of Christ'. A
cross hangs around her neck and
may show which order of nuns she
belongs to.

Religious orders which
concentrate mainly on prayer and
worship are known as
Contemplative Orders. Today, one of
the problems which faces religious
communities is whether they can
achieve more for God as
contemplatives or by being active in
the world. This is sometimes
reflected in the clothes they wear.

Some monks and nuns wear
ordinary clothes and maybe a large

This nun, like many today, goes about
her work in 'mufti'.

Sister Bede, wearing her traditional habit, works on an
icon at St Cecilia's Abbey, Isle of Wight.

cross around their necks. In
particular, some orders of active
nuns feel that their traditional robes
mean that people might think that
they are rather odd! They feel that if
they wore jeans and sweatshirts
they would be able to go more
easily into areas where people
would not accept nuns. For
example, some orders of nuns work
in the red-light districts of
Amsterdam, amongst prostitutes
and drug addicts.

Mother Teresa

Nobel Peace Prize winner and founder of the Missionary Sisters of Charity, Mother Teresa has become famous for her work of caring for the poorest and most destitute people in Calcutta – and in other cities across the world where her Sisters share her love for those who are shunned by society. She is perhaps the most famous nun of our age.

Christians admire her and are inspired by her example. But what do non-Christians make of someone like Mother Teresa – someone who has given up everything to work with the poor of society; someone who tries to live the life of Christ as a nun?

Francis Shennan is a writer and journalist based in Glasgow who has worked for many UK newspapers and magazines. Raised as a Catholic, he is now an atheist, but feels his beliefs are closer to Buddhism than to any other religion. Here, he recalls his impressions of Mother Teresa, whom he interviewed during one of her rare visits to Britain:

"Happiness after seeing the worst of human suffering, joy without the security of knowing where the money, food and medicine you need will come from, is an impressive personal achievement. And meeting her made me realise something about the nature of goodness. Genuinely good people are happy because they are in tune with themselves. You can almost sense it, like knowing when a guitar string is in tune. It has nothing to do with the long-faced Christianity of some well-known writers, nothing to do with obeying rules.

The challenge for the non-Christian is: can that kind of life of heroic goodness in action ever be achieved without an all-consuming belief in a personal God? My answer must be that it would be next to impossible to achieve without the constant mental and emotional nourishment of that kind of belief.

If all Christians were Mother Teresas, I might be tempted to say: 'It doesn't matter if there is a God or not, the effect of believing outweighs the questions about the truth.'

But, in fact, Mother Teresa is just as much an exception among Christians as she is among non-Christians. Her faith, though essential to her, does not explain her existence.

Nor will she let any of us off the hook. 'Sanctity is not the luxury of the few,' she told me. 'It is a duty for each one of us. The way for you as a journalist to be sanctified is to write the truth.'

Mother Teresa gave me a glimpse into the real meaning of goodness and happiness. But seven years after meeting her, I probably still have more questions than answers. **"**

Apparently he came here to get away from it all.

Simeon the Stylite

If you had been alive in AD450 one of the places you might have visited on a pilgrimage was a place in Northern Syria – near the border with Turkey. Even in the fifth century AD people would have made the journey from as far away as Britain, although that journey would have taken many months and would have been extremely dangerous.

What you would have visited was a stone pillar. Or, more precisely, you would have visited the man who lived on top of the pillar. His name was Simeon and he spent the last twenty years of his life (until AD459) on top of a pillar. At first it was quite a low pillar but gradually the height was increased until it was twenty metres. It had a railing around the top to prevent Simeon from falling off. Presumably people passed food up to him but history doesn't record how he coped with his other bodily functions . . .

Simeon the Stylite (a pillar dweller) was like a very early version of an agony aunt. People would visit the pillar and shout up all their problems to Simeon and he would shout back his advice. Living on a pillar became quite popular for a while, and Simeon had disciples who followed his way of life. Even today there is the occasional person who chooses to spend time as a stylite on top of a pillar.

Simeon and his disciples were part of a movement of people – usually men – who wanted to try to achieve a purity of Christian life which they did not think was possible in the ordinary world. They were the beginnings of the movement which eventually led to our modern-day monasticism.

St Benedict

Probably the most important person in the development of monasticism is St Benedict. He was born in Nursia in Italy in about AD480. Benedict started his religious life as a hermit – he lived alone for three years in a cave at Subiaco near Rome. Then he joined a group of fellow hermits who wanted to live in a community together. This was not a success, and Benedict was forced to leave. One story suggests that Benedict discovered that the other hermits were putting poison in his food!

Benedict founded another community on Monte Cassino in central Italy. This community was more successful and eventually a monastery was built there. Benedict became the abbot, and wrote a list of rules by which all his monks must live. An abbot is the head of the community. When a monk joins the community he has to accept the discipline and authority of the abbot. Benedict wrote that his new rules were to be 'a school of the Lord's service in which we hope to order nothing harsh or rigorous'.

These rules have become the basis of monastic life today. Collectively they are known as the Rule of Benedict. The Rule is based on two activities – prayer and work, and can be summed up in a phrase which Benedict used *laborare est orare* – 'to work is to pray'. Benedict stressed that worship in church was doing the work of God.

As a result of Benedict's teaching a pattern of worship was introduced which is still followed by many monastic communities today. Benedictine communities developed a cycle of seven periods of prayer and worship each day, from a verse in one of the Psalms in which the psalmist stated: 'seven times each day I thank you' Psalm 119:164.

Lauds
(praise):morning prayer.
Prime
(first hour): 6a.m.
Terce
(third hour):9a.m.
Sext
(sixth hour):midday.
None
(ninth hour):3p.m.
Vespers
(evening):evening prayer.
Compline
(complete):final night prayer.

This looks like a fairly exhausting timetable, but the monks usually went back to bed after Lauds for another three hours' sleep. Each service was different but included prayers and intercessions, the reciting or singing of psalms, and a set reading from the Bible.

Basil the Great

Basil set up his own community as a monk but decided to become a priest as well. He was made a bishop in AD370 and believed that all monasteries should come under the authority of a bishop. His own community provided medical help, relief for the poor and did some work in education. They were also strictly disciplined to only eight times of prayer a day.

Basil developed two rules for community living in a monastery or convent. These rules are still used by religious orders in the Eastern Orthodox church today.

FOLLOW UP

You are a Roman Catholic and you have decided to become a monk or a nun.

1. Write a letter to each of the following people explaining your reasons for wanting to join a religious order:
- your mother
- your boyfriend or girlfriend
- your priest.

2. Write a letter which you might receive from one of the above people in reply to your letter.

Community and Fellowship

A famous religious community was founded by Roger Schutz at Taizé in France. Brother Roger, as he is now known, acquired a house at Taizé in 1940 and sheltered Jewish refugees there until 1942.

Taizé

When the Germans occupied France, Roger moved to Geneva and started living a community life with several friends. In 1944 they moved back to Taizé and seven of them took solemn vows as monks in 1949. In 1952 they composed the rule of Taizé which was similar to the Benedictine rule, except that the monks were to dress in ordinary clothes and have only three services a day.

Today Taizé has become a place of pilgrimage for young people from all over the world. Its special role is as an

Everywhere Christians form communities, some formal, some informal.

Here is an extract from the information given to pilgrims when they arrive:

'As you arrive at Taizé, understand that it is part of the community's vocation to welcome you, so that you can reach the sources of God through prayer, through the silence of contemplation, through searching. To listen to you, if you want to speak about something which hurts you or which obstructs the paths of a search for the living God, some brothers remain in the church after the evening prayer: *perhaps being listened to in the church is a way for you to break through what blocks you or to discover a path for your life.*

You have come to Taizé to find a meaning to your life. One of Christ's secrets is that he loved you first. There lies the meaning of your life: to be loved for ever, to be clothed by God's forgiveness and trust, as if by a garment. In this way you will be able to take the risk of giving your life.

It is good, if you can, to finish your week at Taizé in silence, on Friday or Saturday. For many young people, a second week at Taizé, spent entirely in silence, proves to be a vital experience.

In the evening, silence, in the areas around the church, tents and huts, begins at the end of the evening prayer. . . '

ecumenical community which tries to break down the barriers between different denominations and branches of the church. Many young people camp out in the fields nearby and join in the daily worship of the community and the practical work of the kitchens and the farms.

The worship at Taizé has become famous for its simple songs in Latin, French, German and English, with which everyone joins in. An 'Easter vigil' is held every Saturday evening, when everyone is given a candle to hold during the service.

Taizé is like a halfway house between the life of traditional religious orders and the life of the majority of Christians today. It is a place where Christians can go for a time and live a monastic life. Many of them receive spiritual strength while they are there to go back to their normal life and be effective witnesses to the power of God in their lives.

Community life

Today there are many communities of people who live together and share their possessions without having taken monastic vows. The early church, which we read about in the New Testament, was the first of these Christian communities. We read this about them:

'All the believers continued together in close fellowship and shared their belongings with one another. They would sell their property and possessions, and distribute the money among all, according to what each one needed. Day after day they met as a group in the Temple, and they had their meals together in their homes, eating with glad and humble hearts . . .'
Acts 2:44–46

There are many Christians today who are trying to recapture the kind of life which those early Christians lived. Several families may pool all their possessions and maybe buy a large house where they can all live together. They actively try to live a communal life – no one has the right to say 'that is *my* stereo' or 'those are my books'.

There are all kinds of different communities. Some are made up of families. Others are groups of single people. And others still a mixture of clergy and lay people. Steve, who is now a Methodist minister, lived for two years in a community.

" At first I thought that living in a community would be the answer to all my problems! As a single person I thought it would be fantastic to have a ready-made supply of company. What I soon discovered was that it was quite hard not to have anything of my own. I also found it very hard to have my salary paid into a communal account and then have to ask for any money I might need.

I soon discovered just how much money I spent on non-essential things like magazines and sweets. It became embarrassing to ask for money for sweets each week at the house meeting! What was good, however, was being able to talk to people at any time without feeling you were getting in their way.

I think my worst experience of community life was when I spent two months in an American community. They had several community houses including one for single men. As a mark of everyone sharing everything there were no locks on the doors – including the bathroom! I found it very difficult to be shaving and have some guy stroll in to sit on the loo . . .

To non-Christians we appeared very strange until they got to know us. Then they were amazed at how we shared everything in the house. People began to realize that our Christian faith was real – not just something which existed on Sundays and was then put away until the following week. While I lived there about fifteen people became Christians because of the fellowship they found in our mini-community.

I only left because I went to theological college to train to be a minister. Otherwise I think I would still be there. I am hoping eventually to open my home here as a sort of community but I haven't yet found a group of like-minded people in my church. Maybe they think it would be threatening to live with the minister? I think some people assume that our family must sing hymns at breakfast time . . .

The people in this town need to know that Jesus is alive and well today. They're not going to do that while we live in separate little boxes and only meet together for an hour each Sunday; they need to see us make room in our homes for the down-and-outs and the drug addicts who sit in the town square every night. "

Different people join communities for different reasons, and for different periods of time. Some communities accept people only for a short time, whereas others take people for life.

Some communities were formed as a result of religious persecution. For example the Anabaptists founded a very long-lasting form of economic community in Europe called the *Bruderhof*. The Anabaptists decided that infant baptism was meaningless, and re-baptized people who joined their movement. They were persecuted by the Catholic authorities in the Tyrol, who thought they were dangerous heretics, and they fled from Zurich. Eventually they found refuge in Holland, the USA and Canada. It was easier to survive as a group than as individuals. In their community they aimed to follow the pattern of the early church (see Unit 20), and lived a very simple lifestyle.

There are still Anabaptist communities today, but now they are known as Mennonites, from one of their early leaders, Menno Simons. Their life is characterized by an emphasis on personal faith, a rejection of anything that is not scriptural (including electricity for some of the groups), study of the Bible, and pacifism. One of the better-known Mennonite groups is the Amish community in the USA (you may have seen them in the film *The Witness*).

House- or home-groups

As well as people who actually live in community together, there are other Christians who spend a lot of time together apart from their Sunday worship. Many groups in all churches meet together weekly for Bible study and prayer and to share both joys and problems.

Pat Shackleton belongs to a group of eight women who meet each week.

> 66 We always mean to do lots and lots of Bible study, but we spend a lot of time talking! It's good though, because it means that we can share the concerns we have. We are a mixed group, although five of us are teachers. You can share some problem in your life and know that the group won't talk to anyone else and that they will all pray for you, help and support you.
>
> We have a meal together with all our families every six or eight weeks and we go out for a meal together occasionally. Other housegroups in our church do different things – one of them had a group day out at Alton Towers the other week. The groups are a good way of getting to know people in the church better. 99

House or community churches

The housegroup which Pat belongs to is part of the structure of an Anglican church. During the week, most of the congregation meet in housegroups, and then on Sunday they meet together for a traditional Anglican Communion service.

There are some people, however, who find that the structure of the traditional churches is too restrictive. They do not like having a particular pattern of worship which is repeated every week, and they want everyone to be able to take part in the leadership.

Some of these Christians meet in

A Christian house-group gets together for a family meal.

houses rather than in churches and, for obvious reasons, these groups are called 'house churches'. House churches started in the 1960s as a result of what has become known as the charismatic movement (see Unit 53). Some of them have now organized themselves into groups to provide support and encouragement and to give overall leadership. Some of them have also grown so big that they now have to meet in rented halls or church buildings no longer used by the traditional denominations.

Usually there is a house church leader or 'elder' who has overall responsibility for the group. House churches want to get back to the simple lifestyle of the early church and many of them also live in community, where everyone pools their resources, which are then shared out equally.

Some house churches have grown so big that they have several 'branches' and some have set up their own Christian schools and enterprises.

FOLLOW UP

1. Imagine you are spending a week at Taizé. Write a letter to a friend describing the life there. Are you enjoying yourself? Why?

2. List five advantages of living in community like Steve.

3. List five disadvantages of community living.

4. Why would someone want to join a house church rather than one of the traditional churches?

The Charismatic Movement

The 'charismatic movement' began with the realization by many people that the kind of Christianity they had did not match up to the kind of Christianity they read about in the Bible.

For example, they read this about the early church in Jerusalem:

'Many miracles and wonders were being performed among the people by the apostles . . . sick people were carried out into the streets and placed on beds and mats so that at least Peter's shadow might fall on some of them as he passed by. And crowds of people came in from the towns around Jerusalem bringing those who were ill or who had evil spirits in them; and they were all healed.'
Acts 5:12,15,16

'When the day of Pentecost came, all the believers were gathered together in one place. Suddenly there was a noise from the sky which sounded like a strong wind blowing, and it filled the whole house where they were sitting. Then they saw what looked like tongues of fire which spread out and touched each person there. They were all filled with the Holy Spirit and began to talk in other languages, as the Spirit enabled them to speak.'
Acts 2:1–4

In the 1960s people in the traditional churches such as the Roman Catholic and the Anglican churches began to ask God to baptize them too in the Holy Spirit. Jane Morton was a student when she learned about the baptism of the Holy Spirit. I asked her what happened.

There was a feeling among many people that the Christian church should still be able to offer healing to people. Further study of the New Testament led to the conclusion that the early church had power to perform miracles because they were 'baptized in the Holy Spirit'.

In the days following the ascension of Jesus, his disciples were very frightened men and women. They thought that the Roman authorities would turn their attention on them very shortly. But Jesus had told them to wait in Jerusalem until the Holy Spirit came upon them, filling them with power.

This is how Luke, in the book of Acts, describes what happened:

When did you become a Christian, Jane?

I committed my life to God when I was confirmed at the age of twelve, but I didn't really make a success of being a Christian during my teenage years. Although I knew Jesus to be my Saviour, I didn't really have very much idea of him as Lord. When I was nineteen I re-committed my life to God at university.

When did you first hear about the baptism of the Holy Spirit?

Again at university. In my Christian Union there was a very quiet first-year student who started to talk to me about the Holy Spirit. Looking back, I realize that he was probably praying for me because he thought there was something missing in my life.

So when were you baptized in the Holy Spirit?

I went away to France for a year of language study. When I came back to university I thought I would be the Grand Old Lady of the Christian Union – showing and ▶▶

The name 'charismatic movement' comes from the Greek word for gifts – *charismata* – because the charismatic movement emphasized the gifts of the Holy Spirit which are described in the New Testament.

God's grace (*charis*) is the quality in his character which gives freely. Through his Holy Spirit he gives gifts (*charismata*) to the members of his church, which they are to use in serving each other and the world. Each member has a different gift, a different role. They are to honour each other's gifts and use their own.

Paul and Peter both give lists of gifts. Among the most important are:

- **Teaching:** explaining and passing on God's revealed truth.
- **Evangelism:** passing on the gospel to those who do not know it.
- **Pastoring:** caring for people in their personal and spiritual needs.
- **Healing:** praying effectively for those who are physically or emotionally ill.
- **Prophecy:** passing on messages from God, which should always accord with the Bible.
- **Speaking in tongues:** using unknown languages (always explained by someone with a gift of interpretation).
- **Discernment:** knowing when a spiritual claim is true and when it is false.

▶▶ telling everyone what to do. There was a group of students in the Christian Union who went to a house church in Oxford, and they held some meetings for people who wanted to receive the Holy Spirit.

I went to the first of these meetings and found myself being very, very angry about what was said. I thought they were saying that anyone who wasn't 'baptized in the Holy Spirit' wasn't a Christian. I decided that I didn't want any more to do with these 'charismatics', but as I read my Bible and other books about the baptism in the Spirit, I decided that I would ask God for whatever he wanted to give me.

One night I knelt in my room and asked God to fill me with his Holy Spirit – and he did. It was the most wonderful feeling and for about three weeks afterwards I felt like I was walking on cloud nine!

What difference has it made in your life?

There are three major changes, really. Firstly, I am much more aware of the differences between the Father, Son and the Holy Spirit in the Trinity. I am very aware of the presence of the Holy Spirit with me at all times.

Generally my whole life is now much more God-centred than self-centred. And worship has become much more important to me too. I find I am no longer inhibited in what I say or do to worship God.

'Charismatic' churches

Many churches in the traditional denominations such as the Anglican Church and the Roman Catholic Church have been affected by the charismatic movement.

These churches are often characterized by a different style of worship. Some features you might expect to find in a charismatic church are:

- simple, modern songs, often accompanied by clapping;

- people raising their hands in the air in worship;

- some of the gifts of the Spirit being used (see the end of Unit 22)

- a joyful style of worship;

- a fairly informal type of service;

- dancing – either by a trained group or with everyone joining in.

St Andrew's Church, Chorleywood is a 'charismatic' Anglican church. In this extract, the vicar, Bishop David Pytches, explains the use of the gifts of the Holy Spirit in their Sunday worship.

With a morning attendance of about 500 including children, it is difficult to be too flexible. 'But there is still an opportunity for words of knowledge and prayer ministry after the blessing each Sunday. In the evening, with a similar sized congregation, we have much more time, however, and can have prophecies, tongues and interpretation, etc.'

Only regular members are allowed to use the gifts.

'We try to protect ourselves from the lunatic fringe who are not allowed to prophesy in their own church and are looking around for a place in which they can.'

Members prophesy from where they sit or stand in the wooden pews, which span out from the platform of the church. Then David or whoever is leading the worship will 'reflect the gist of it back to the microphone. We have to recognise that in the exercise of a gift we could be wrong and people could continue to speak "in the flesh." I usually wait for two or three prophecies and reflect back the burden of them – what I prayerfully sense in my spirit is from the Lord. Then we like to have silence to allow the Holy Spirit to apply the prophecies to our hearts.'

Another characteristic of many charismatic churches is a warmth and friendliness and a sense of community. Here are some people's descriptions of their charismatic churches.

I haven't always loved my church. When I moved to Ipswich just over five years ago I didn't like it at all! It hadn't moved to the place it is in now, and was so different from my previous church it was like a culture shock. I knew it was where God wanted me, but I was a mass of criticism and rebellion. I couldn't adjust to the move and couldn't cope with myself or my circumstances. I just fell apart. I realise now I must have been a very difficult person to deal with – angry, prickly, defensive and critical. Yet people in the church were patient and loving. Hours of prayer counselling time were given to me over about two years, and gradually the Lord ministered to me and gave me an enormous amount of inner healing. Anger and criticism were replaced with love and acceptance for the church and for myself.

If it were not for the forgiveness, patience and ministry of the St Matthew's family in Ipswich I don't think I would be experiencing the joy, peace, love and security in Jesus and his family that I rejoice in today.

Chris Sharples

I love my church – the Harrow Corps of the Salvation Army – because there I am loved and accepted for what I am.

In worship I can raise my hands, dance, play a tambourine, clap or just be quiet and undemonstrative. The love given is not conditional on my success as a Christian. There is no need to put on a front or pretend to be what I am not. I can be honest and open about how I feel. I am loved without condition and through the depth of love experienced I have learnt more about the love of God in the last few years than in the whole of my earlier life.

I could tell you of the support and care received two years ago when I was desperately ill with a lung abscess, or of two years prior to that when I went through a long period of depression. The love I receive doesn't just operate in crises – it operates (like God's love) 24 hours a day, seven days a week.

Norma Knight

▶▶

Christian celebration. Scenes like this are common at charismatic gatherings.

▶▶ I love my church for its preaching, pastoral ministry and evangelism. I have been worshipping at Holy Trinity, Eastbourne, for the eight years of my married life.

Ken Blythe, the present vicar, came to us six years ago and almost straightaway I felt a fresh breath of the Spirit. I have a precious memory of one of the ministry team, the then curate Ross Tully, preaching on the theme, 'I was in the Spirit on the Lord's day, when I heard and I saw'. Somehow that vision of John in Revelation remains with me Sunday by Sunday.

Martyn Pedley

Helsby Methodist Church: I used to think this name was prosaic, and was envious of churches with names like Holy Trinity. But not any more.

Helsby is seven miles along the A56 from Chester and the church building is on the main road. Our church's name is there in big white letters for all to see. For many in the village the name means no more than the building, but when I think of Helsby Methodist, my heart warms. I think of the 150 or so people who worship there, my brothers and sisters, some of whom know almost all there is to know

Ian Watson

about me. Within this fellowship the once-superficial relationship with my wife was put right.

In the 21 years since we have been here, our church has grown greatly in spiritual terms. Ten years ago we went to live in Holland for four years, and when we came back it was not only the children who had grown up. To see how the Lord had changed people was breathtaking: shy people had become bold; grumpy people had become radiant; the Spirit of Jesus shone all around.

Not all Christians are in favour of the charismatic movement, even though it is a fast-growing sector of the Christian church. They disagree with the idea of a baptism of the Holy Spirit which is separate from conversion, preferring to emphasize the need for continual filling of the Spirit, and the 'fruit' which that produces in lives marked by love, peace, joy . . .

For some people it has felt as if their whole church has been turned upside down! Other people think that there is too much emotionalism, that people get carried away and rely on feelings instead of mind and faith.

Some charismatics believe that everyone should act and feel as they do. This puts tremendous pressure on people who don't like jumping up and down in a church service. However, it is very easy to be critical of things you don't like . . . For some people the baptism of the Holy Spirit has transformed their lives and made them into dynamic and active Christians.

▲ FOLLOW UP ▲

1. The Anglican church down the road from your school has become 'charismatic'. As the local newspaper reporter you have been given an assignment to run a front page feature on the changes taking place in the church.

Design and write your front page. It should include:

● a description of the church
● a description of the changes which are supposedly taking place
● an interview with the vicar
● an interview with Ada Perkins, who has been a member of the church for the last 64 years
● A comment from the vicar of the next parish who has a very traditional Anglican church.

2. You are a television personality, particularly famous for doing 'in-depth' investigations.

You have visited a number of Christian churches to investigate occurrences which you have heard described as 'the gifts of the Spirit'.

Prepare a five-minute feature on what happens in these churches.

Also record interviews with three people who claim to be able to use these gifts of the Spirit.

Finally, take your crew to a healing service at one of the local churches – they will not allow you to film the service so you will have to describe what happens to your audience.

(You may need to look back at Unit 22 for further information.)

The Ecumenical Movement and the World Council of Churches

Although Christianity is split into its various denominations – for historical reasons concerned with differences of belief and emphasis – these days the main denominations believe in getting together and working together wherever possible. It happens a great deal at the local level, often ahead of 'official' policy.

This 'togetherness' across the old barriers is referred to as the 'ecumenical movement', from the Greek word *oikumene* meaning 'whole world'.

From the time of Jesus Christians have tried to obey his command to go out into the whole world and tell others about him. The ecumenical movement began for the very best of reasons – Christians who were anxious to spread the gospel throughout the world realized they were being hindered by the image of a divided church. By the eighteenth century Christianity had reached a low ebb in Britain. Then came the 'Awakening' or 'Revival' led by the Wesleys and others, and Christians once again began to spread the Good News. In the nineteenth century many missionary (gospel-spreading) societies were founded, and it was when some of these societies began meeting and planning together that the need for a united front first became an important issue.

In 1927, an inter-denominational conference on 'Faith and Order' was held at Lausanne in Switzerland, to explore ways of overcoming the differences between the denominations. Things moved slowly and progress was halted by the Second World War, but eventually a 'World Council of Churches' was established in 1948, at an Assembly in Amsterdam.

At first, the Roman Catholic Church, the Eastern Orthodox Church and the various Pentecostal churches were not represented

FACT·FILE

The World Council of Churches calls itself: *'a fellowship of churches which confess the Lord Jesus Christ as God and Saviour according to the scriptures and therefore seek to fulfil their common calling to the glory of God, Father, Son and Holy Spirit'.* It has held Assemblies at:

– Amsterdam	1948
– Evanston (US)	1954
– New Delhi	1961
– Uppsala	1968
– Nairobi	1975
– Vancouver	1983

on the World Council. The Orthodox Church has been fully represented since 1961. In the same year the Pentecostalists began to become involved. The Roman Catholic Church has been sending 'official observers' since the 1968 Assembly.

The Assemblies of the World Council of Churches have tackled a number of difficult issues, including:

● the need for aid to war-torn countries and to refugees
● political tensions between the world super-powers
● racism
● advances in technology
● theological differences between the churches
● evangelism and education.

But always, the WCC has had two main aims:

to bring Christians together

to help those in need.

In addition to its Assemblies the WCC has an on-going programme of aid and relief work. It supports aid to refugees, other emergency relief, development and church expansion projects.

Just as important, the WCC recognizes that true justice depends on the attitudes of individuals and governments, so it works for changes in policy which will actively help those in need.

Sometimes, the decision about which people really ought to be helped causes tensions within the WCC and raises opposition from governments. One example was when when aid (but not arms) was sent to illegal anti-apartheid groups in South Africa.

Bringing Christians together

Christian denominations committed to the ecumenical movement explore their oneness in three ways:
- agreeing together
- worshipping together
- joining together.

The World Council of Churches aims to bring the churches together in work and worship.

● **Agreement.** One way in which the barriers of old differences are broken down is by denominations agreeing on what they have *in common* with each other.

For example, the Church of England and the Roman Catholic Church have an ecumenical group called the 'Anglican-Roman Catholic International Commission' (ARCIC). This group meets to discuss beliefs and liturgy (forms of worship), and it publishes reports on the various areas of agreement between the two branches of the church. This helps their members to see that there is more that *unites* their two churches than *divides* them.

● **Worship.** Some Christians have expressed their commitment to ecumenism by deciding to worship together. In some places, one church building is used by more than one denomination. The congregations may still worship separately, but the shared use of facilities and meeting for social occasions is seen as a first step in bringing churches together. Some churches that share buildings have actually merged their congregations, bringing together members and ministers from two or more denominational backgrounds.

The idea of shared worship across the denominations is the moving force behind 'inter-denominational' religious communities, such as the monastery at Taizé in France, where young people from many denominations gather together for a time, to pray and grow in understanding of each other and of God (see Unit 52).

● **Unity.** Sometimes, when denominations get together they discover that their differences are so few that they can forget them and become a new 'united' church.

Neither the Roman Catholic Church nor the Eastern Orthodox Church has, as yet, been part of the forming of a new 'united' denomination in this way. But the members of the Church of England living in India became part of the new 'Church of South India' in 1947, along with the Methodist and Reformed denominations there.

In Britain, the Presbyterian and Congregational denominations united in 1972 to form the 'United Reformed Church', which was joined in 1981 by the 'Church of Christ' denomination.

Official talks in the 1960s about unity between the Church of England and the Methodist Church failed to bring about a united denomination when the ruling assembly of the Church of England

These are some of the questions which make unity a difficult process:

● What makes a person a Christian? Infant Baptism? Adult Baptism? Personal repentance and conversion? Living a good life?

● Which has the greater authority, the church or the Bible?

● What is the qualification for leadership ministry? Ordination by a bishop ordained by a previous bishop? Recognition and commission by a national body? Recognition and commission by a local congregation?

● Can women become ministers/priests?

● Can homosexuals be welcomed as members of the local church? As priests and ministers?

● Can it ever be right for Christians to go to war?

● What kind of worship is most pleasing to God? Well-planned services published in a book? Spontaneous prayer and praise inspired by the Holy Spirit?

(General Synod) voted against the idea by a narrow margin.

But the Ecumenical Movement expresses the desire of individuals to come together, so local Anglicans and Methodists worship happily together at 'ecumenical project' churches in many places, sharing at a local level what is still to be achieved at national level.

That is not to say that there are no difficulties when Christians of different denominations consider some form of unity. One reason why there are different denominations is that some Christians groups hold some beliefs so strongly that they have been prepared to die for them.

⬆️FOLLOW⬆️UP⬆️

1. The two main aims of the World Council of Churches are to:
● bring Christians together
● help those in need.
   Which of those two aims do you think is the most important? Why?

2. Find out about any activities in your area which are run by churches of different denominations working together.

3. In what ways do you consider the differences between the churches to be:
● negative
● positive?

Helping the Hungry

Throughout the centuries since the time of Jesus, Christians have followed his example in caring for people's spiritual and physical needs. Christians have been pioneers in providing medical aid, food, water and education, wherever Christianity has flourished. In the modern industrialized countries of the world, these needs are now more usually met by the state, but in the countries of the Third World it is still very often groups of Christians who offer the necessary relief and help.

In the years following the Second World War, the emphasis was on Christians in rich countries sending or taking food and other supplies to poorer countries – offering 'relief' or 'aid'.

The member churches of the British Council of Churches (part of the World Council of Churches – see Unit 54), for example, undertook this kind of overseas support under the title *Inter-Church Aid*. Since 1964 this has been renamed *Christian Aid*.

From 1962, similar overseas relief work has been undertaken by the Roman Catholic Church (not a member of the British Council of Churches) under the title of the *Catholic Agency for Overseas Development* (CAFOD).

'I am puzzled about which Bible people are reading when they suggest religion and politics don't mix.' Archbishop Desmond Tutu

Christian Aid

This poster is one produced by Christian Aid.

But Christians in the developed countries of the world have come to realize that the poorer countries need more than just imported supplies. There is growing

CAFOD

The Catholic Fund for Overseas Development supports 500 projects in 75 countries, working where possible through the Catholic Church at national, regional and local level – a network which makes sure that the help offered reaches the people who need it.

The main project categories are food production, water development, preventive health care, agriculture, leadership training, adult education and literacy programmes.

CAFOD's work is a two-pronged response to the Bible's command to 'love your neighbour' –

● in sharing resources (over £11 million a year is raised for CAFOD)
● in making Christians aware of the changes required to alleviate poverty and injustice.

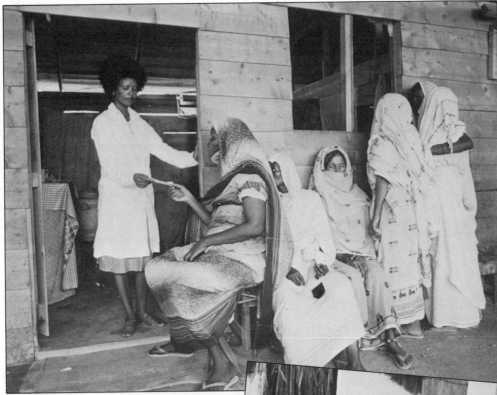

CAFOD workers give medical aid in the shanty town of Port Sudan.

concern about the way government policies can affect levels of poverty in the Third World, and Christians in rich and poor countries alike are involved in campaigns to change their own government's policies so that the world's resources can be tapped and shared efficiently and fairly.

Traidcraft

Traidcraft is a Christian organization which buys craft goods and other products in developing countries and sells them in the UK.

Rather than raising money and then giving aid, Traidcraft helps people in developing countries to work their own way out of poverty. This is done by purchasing their

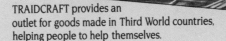

TRAIDCRAFT provides an outlet for goods made in Third World countries, helping people to help themselves.

products, trading fairly and encouraging local skills in design, marketing and quality control.

Craft goods are bought directly from the people who make them, or through organizations which the craftspeople have set up or approved of for the selling of their goods. Foods are purchased from groups where the growers or processors themselves benefit from fairer prices and better working conditions.

Traidcraft sells its purchases – furniture, clothing, jewellery, handicrafts, recycled paper products, teas, coffees and food – through a mail order catalogue, voluntary sales reps. and Traidcraft shops.

Traidcraft is a response to the Bible's command to 'preach the good news to the poor . . . proclaim release to the captives . . . set at liberty those who are oppressed'. So the organization also aims to create awareness amongst its customers of those unfair trading practices which make – and keep – people poor.

World Vision

World Vision is an international Christian relief and development agency with offices around the world. It was founded in 1950 to help orphans and displaced children during the Korean War. Today it helps the poor, the hungry, the homeless and the sick in over seventy countries.

Thousands of people are involved in the work of World Vision by sponsoring children in Third World countries. The sponsor pays so much a month for individual children to be given help with their food, clothes and schooling. Sponsors are encouraged to write to 'their' children and even – if possible – to visit them!

▲FOLLOW UP▲

Write to one of the Christian relief organizations and ask for details of their work. The unit mentions Christian Aid, CAFOD and Traidcraft. Other organizations are TEAR Fund and World Vision.

When you receive the materials, try to find the answers to the following questions.
● When was the organization founded?
● Why was it founded?

● What is its annual turnover?
● What percentage of that is used for administration?
● List some of the ways in which the money is used.
● How much of their work is specifically Christian, and how much is similar to that done by non-Christian organizations such as Oxfam or Save the Children Fund?

Main Movements in the Roman Catholic Church

Because of the many changes taking place right across the world in the nineteenth and twentieth centuries, Pope John XXIII called a special council of the Roman Catholic Church in 1962 to 'update the church'.

So, in the years from 1962 to 1965, 2,450 bishops met for four long sessions at St Peter's Basilica in the Vatican City, in the centre of Rome. These sessions were the 'Second Vatican Council' (the first was held in 1869–70).

Vatican 2 produced sixteen major statements, which together make up the new, authoritative teaching of the Roman Catholic Church. They cover a wide range of issues. Because it was an 'up-dating' exercise, many changes were made. The most notable changes made since Vatican 2 relate to:

● **the church itself.** Although still organized on a 'hierarchical' basis – in levels, one above the other, the most important at the top – the Church recognizes that all baptized members are equal in membership and responsibility. This allows the 'lay' people (those who aren't priests) to play a much fuller part than previously.

● **the lay people.** Ordinary church members are encouraged to understand that they *are* the church, whatever work they do, and encouraged to share the priests' work of teaching and caring for people both in the local church and in the community.

● **liturgy** (forms of worship). The use of Latin for the Roman Catholic Mass in services throughout the world has been dropped in favour of using the local language. The Bible plays a greater part in services and there is more detailed instruction of members about baptism, confirmation, reconciliation (formerly called 'confession') and marriage.

● **the Bible.** As well as becoming a more important feature of public worship, the Bible is read more widely than before by individual Catholics in private or family

Anglican Bishop David Sheppard and Roman Catholic Archbishop Derek Worlock work together for the people of Liverpool. This represents a great movement for change within the Catholic Church.

prayer and worship, by groups meeting for Bible study, and in Roman Catholic schools.

● **consultation.** Bishops, who used only to meet each other at great events, now get together in area conferences to discuss the welfare of their churches. Some local areas (dioceses) have councils made up of clergy and lay people. The underlying principle (known as 'collegiality') is that the whole Roman Catholic Church is a family made up of all the local churches.

● **ecumenism.** There has been a growing willingness to be associated with the work of the World Council of Churches (see Unit 54), and there are now also regular dialogues between Catholics and 'Christian brothers and sisters' in other denominations – who were formerly seen as strangers or even enemies.

Roman Catholics working in the poorest parts of South America in the years before the Second Vatican Council had to look to economic aid as the only way to alleviate the plight of some of the poorest people in the world – the inhabitants of the shanty towns around the great Latin American cities, and the Indian tribes in the mountains and jungles, who were losing their land and their lifestyle in the wake of development or exploitation.

However, the 'reforming' atmosphere that pervaded the Roman Catholic Church after Vatican 2 encouraged new ways of thinking about things like poverty, exploitation and social injustice. And it was

particularly in South America that much of this new thinking evolved, growing out of new ways of looking at **the Bible**, **theology** (study of God and religion) and **political theory**.

● **the Bible.** Arising directly from Vatican 2 there was a new interest in the relevance of the Bible to people in today's world. Four great biblical themes seemed to have particular relevance in Latin America:
– the Exodus – Israel's escape from slavery in Egypt
– Jesus' teaching on social issues
– God's love for the poor
– the Old Testament prophets' demands for justice.

● **theology.** At the time of Vatican 2, some Catholic theologians were exploring the

In South America many Roman Catholic priests lead the liberation movement on behalf of the poor.

idea that all Christians are on a pilgrimage of hope, a journey towards better things. They should therefore be committed to action which will bring the hope of better things nearer to those who need it.

● **political theory.** To priests actually living and working among the poor, the exploited and the oppressed, it seemed that the real need was for political and economic 'liberation' ('exodus') for their people. The European capitalist system which came to South America with the European settlers had not brought this about. So these priests became attracted to some aspects of Marxist Communism as a way of closing the gap between rich and poor – by violent revolution if necessary.

All these ideas – the Bible's teaching, the 'pilgrim' church's responsibility, and the models of Marxism – gave rise to a new way of thinking called '**liberation theology**', the study of how God sets free oppressed people today.

Because the Roman Catholic Church had had close links with the power structures that had grown up in South America under European capitalism, many priests found themselves opposing both church and government in their fight for justice for the poor. One such priest was Camilo Torres, who insisted that 'the Catholic who is not a revolutionary is living in mortal sin'. He was shot dead in 1966.

The liberationists won some ground as socialist governments gained control in several South American countries. But many of these governments have in turn been overthrown by right wing, often military, even fascist regimes. And at the same time as the whole Roman Catholic Church has gradually been influenced by the claims of liberation theology, tension has increased between church and government in Brazil, Argentina and Chile.

The arguments surrounding the 'liberation theology' debate continue within the Roman Catholic Church. Many recognize the need for drastic action on behalf of the poor. But many, too, are suspicious about the validity of using Marxist means to achieve it, particularly the use of force in the name of Christ.

◆FOLLOW✋UP◆

1. In your own words describe what difference the Second Vatican Council will have made to an English Roman Catholic Church in the following areas:
● leadership
● worship
● the Bible
● consultation
● ecumenism

2. Don't copy paragraphs out of the unit – think about what 'ordinary church members are . . . encouraged to share the priest's pastoral and teaching ministries . . .' actually means in practical terms.

Write an account of how these differences are reflected in a Sunday morning service.

Do you think all Roman Catholics would welcome these changes? Give reasons for your answer.

Some of the issues connected with liberation theology are quite difficult to grasp. Here are some questions to help you to get inside the issues.

3. What would you say to a Christian who was sure that it was right to overturn a harsh government by use of force?

4. What would you say to a Christian who lived in a South American slum without any means of support because of government policies?

5. What would you say to a South American priest who had been offered money by a Marxist group but had been ordered to refuse it by the Catholic hierarchy?

6. What would you say to a Christian, living in Northern Ireland, who gave money and support to the IRA?

Culture Clash

By now you probably know quite a lot about Christianity, the beliefs and practices of Christians. Read through the following list of statements and see which you think most Christians would agree with and which they would disagree with.

> Christians should read the Bible every day.

> No Christian woman should go bathing topless on holiday.

> A Christian man should have only one wife.

> Christians should be teetotal.

> To be a Christian you have to believe in the physical resurrection of Jesus.

> The men in the early church were all circumcised Jews, so Christian men today should also be circumcised.

> Christians should go to church every Sunday.

> Jesus' twelve apostles were men, so only men should be ministers in the church today.

> You can't be a practising homosexual and a Christian.

Now compare your answers with those of the rest of the people in your group. Are there any differences? There should be. Those statements were deliberately chosen because they are some of the 'problem' areas for the Christian church worldwide today. There aren't easy answers to any of them. However, if you asked different Christians they would probably be quite definite in their answers and not necessarily be aware that other Christians

Like other people, Christians can disagree! There is plenty of lively argument, especially where cultures differ.

might give different ones. Let us have a look at them one at a time.

● **Christians should read their Bible every day.** There is no place in the Bible which says that Christians should read their Bibles every day. Some Christians do make sure that they read the Bible every morning before they do anything else but others only listen to the Bible readings in church. Both groups of people would consider themselves to be Christians. Which ones are right?

It is only in the twentieth century in Western society that it has been possible for most Christians to have their own copy of the Bible. In many areas of the world Bibles are very scarce and a family may only be able to borrow a few pages at a time. Also there are many people who can't read at all. If reading the Bible every day is a part of being a Christian, they can't be Christians (nor could people in Jesus' day!).

● **No Christian woman should go bathing topless on holiday.** What did you put for this one? Some sections of the church are very strict about how much of the body their members expose – in some churches wearing a bikini would be frowned upon.

When some missionaries went to a tribe in Central Africa in the last century they were shocked to find that all the women walked about topless! The missionaries insisted that if a woman was to be baptized as a Christian she must agree to wear a blouse or something else to cover her breasts. Now it was the turn of the husbands to be shocked. The only women who could afford to wear blouses as well as pieces of cloth for skirts were the prostitutes – and here were the missionaries telling their wives that they must dress like prostitutes . . .

● **Christian men should have only one wife.** It would probably make the front page of one of the tabloid Sunday papers if a vicar was discovered to have two wives! In many countries, as in Britain, it is illegal to have more than one wife at any one time and the church teaches very firmly that a person should be committed to only one other person for the whole of their married life.

But again it is different in different cultures. A problem which some missionaries have had to face was what to do about polygamy. They would arrive at a village and discover that most of the men of the village had two or three wives. When the men wanted to convert to Christianity the missionaries told them that they would have to get rid of all their wives except one.

The men would accept this and keep their youngest and prettiest wife. The other wives would be turned out of the home and have to support themselves. But there was no way for these women to support themselves in those societies – which was why the men had two or three wives in the first place. So the abandoned wives had to become prostitutes or starve unless they could find another man who would marry them.

● **Christians should be teetotal.** This is a statement which would provoke a lot of discussion amongst Christians of different denominations. Some believe that when you become a Christian you have to give up drinking alcohol, and that if you don't you are not really a 'new creation in Christ Jesus'.

Other denominations don't think it matters whether you drink alcohol or not. If you look back at the section on Communion (Unit 37) you will see that some churches use wine for Communion and some use grape juice.

But even within denominations there are differences. Most Pentecostals in Britain and America are teetotal. But Pentecostals in France don't have the same views – many of them would drink wine with their meals.

● **To be a Christian you have to believe in the physical resurrection of Jesus.** This is a difficult one . . . You have probably seen comments made in the Press about the Bishop of Durham. According to some newspapers he doesn't think it is important whether there was a physical resurrection. And yet he is a bishop of the Church of England. Can you believe anything and be a Christian? If not, what do you have to believe?

● **The men in the early church were all circumcised Jews, so Christian men today should also be circumcised.** Not many men in the Christian church today would agree with this statement – but some would. One group of Christians called the British Israelites believe that God has chosen some British Christians to replace the Jews as his chosen people and they observe as many of the Jewish laws as possible.

● **Christians should go to church every Sunday.** In countries with a Christian tradition the churches all hold services on a Sunday. But what about Christians in other parts of the world? In Muslim countries the holy day is a Friday, when everyone goes to the mosque. Sunday is an ordinary working day. What should Christians do? Celebrate Sunday on the Muslim holy day or lose a day's pay to keep Sunday as their holy day?

● **Jesus only chose men as his disciples so only men should be ministers in the church today.** This is a problem which is dividing the Church of England at the moment. Some Anglicans believe that only men can be priests because they are part of the apostolic succession

which goes back to men – the twelve apostles. Also, St Paul wrote that women should be silent in church (though this can be understood in a number of different ways). These people believe that the general teaching of the Bible is that men should have authority over women. They also hold a particular view of the priest's role, and the debate is about this as much as it is about the role of women.

Others believe that Jesus chose men because in the culture of that time women stayed at home and didn't usually go, for example, to the synagogue. Today men

Barbara Harris, the first woman bishop, after her ordination at Boston, USA.

and women have equal opportunities for education and equal roles in society, and so it is argued that women should now be allowed to be priests.

Also, the gospel message which the apostles preached was that everyone was equal in Christ Jesus – men and women, slave and free, Greek and Jew. Throughout the New Testament there are examples of men and women working together in Christian ministry.

Both sides, of course, believe that they are right and the others are wrong. The argument has become much more heated since a woman was consecrated as a bishop in America. Even some of the people who were prepared to accept women as priests are having problems with the idea of a woman bishop.

● **You can't be a homosexual and a Christian.** This again is an issue which threatens to divide Christians. Some Christians believe that a person is born with a sexual preference either for people of their own sex or for people of the opposite sex. Because God created them in that way it is part of his plan that homosexuals should enjoy loving sexual relationships in the same way that heterosexuals do. There are some churches specifically for homosexuals and the ministers of these churches will perform a wedding ceremony for homosexual couples.

Other Christians believe that heterosexuality is the pattern that God intended and any other form of sexual expression goes against his laws. Some of these people would say that AIDS is a punishment from God against homosexuality.

▲FOLLOW✋UP▲

Choose one of the nine statements at the beginning of this unit.

1. Find out what the Bible says about that topic. (Use a concordance to help you!)

2. Interview a Christian minister and find out his opinion on that topic.

3. Ask two or three other Christians what they think.

4. Discuss what they – and you – think with others in your group.

Living Out the Faith

From time to time, particular Christians come into the public eye because of the way they live out their Christian faith. They stand out as 'good examples' – or 'exemplars' – of what Christianity ought to be. You can perhaps think of some famous Christians already – people like Martin Luther King, Terry Waite, Desmond Tutu, Mother Teresa. Perhaps one day some of them will be called 'saints' and remembered on particular days in the church's year. (Though they would probably protest. Those who are closest to God are usually most aware of their own failings.)

Here are five other 'exemplars of the faith':

- Charles Bester
- Sheila Cassidy
- Kriss Akabusi
- David Wang
- John Smith.

Charles Bester

Charles Bester is a white South African who, at eighteen, was jailed for six years in December 1988 for refusing to do military service. He insisted that as a Christian he could not join a force which upheld apartheid.

'I am fully aware that I am breaking the law of the land,' he said, by way of explaining his actions. 'I cannot obey both this law and God.'

Bester's stand has won support both in South Africa and further afield. Black South African Archbishop Desmond Tutu said, 'We are proud of Charles' stand and witness. We are appalled at the vicious sentence he must serve for taking a moral stand, condemned when he should be commended.'

British MP David Alton tabled a motion in the House of Commons and presented Parliament with a 50,000 signature petition calling for Bester's release. Sir Richard Attenborough, who made the film *Cry Freedom*, also praised his 'extraordinary courage, for refusing to participate in the process of violence that is aimed against black people in his country'.

Sheila Cassidy

Someone else who came to the public eye because of her Christian faith is Sheila Cassidy, a doctor who today is head of a hospice in Plymouth, caring for the terminally ill. You may have heard of her or seen a television programme about her work in the hospice.

We would probably not have heard of her at all, except for the fact that she made news headlines around the world when she was expelled from Chile on Monday 29 December 1975.

And that would probably have been all the news that most people would know; except that Sheila has written an account of the four years she spent in Chile and the reasons for her abrupt departure.

In her book *Audacity to Believe* Sheila Cassidy tells the story of her life which led her, as a doctor, to Chile, to work with the poor and the underprivileged.

At first she had only brief contact with the poor and with the revolutionaries who were trying to overthrow the government and bring democracy and freedom to

▶▶

the country. But on 15 October 1975 all that changed. In a gun battle between the security forces and the revolutionaries one man was killed and another received two bullet wounds in the leg. It was just one of many such events – except that Sheila Cassidy was asked by a Roman Catholic priest if she would treat a man with a bullet wound in the leg . . .

Sheila knew that if she treated this man she was siding with the revolutionary forces against the government. She knew that she ran the risk of imprisonment if it was discovered that she had helped this man but she says simply in her book: '. . . it was not my place to judge this man but to treat him.'

It was discovered that Sheila had treated the wounded revolutionary. She was arrested and brutally tortured. After two months in prison she was released because of pressure from Britain and other countries, and deported from Chile.

At first she wanted to wipe out the memory of what had happened to her. But gradually she realized that if she didn't say anything, people in Britain might not know what it was like to be fighting for freedom under a repressive regime. They might not know what torture and imprisonment meant in countries like Chile. So she wrote her book. It is dedicated to the people of Chile and in her preface she says this:

Sheila Cassidy, following her release from prison in Chile.

On the day that I left Chile, one of my fellow prisoners told me that since she had known me her opinion of Catholics had fallen even lower than it had been before. This hit me especially hard not only because she was a woman whom I deeply respected but because I had secretly imagined myself to be living a life of splendid Christian witness among the Marxists. She said that when I decided not to speak about my prison experiences because of the risks involved she could hardly bring herself to speak to me. Her condemnation of me was for professing to be a Christian without having the courage to act like one.

It was then that I realized that I owed it to the members of the camp to speak out on their behalf; it became clear to me that, 'whatever the diplomatic or personal repercussions, I must speak the truth quite openly to those who were prepared to listen.

Throughout the book Sheila struggles with her Christian response to, what appeared to her to be an evil government which oppressed and persecuted the people of the country. Is it right for a Christian to fight, maybe literally, for freedom, peace and love? And is it right for a Christian to work with Marxists in that fight for freedom? Sheila concludes that it is, whatever the cost. She was tortured, beaten and imprisoned – she knows she is very fortunate to have left Chile alive.

But she has this to say: 'There is a phrase much used in these times of hardship in Chile: *entrega total* – total commitment. It is a phrase which links Christian and Marxist, for they have both answered the call of that Greater Love whereby a man is granted the strength to lay down his life for his friends.'

David Wang

David Wang is the Vice President of Asian Outreach International – a missionary society which provides support for Asian Christians in their efforts to introduce other Asians to Jesus Christ.

Although he was born in China, David and his family were forced to flee to Hong Kong when the communists took control of China in 1949.

In their flight the family lost everything they had ever owned and had to start a complete new life in Hong Kong.

David went to school in Hong Kong and when he was seventeen he was invited to join Asian Outreach in ministry to China.

Today David visits China whenever possible,

Kriss Akabusi

In August 1989 Kriss Akabusi hit the headlines with a blistering performance in the European Games which brought him two gold medals. These two wins, following his successes at the Seoul Olympics, brought Kriss to the forefront of world athletics. At Tokyo in 1991 he brought home a bronze in the hurdles and gold in the relay.

A magazine interviewed Kriss just before the Olympic Games:

'I'm going out to the Olympic Games because I'd love to be Olympic champion. But it's not the sole thing that's driving me.

'I'll do the best that I can do with the talent God has given me and hope he uses it to his glory. I am competitive, but I can't take the glory, because it's not me, it's the Holy Spirit.'

Akabusi's competitive spirit stems from a broken and lonely childhood spent in innumerable foster homes and finally a children's home. When he was only three years old Akabusi's Nigerian parents returned to their homeland leaving their two sons in a foster home.

'When I was eight the Biafra war started, so I went to a children's home because all the money my parents sent dried up,' he says.

'You miss your parents. You think that love is just owning things. Everyone would think, "That's the kid from the children's home," so in everything I did, I would be competitive to be as good as them.

'In my sports there's always been an ulterior motive – "I'll show these guys that I'm as good as them". That's been in everything in my life – wanting to have fast cars, nice clothes and find my security in things.

'Now I've lost that hang-up because I've become a Christian, I have stopped having to prove that I am as good as everything else. After all, you can never prove that you're the best.

'So now it isn't the prestige of being Olympic champion that drives me to go on. I just enjoy pitting my body against someone else's,' he smiles.

Despite his sporting success he says that before he became a Christian he felt dissatisfied. 'I was searching for something, but I didn't know what it was.

'I wouldn't say I was a male chauvinist pig,' he

sometimes visiting very remote areas of the country. He is a Chinese speaker and since 1968 has supervised a completely new translation of the Bible in today's Chinese language. This new Chinese Bible was designed to reach the young people of China by using a modern up-to-date translation.

As well as the work in Asia, David and his wife Alice travel around the world telling people about the church in China and asking for prayer support for Chinese Christians.

frowns, 'but I was a man's man. I liked to think I was a roughy-toughy, scared of no one.

'For a man to say that he hasn't got all the answers isn't macho. You've got to put your trust in Jesus, but a man says "I don't need anybody. I can do it on my own." '

Arriving in Edinburgh for the Commonwealth Games he was greeted by a Good News New Testament on his bed. 'I read through the whole lot while I was at the Games because I was so spiritually hungry,' he says.

'For the first time the Bible was more than just a story. I realised that this guy Jesus had actually lived . . .

'I prayed to Jesus to reveal himself to me, so that I would know what was the right way to go. I said, "All I want is to follow you." '

At 3am on the night of April 1987, Akabusi had a clear vision in which he was swimming towards a voice which said, 'Come to me, all who are weary and heavy laden and I will give you rest.' The struggle was intense, and many times he considered turning back. Then he saw 'a giant configuration of Jesus like a waterfall with his arms held out wide.

'I entered Jesus' kingdom and cried out his name loud and hard . . .

'I felt so happy and tranquil. I felt I was born again (although that was a phrase he had never heard) and forgiven for my sins.

'That morning I felt so great,' he says, punching the air with uncontained enthusiasm. 'I knew I'd just experienced my salvation. I knew that if I died tomorrow, Jesus had claimed me.'

The impact of this vision was life changing.

'Everyone knows that there's someone superior to themselves,' he says. 'It's just not manly to say it. I'm going out to the Olympics to do my best. If that's good enough for Jesus . . . It's whatever he feels will do the job well enough.

'I'm looking forward to the Olympics very much because it's the pinnacle of an athlete's career. To be an Olympiad is extraordinary in itself. To make the Olympic finals is something super-lative. If being an Olympic champion will spread the gospel, that's what I'll be.'

John Smith

What do you call a church minister who rides a Harley Davidson motorbike, heads up a team of biking evangelist/social workers called 'God's Squad', quotes freely from Pink Floyd, U2 and Bob Dylan and speaks out against injustice and Western values?

To young people in Australia, he's known as 'Smithy'. More accurately, he is Methodist minister, the Rev. John Smith – pastor of St Martin's Community in Melbourne, Director of 'Care and Communication Concern', a Christian counselling organization, and President of 'God's Squad', the Christian motorcycle club working amongst Hell's Angel gangs and others like them.

Although John Smith began his career as a conventional minister, the youth movement of the 1970s, with its 'flower-power' rejection of Western culture and values, challenged his traditional presentation of Christianity as a respectable lifestyle where make-up, rock music and dancing were 'taboo'. Acknowledging that Christianity was 'not necessarily a set of cultural rules', Smith found himself identifying with the young people who were turned off by respectable Christianity, especially the biker gangs.

His eventual acceptance by the motorcycle gangs was hard won. At first, he fell off his huge new machine so many times he was known as 'Autumn Leaves'! More seriously, his Christian message provoked verbal and physical violence. But John Smith persisted in befriending the bikers, becoming one of them, opening his home to them and helping them with their problems, basing his new-found ministry on the teaching of the Bible: 'In my understanding, the emphasis in Scripture is towards the poor. Not because God has favourites, but because society is administered powerfully in the interests of élite groups and it is an unjust system.'

But Smith prefers not to quote the Bible outside of church circles. A wide reader, he gains respect from non-Christians when his message is based on his knowledge of Freud or Sartre, Woody Allen or Pink Floyd.

John Smith's ministry to motorcycle gangs and other 'street kids' is now shared with the twenty-five converted gang-members who form 'God's Squad', giving him more time for regular radio shows and visits to schools and universities, where he challenges all kinds of social injustice and warns against accepting the secular humanists' view of human existence: 'You are more than what you own, where you live, what you drive and how you look.'

Such an unconventional ministry is not without its critics. Smith's wife Glena was once advised by a Christian leader to take her

husband to a psychiatrist; angry whites threatened his life when he championed the Aborigines' land rights cause; some see his message to students as anti-Australian and subversive; he unsettles traditional Christians with his support of 'liberation theology', using Marxist principles to analyse the weaknesses of Western capitalism.

However, the Anglican Archbishop of Melbourne refers to the man responsible for the Christian conversion of thousands of Australians as 'my favourite evangelist'. And a cabinet minister has said of him: 'I can think of no other Australian who has earned the admiration and respect of so many, in spite of constantly challenging the assumptions and practices of their lifestyle.'

(NB – you can read about John Smith in his book, On the Side of the Angels, Lion Publishing.)

FOLLOW UP

In addition to this unit, you will need to refer back to Units 23, 52, 55 and 56 in preparation for this work.

1. Name five people whom you consider to be examples of the faith for Christianity.

2. Choose one of these examples and write a brief outline of his/her life and work.

3. Why have you chosen this particular person as an example?

4. *Entrega total* – total commitment. To what extent does your example show the person's total commitment to his/her faith and beliefs?

Index

INDEX

INDEX